Norman Cresswell describes himself as 'an old Catholic hack'. He has been involved in religious journalism since 1960 when he founded the *Catholic Pictorial*, first in Birmingham and then in Liverpool, where it is still published. In 1993 he was asked to edit the re-launched *Catholic Times*, which he did for three years until the weekly was firmly re-established.

Once a Palestinian policeman, he returned to Palestine for a while to produce programmes for the BBC and later travelled extensively in Africa. For ten years he was a documentary writer with BBC Midlands. Among the programmes he compered was the long-running religious radio series 'In Search of the Truth'. An apt title, for he still continues that quest.

THROUGH THE YEAR WITH THE CATHOLIC FAITH

Norman Cresswell

Fount

An Imprint of HarperCollins*Publishers*

Fount is an imprint of
HarperCollins*Religious*
part of HarperCollins*Publishers*
77–85 Fulham Palace Road, London W6 8JB
www.christian-publishing.com

First published in Great Britain in 2000 by Fount

1 3 5 7 9 10 8 6 4 2

A catalogue record for this book is
available from the British Library

ISBN 0 00 628159 1

Printed and bound in Great Britain by
Omnia Books Limited, Glasgow

For my sons Nicholas and Mark
and their mother Mary –
the only legacy an old hack can leave

CONTENTS

FOREWORD BY ANN WIDDECOMBE

When I was a bridesmaid at my brother's wedding, I was given a *Daily Light*. This was a small book of meditations and Bible readings, designed for daily use. From then, which was in the mid-1960s, until now, I have seen very little to compare with it. Sadly, for too many the practice of daily reflection has now become submerged beneath the tide of modern life.

At the beginning of the second millennium England was covered with monasteries whose inhabitants stopped work five times a day for prayer. At the beginning of the third millennium there are few monks or nuns left and everyday life is lived under such pressure that no one can even wait for the post: everything must be faxed, all reactions must be instant and mobiles and pagers ring in church. Small wonder that prayers are now hurried one-way conversations squashed into a few moments first thing in the morning or last thing at night. It is rare indeed now to find anyone in the working world stopping for the Angelus.

What is needed is a thought, simple, easy to understand and memorable, which can form the basis of contemplation at odd moments during the day. This book provides such daily meditations and is a veritable treasure. Norman Cresswell used to produce similar stimuli to meditation when he edited the *Catholic Times* but that, of course, was on a weekly basis.

The meditations are relevant to the particular Saints whose feasts fall on the days in question and thus the book also keeps the user in touch with the Church's year where daily attendance at Mass is not possible. As each day's contemplation is complete in its own right you do not lose the thread if you miss a few days – or lots of days.

The book will appeal to all ages and is leavened with humour. You do not need a degree in theology to get the maximum benefit from this down-to-earth communion with the Saints in Heaven. Nor do you need to be feeling especially holy to embark on a meditation. It is reassuringly practical, modern and in touch.

The Christian journey is one which should bring us closer to God as we progress through our lives, but for most of us it is a path which we tread in small steps not great leaps. Each of the meditations in this book enables us to take one of those small steps. Every so often one strikes a chord which might facilitate a great leap.

Whether used every day or only occasionally, this book will fill a spiritual gap. It may not be a substitute for monastic contemplation but it is certainly a buffer against too much worldly stress. It brings God back into daily life and it reminds us of those who have trodden imperfectly but fulfillingly a long time ago the same essential road we tread today.

Ann Widdecombe

PREFACE

L et's face it, what you will read here is something of an imperti-
nence. We're told there are now more than one billion Catholics
– a staggering potpourri of often very opinionated folk whose
prejudices are unlikely ever to coincide. Each one is an individual;
each one bears a highly personal view of God, largely the result of a
mother's love and a parish environment that differs hugely even
within the same diocese.

So, to capture this vast tapestry is not just impossible – it is incredibly cheeky. And I ask your forgiveness even before you start charting
the Catholic year with me.

As even the role of the Pope is increasingly challenged, Catholics
have just one vital belief in common – they wholly believe that the
wafer that sits upon their tongue is the actual Body and Blood of
Christ. As they pad back to their places – gentry and peasants, the
tutored and the ignorant, the proud and the humble – each knows
that within them is the physical Christ. No doubt they understand
this in proportion to their intellect, this cannot be denied. But the
certitude is the same for everyone, and this is the mark of the
Catholic; and, moreover, the point at which this book commences
and ends.

We all, Catholics, come to our Faith by different paths. The cradle
Catholic no less than the convert Catholic is subject to external
influences, since they will always exert a compelling dictat on the
manner in which the Faith is regarded. It is only fair that before
venturing into my version of the Catholic year you should be aware
of the circumstances that moulded my Catholicism.

Paternally, my family was part of the Plantation of Ulster –
strongly Protestant for over 300 years in the same spot in Donegal,
not just disliking Catholics but actively terrified of their beliefs. My
father was destined for the ministry until he served four years in
France. After that, he studied medicine and met Anna, daughter of
Catholic Bavarians who had fled German militarism like so many

others in the 1870s. It was a strange alliance made no easier when my grandmother in Londonderry refused ever again to see her only son and certainly not his wife and child who, naturally, was brought up a Catholic.

I like to think that the violent contrast of my heredity produced some sort of balance. But that, of course, is for you to find out now as you join me in an admittedly prejudiced pursuit of the Catholic year.

HOW TO USE THIS BOOK

*T*hrough the Year with the Catholic Faith is based on Year C of the liturgical calendar. At certain moveable feasts it will be necessary to either read the day as it is or switch it with another. (For example, at Easter simply go to the entry for April 12 and read the other date when you reach it during the year.)

The moveable feasts are marked on the relevant days in this book and are also listed below:

Year	Sunday Cycle	Weekday Cycle	Ash Wednesday	Easter	Ascension	Pentecost	Corpus Christi	First Sunday of Advent
2000	B	II	8 Mar.	23 Apr.	(1) 4 June	11 June	(22) 25 June	3 Dec.
2001	C	I	28 Feb.	15 Apr.	(24) 27 May	31 May	(14) 17 June	2 Dec.
2002	A	II	13 Feb.	31 Mar.	(9) 12 May	19 May	(30 May) 2 June	1 Dec.
2003	B	I	5 Mar.	20 Apr.	(29 May) 1 June	8 June	(19) 22 June	30 Nov.
2004	C	II	25 Feb.	11 Apr.	(20) 23 May	30 May	(10) 13 June	28 Nov.
2005	A	I	9 Feb.	27 Mar.	(5) 8 May	15 May	(26) 29 May	27 Nov.
2006	B	II	1 Mar.	16 Apr.	(25) 28 May	4 June	(15) 18 June	3 Dec.
2007	C	I	21 Feb.	8 Apr.	(17) 20 May	27 May	(7) 10 June	2 Dec.
2008	A	II	6 Feb.	23 Mar.	(1) 4 May	11 May	(22) 25 May	30 Nov.
2009	B	I	25 Feb.	12 Apr.	(21) 24 May	31 May	(11) 14 June	29 Nov.
2010	C	II	17 Feb.	4 Apr.	(13) 16 May	23 May	(3) 6 June	28 Nov.

1 January

SOLEMNITY OF MARY, MOTHER OF GOD

If only every minute we lived was as valued as the one last night that preceded midnight. We marked its approach, we wrapped it in purpose, fondled its mystery, heralded its approach. Every second of that minute was savoured, matched to our own heartbeat. When midnight came it was greeted with laughter, tears, song, nostalgia, joy. That minute didn't pass – as so many do – in anonymity. That minute was lived to the full.

Some spent the minute in prayer; they were few. Some in an alcoholic haze; they were many. But all in apprehension, which is puzzling. For isn't it the truth that every minute given to us is equally precious, just as challenging as the one that has just slipped into the past like a gauntlet we didn't bother to pick up?

In its mercy the Church decided not so long ago that today was no longer a Holy Day of Obligation. Only those old enough to recall the agony of creeping to early Mass after a night spent welcoming the New Year can appreciate the kindliness of this dispensation. But we'll see as we slide through the year that this was only one of the fruits of the Second Vatican Council intended to soften the sometimes masochistic practices that tormented Catholics down the centuries. This Council, in the mid 1960s, carefully changed the image of God from He whom we feared to He whom we loved, and His Church from what some saw as a fortress to what all would see as a home.

Hopefully we're going to walk through this home in these coming days. We'll find, I think, a similarity with the celebration of New Year – there will be much in the one passing both to regret and to love. But, as ever, there is more to celebrate on the voyage into the future. Happy new year, happy new Church.

SS BASIL THE GREAT AND GREGORY NAZIANZUS

A t the tail's end of the last millennium the English Church sadly mourned the loss of its very own Basil the Great – a description that George Basil Hume, Cardinal Archbishop of Westminster, would have despised. Yet should you mingle today's saints you would end with a flavour of the Benedictine monk who led the English Church for the 23 years prior to the close of the twentieth century.

Like St Basil his namesake, our Basil cared hugely – and to purpose – for the poor of spirit and the poor in fact. Like Gregory of Nazianzus, he never ceased to be at heart a contemplative.

A mark of the Church, perhaps its most vital one, is that it produces a constant stream of good people. It's the tree you truly recognize by its fruits. And like any tree the Church has its off-seasons.

It would be different, of course, if the Church – and that's us – was genetically engineered. Each fruit would be rosy red, maggot free and of a precise diameter. Each fruit – us again – would be of a standard pre-ordained and precise. A clone, one of the other.

Thank God that He never intended things to be that way. So, for every saint the Church produces it has the balance of a crateful of sinners like us. Few of us are spectacularly evil – great sinners are as rare as great saints and almost as treasured in history's annals.

Our Church, then, is the Church of sinners. Or, as the Litany has it, the refuge of sinners. To understand the Church you have to realize that for every holy person it grows it nurtures a thousand like us.

3 January

ST GENEVIEVE

———

It's that time of year – shortly after Easter is the other – when your priest might gently announce that he is leaving for another parish. Sometimes it's done between calling the banns and announcing the bingo. Alternatively it's a few muttered words sandwiched between the Blessing and the scamper for the door.

It's seldom news to the parishioners, who have known about it long before the priest. There's no more fluent a means of communication than the parish grapevine. Yet they play the game. There's an intake of collective breath, a surprised glance at the neighbour and then the universal sigh.

For Catholics hold their priests in possessive affection. If he has an evil temper he is a 'character'. If he is lazy he is 'frail'. If he is unpunctual he is 'unworldly'. If he is greedy he is 'a proper lad'. If he is a tyrant then he is 'one of the old school'. Should he possess all these qualities he is still 'our priest'.

So the transfer of a priest is inevitably a sad moment in the life of the parish. More importantly, the people sense a momentum will be changed. They have grown accustomed to eccentricities in the performance of the Mass. Creatures of habit, parishioners sniff change in sanctity's odour. And they are restless.

To fill in the time they start a collection – the Catholic's first instinct at moments of stress. They lure the departing priest to a farewell party which is at best a wake or at worst an embarrassment. But all accept it as a vital rubric of departure.

The melancholy is genuine but transient – just as it has to be for the priest who is, after all, his bishop's vassal pilgrim. Next Sunday both priest and people will face strangers – strange in everything except the Faith they share.

4 January

St Elizabeth Seton

A head of me in the 'eight items only' queue was an elderly lady buying her rations for the day. 'Ping' went the machine for a single chicken breast; a double 'ping' for two apples; 'pong' for a slightly battered tin of rice pudding I had spotted on the bargain tray. And there it was – her day's feasting.

The checkout is highly educational, and can be almost as revealing as a place in the pew. Almost – but not quite, because in the pew we tend to disguise ourselves. Not from God, of course – even the dimmest of us know we cannot do that. But we do conceal what is 'us' from our temporary neighbour.

Sure, we offer our hand in peace when called upon to do so by the priest. But we do not show our hearts, or even hint at what is making them ache. We are oddly reticent folk, ensconced on our benches, lives hidden under anoraks. Our feelings are muted to the rhythmic demands of standing, sitting, kneeling. Our voices are mute but for the familiar responses jerked from us through long-established habit.

Sometimes I wonder if God isn't more interested in us when we queue with our baskets in the supermarket. At least then we are revealing more of ourselves than we are in His church.

But that is to underestimate God. And ourselves. Invisible it may be but we each have tacked to our souls one of those tricky little labels that tell Him instantly our worth, our value and, yes, even our sell-by date.

It's certainly not too much to hope that we are as individual to Him as the box of remaindered dates that merit a special 'ping' at the checkout.

Asda's attempt one year to take the Christmas message to the shoppers was rated a failure. Could it be that the organizers had overlooked the fact He was already there – in the mute needs of His people?

St John Neumann

Thanks to the courtesy of a Missionary of the Sacred Heart I have a new calendar on my desk. Small it may be but challenging all the same. Twelve clear months and only four days gone. From today the Church creaks back into the pilgrimage we call life. In kindly fashion she fleshes out the year using the devices of liturgy. Lent, Easter, and Ordinary days that can be so extraordinary. Throw in a host of saints' days and you have the map we pilgrims are expected to follow.

It should be a comforting safari. But it isn't. For the chart is a minefield — scattered there are days when we'll have to tread warily, awkwardly, even dangerously. Days to fast, days to give, days to sacrifice, days to acknowledge the peculiarities of our Faith. Miss them — even one — and we've blown it.

At best our belief will be maimed. At worst we'll run right off the map into regions designated 'Here be dragons'. But if there are mines then there's shrapnel too. Plenty of flack for the Catholic living by standards now derided and, worse, ignored.

No, it's not easy. But whether we're born Catholics or have come to the Faith by grace then, like it or not, the blueprint for the year ahead is designed for us.

The secular diary I have gives the rate of exchange current and predicted for the dollar, the yen and the punt. But it gives no indication of what collateral I might have in Heaven. It tells me the phases of the moon and the times of the tides. But it doesn't locate Paradise nor when my own tide may ebb. It tells me the miles between Cairo and Adelaide but fails to tell me the distance I must still travel to meet my God.

On balance I prefer the little calendar, the gift of the Missionary of the Sacred Heart.

6 January

THE EPIPHANY

Wise men, kings, astrologers? Travellers certainly, men from far lands because they seemed ignorant of Herod's reputation. Naive, perhaps, for all their learning. It did not occur to them that their joy searching for a king of the Jews would hardly be shared by the one holding that title.

These were not the Holy Family's first visitors, of course. The shepherds had that honour. And we can assume that the innkeeper and his wife would have been curious enough to inspect their guests in the barn. Then the maids from the inn – they could hardly have resisted a peep or two at a new baby. They would have brought gifts too. The shepherds must have shared their food, the people from the inn a morsel or two from the larder.

The Magi, we are told, brought rich gifts: luxuries carefully selected even before they began their search. Perhaps it was the thought rather than the value that made their gifts no less memorable than the scraps from the maids.

The notion of gift-bearing is as much a part of the ethos of the Church as is hospitality. Gifts are an integral part of all the sacraments – from the presents given at baptism to the giving of the oils at the sacrament of the sick.

Of all the sins the Church can have laid at its doors, avarice must be the most shameful. But here we must distinguish between the Church and the individuals who have from time to time manipulated her. Like the harlot, the Church may have loved too much from time to time. But seldom too little.

Pope John Paul II reflected something of this open-handedness when he told the English Church at the time of the exodus of Anglican ministers: 'With such men you must be generous'. It was an instruction treasured by us on this island. Perhaps because it reflected the liberality of the three wise men. And something of their sagacity too.

7 January

St Raymond of Penyafort

T he crib is down. Where it stood, the space looks lonely, forlorn. At home it is the same. The dust hidden by the gee-gaws of Christmas is now again apparent. The Hoover whisks away the last traces of our celebration. We sit back and relax, a strange torpor gripping us.

But, whilst we may doze, our bishops don't. This is the week when Catholic bishops are missing – to be found together in quiet retreat taking advantage of one of the few occasions during the year when they are not carried upon the round of meetings, interviews, confirmations; when they are not badgered by accountants, cornered by architects, hectored by Rome.

When there were curates, they were said to be mice in training to be rats. Bishops are so often camels in transit to their next burden. A bishop confided to me once that as a parish priest he was able to plan a school, envisage a church, and see them both built. As a bishop he could only pass from one problem to the next without the satisfaction of completion.

Perhaps, in the not so distant past, there were priests who coveted the mitre. But it's no longer the case. Today, the one consecrated abdicates most of the joys of priesthood in exchange for a task that will alienate his friends, and insulate him from the compassion a priest so often needs.

This little band then – no more than 30 – will gather together quietly enough. Their ages may well be disparate but the difficulties they share are not. This time will be precious for them; the chance for like to confide in like, when the wounds of office – which cannot be revealed – can at least be shown and perhaps healed. For those whose public duty has to be compassion it's an opportunity to be a recipient.

As in big business, it's tough at the top. Tougher still when you appreciate that the good bishop knows he is the servant of all and the master of none. And that his boss is God.

SS NATHALAN, PEGA AND WULSIN

It was a very, very long time ago – even in Church terms; '1066 and All That'. Amongst 'all that' was the total transformation of the Church in the British Isles. The Norman Conquest was more than a military coup, it redesigned the Faith in Britain, changing it from a loose, merry democracy into a Romanized organization.

The saints honoured today may be obscure but are worth remembering as representative of what was best in the Old Church of the Britons. Nathalan was a Scot, a nobleman wealthy enough to share his carefree generosity with his tenants – something the old saints did so well before being encased in the straitjacket of Norman conformity. He turned farmer, not for profit but to feed the people on his land. Pega was an anchoress in Northamptonshire. Saxons delighted in having eccentrics in their midst and a hermit was someone to be especially treasured.

Wulsin, the first Abbot of Westminster, died 64 years before the Conquest and the arrival of churchmen like Lanfranc who swiftly tamed the well-meaning but ill-disciplined charity of the native clergy.

It took almost an entire millennium for the English Church to return to the gentle compassion which existed before William I. It's true, of course, that Saxon enthusiasm probably created more saints than there was piety. It's unlikely that Edward the Confessor would have reached the ranks of the blessed in a later age.

Yet our Saxon heritage – race memory, if you like – did assuage the brittleness of Norman rule. And later it gave a gentling to the great monasteries. Saxon contentment with home and hearth, Saxon gaiety with simple celebration was never eradicated but persisted down the centuries. In Britain as nowhere else there was always to be a special affinity with Our Lady of the May, a gentleness that slipped unseen between the chainmail of the conquerors.

SS BERHTWALD AND FILLAN

Sure, it's the time of year we all hate. Surfeited, the children are herded unwillingly back to school. Grown indolent, their parents are just as reluctant to take up the reins. Momentum is all. And over Christmas and the New Year we've lost it. Even at Mass our furtive quest for a spot near the radiators implies a loss of dignity. And dignity matters when we place ourselves before the Lord of Hosts.

It's dignity that the poor lose last. When it's gone – either stripped away or surreptiously stolen – there's nothing left. Queuing for assistance, signing on, waiting hours in a corridor for an X-ray, buying your children's clothes at Oxfam – we've invented hundreds of ways in which folk can lose their dignity.

I've a theory that dignity died with the invention of the anorak – that drab symbol of the classless society designed to remind us that we are all members of the same herd. Yet at Mass, anoraked or not, we have the opportunity to recover our dignity. Before Him – who recognized the uniqueness of every sparrow – we're not shapeless beige blobs of the same jelly. Before Him we are individuals, alarmingly different, brilliantly original. We did not arrive via incubation, experimentation nor test tube. We are not cloned. We are us. We have dignity.

The Church is conscious of this need. Commenting on an experiment in which a girl had brought to term another's fertilized egg, the Vatican newspaper, the *Osservatore Romano* said: 'She had been used as an incubator, the prisoner of the egoism of her mother and of abominable techniques. Her dignity as a woman has been killed.'

Whilst custodian of the supernatural, the Church insists upon the natural – marriage between men and women; recognition that men and women are different but equal; insistence that all life should be created by God and that such life cannot be destroyed at any person's whim.

Simple, natural, and dignified.

10 January

SS DERMOT AND PAUL THE HERMIT

Not far from Inchcleraun, an island on Lough Ree in Ireland where Abbot Dermot founded his monastery, lives my friend Felicity. She told me a tale which reinforced what I had always thought.

It seems that on the Last Day, when all the faithful were celebrating, Peter noticed that Jesus was standing apart, looking beyond the Gate. He was silent and clearly sad. Peter asked why. 'I am waiting for Judas,' explained Jesus.

The story's a nod to predestination, a knotty problem which has absorbed the great brains of the Church over the centuries. Put simply, how can a good God, who knows all things, create a person He knows will be ultimately damned for all time? Approach the query one way, and God comes out cruelly. Approach it another and you must come to the conclusion that it is inconceivable that anyone – even the most bestial – can ever be condemned to Hell.

Most of us trot off dutifully to Mass each Sunday, say our prayers and receive the Sacrament. Catholics, even the very intelligent ones, are ever prone to letting others resolve the wobblies circumstances will occasionally throw at us. But from the mid-twentieth century we found ourselves forced to take a stand on matters of conscience rather than affairs of philosophy. From being passive, we were urged to be active. More often than not it was concerned laypeople who harried us from our pews to oppose abortion, euthanasia, and artificial insemination. Unlike predestination, which we could play with or ignore, the new issues demanding our thought were largely concerned with life itself. The challenges came thick and fast with an urgency we could no longer ignore. In their own way they were just as complicated as the complex puzzles the early Fathers had tackled on our behalf. But now we were part of the decision-making process. Contraception, married priests, women priests – big questions posed themselves by the legion. But for the vast majority of Catholics there could be only one answer in the tumult – it was 'follow Peter'.

———————— ⌒ ————————

'I have now come to realize,' Peter confided to Cornelius, 'that God does not have favourites.' So it's a pity that in some places baptism is withheld if parents or godparents are not practising Catholics. At the centre of the furore between intransigent parties lies the baby. The priest's point of view is valid – baptism isn't a social event to bring together relatives, friends and their welcome gifts to the penniless babe. It's the solemn entry of a person to its Faith, and promises made on behalf of the child are serious and binding. So, yes, for them to make promises they neither believe nor intend to keep makes a mockery of a vital Sacrament.

Yet, doesn't this ignore the child's right to become a member of the Church? When John the Baptist demurred to baptize Christ it was Jesus who replied: 'Leave it like this for the time being. It is fitting that we should, in this way, do all that righteousness demands.' And, we are told, John gave in to Him.

Inevitably the 'social' Sacraments are enveloped in an aura of gift-bearing and celebration. Even ordinations are not immune. But at the core of it all there are two people exchanging vows, a man or woman accepting vocation or a baby entering membership of the Church. What happens around the periphery of these actions does not distract from what has happened before God.

Surely, if we accept the notion of grace bestowed by a Sacrament then we cannot deny that a babe baptized is not better than a babe denied baptism.

The letter of the Law, Christ said, kills. As if in proof of this it was His contention with the Law that killed Him. There are moments in Catholic life – and every priest is aware of them – when it is the spirit and not the letter of the Law that must prevail.

12 January

AILRED OF RIEVAULX

~

This Cistercian abbot ruled over a monastery of 650 monks and brothers. Whilst he was never formally canonized it was evident that his sheer goodness was an attraction.

You might say the same thing about our Mollie. I say 'our' but every parish has its own. She is the one who tidies the sacristy, coerces the readers, bullies the servers, arranges the cleaning and the flowers. She marks the absences of the regulars, welcomes strangers, enquires after the sick and is the first to hear when someone has died. Without knowing it she sets the parish standard. Girl servers know better than to wear make-up, the boys' fingernails are spotless, the vestments pressed.

The parish Mollies are neither trained nor elected. They simply emerge from the fabric of the community. Because of this they are wholly representative of the society that produces them. They are the product of trust, familiarity and friendship – often enough the bridge between change of clergy or even liturgy.

It was the Mollies who eased the strange transitions brought by the Second Vatican Council. It is Mollie who always has the time to chat, enquire, sympathize. She is no busybody, no gossip. She doesn't judge. But she does guide and in doing so gives the parish a rhythm. This rhythm of a parish is always a gentle mystery. Inevitably it is centred on the priest. But in the best of parishes the joins between priest and people are scarcely visible – a sensitive stitch produces a seamless whole.

This whole reflects the peculiarities of the individual community. For no parish is exactly the same as another. And the difference – so often the invisible work of its Mollie – is worth preserving.

13 January

ST HILARY

———

A t the newsagent I bumped into my dentist. Without his white coat, his mysterious chair, his assembly of drills, scalpels and eerie implements I didn't recognize him. He knew me immediately. Not because of the white beard and fearful eyes but because of the missing molar top right and broken incisor bottom left.

Perhaps it will be like that with God. Perhaps because I don't find Him on a cloud, sunk into cosy cumulus, His beard being stroked by winsome cherubs, I won't recognize Him. Luckily He'll know me. Not because of some decayed denture but, worse, because of a decayed soul.

Our conception of God is vitally important. Visual aids to understanding are superior to oral descriptions. That's why Pope John Paul II urged artists to return to the great days of religious painting. A shrewd man, he realized that in an age of visual communication the Church – and therefore God – was losing out.

It's also why, in these barren January days, we need some beauty in our churches to remind us that the Kingdom of Heaven is unlike the bleak pavements we've just travelled, that trees do have leaves, that birds sing and that God's hope of spring is only a month or two away.

Over the centuries the Catholic impression of God has undergone any number of visual changes. The clouds and the beard are gone. God the Father is more likely to be depicted through the Spirit – a natural force, perhaps breeze, perhaps tempest. Or through the Son which is why the Turin Shroud alerts both Catholic hope and Catholic faith.

In the past our need to know God's image was so great that a great cult appeared surrounding Veronica's veil. At heart we are all Thomasses – we need to see, to feel, to touch. What we sometimes overlook is that God's resemblance can be as apparent in a child's smile as it is obvious in the magnitude of the universe.

14 January

St Kentigern Mungo

‿

'Charlie is my mungo' sounds odd. But mungo means dar-
ling and Glasgow's very own saint was, as Glaswegians like
to think of themselves, as tough as old boots. As tough
certainly as Scottish Catholics have always had to be.

So much emphasis is laid on the universal Church that it's easy to
forget that every country has its national Church. Or, if national has
become a dirty word, then local Church. The teaching, sure, is universal and so is the primacy of the Pope. But that said, local Catholic
churches can be vastly differing in their ethos. And mostly it's down
to history and experience.

Some, like England, are well defined. Other local Churches, such as
Australia, are a potpourri of straining influences. In the USA there are
almost as many 'local' Catholic Churches as there are states. Even in
Italy the Church of the north is wholly dissimilar to that in the south.

It's the reason, perhaps the best, that so many wanted to retain the
Latin Mass – travel the world, they reasoned, and the Mass is the same
and our brotherhood in Christ is magnified. It led to long debates
during Vatican II about that ugly word which hid so much genuine
sensitivity – inculturization. Or more simply, what do we preserve of
a tribe's, country's original culture when we introduce Christianity?

God bless the old-time missionaries for their courage, their
devotion, their love for their pagan parishioners. But how often
did they destroy the wheat with the chaff? And all with the very
best of motives.

We have learned from our mistakes – learned not to impose Jesus
but to allow Him to take His place naturally with His people.

SS CEOWULF AND ITA

The Irish have strange tales to tell of Ita (or Ytha). But then they always respect a saint plastered in credible legend, unlike the North Britons whose preference invariably was for the stolid tough guy – like today's King Ceowulf of Northumbria who renounced the trappings of power for a monk's cell on bleak Lindisfarne Island.

Saints reflect the people who chose them – Thérèse could only be French; the austere whimsy of Patrick led to his adoption by the Irish; Thomas à Becket, dutiful disciplinarian, had to be English.

Ita is the very stuff of legend – she is, after all, Ireland's most favoured woman saint after Brigid. Like all that island's notables she had royal connections although, truth to tell, there was a lot of royalty around Waterford in the sixth century. Her original name gives the story away, for she was Deirdre, she of the sorrows. In Limerick she founded the convent where she lived in monastic solitude yet is credited with always being available for consultation.

The story has it that the great St Brendan was one of those who made pilgrimage to her cell. When he asked her what three things God especially valued she is said to have replied: 'True faith in God with a pure heart. A simple life with a religious spirit. Open-handedness inspired by charity.'

Counsels of perfection perhaps. But perfections as enduring as the memory of Deirdre herself. Piety as simple as Ita's runs the risk of being platitude, until we realize that it's our own veneer of sophistication which has blurred our ability to accept simplicity at its face value. Ita's gain – our loss.

16 January

SS FURSEY AND HENRY
OF COQUET ISLAND

~

It's virtually impossible for the English Catholic to deny the influence of Irish tradition on his Faith. Catholicism is numerically stronger – as in Boston and Sydney – where the nineteenth-century immigrants first clustered in material poverty with only the richness of their religion to give them dignity.

So in Manchester, Liverpool, Kilburn and Birmingham you'll find subtle interpretations of Catholicism not encountered in Lancashire, Surrey or Norfolk. Irish Catholicism abroad was connotated at an early stage with the diseases of impoverishment – drunkenness, violence, social despair. Little wonder that every instinct of the native Catholic was to distance himself from the incoming brethren. Until, that is, they were forced to look to the vast Irish seminaries to provide their priests for the first half of the twentieth century.

They were priests unlike the English breed; mostly country lads whose parents had welcomed the opportunity to see them become gentlemen. The English priest had often enough been a gentleman whose family unwillingly saw him become a priest.

Cultural clashes were unavoidable despite the care taken by bishops – often enough Irish themselves – to place English priests in predominantly English parishes. It was a process facilitated by the fact that the English upper classes still held the purse strings in their country parishes.

For almost 70 years great seminaries like Maynooth despatched rigid young men, cloned to authoritarian perfection, only to find them mature into what the English loved most – 'characters'. Suddenly, overnight or so it seemed, the supply from 'across the water' dried up. By the mid-1990s the Irish priest was a rarity. The English had to go it alone.

St Anthony of Egypt

Perhaps this St Anthony was the origin of the Catholic love of the word 'little'. It occurs so often in Catholic life – the Little Way, the Little Office of Our Lady, the Little Sisters of the Poor, Sisters of the Little Company of Mary, Sisters of the Little Ones, the Little Red Box, the Little Child Jesus.

In England the runt of the litter, the smallest, was called a tantony, after St Anthony (the same name was given to the smallest peal of bells). But I suspect the Catholic preoccupation with 'little' goes much deeper.

It's a personal type of humility which doubtless owes its origin to the little baby in the crib, but then spreads to embrace so much more. Pascal wrote: 'A little thing comforts us because a little thing afflicts us'. The priest in the confessional knows something of this. We enter the box overwhelmed by the magnitude of our sin. The priest – who has heard it all a thousand times before – puts our sin into perspective. It is, compared to our repentance, a little thing. And it is the little formula of absolution – based on so massive a leap of faith – that puts things right again.

'I will spend my life doing good upon earth. After my death I will let fall a shower of roses,' promised St Thérèse of Lisieux. And the nickname Catholics gave her? The Little Flower.

The whole ethos of Catholicism is littered with little things – the donkey which carried Jesus, the little miracle at Cana done out of love for His mother. These are the reminders that most lives are made up from little events strung together that at death leave the tapestry on which we'll be judged.

Derek Worlock, the late Archbishop of Liverpool, once showed me a homily he was to preach. I suggested that where he had written 'small' he should substitute 'little'. The eyebrows went up. So I explained. After a few moments' thought he scrawled out 'small'. Little was the word he used from then on.

18 January

PRAYER OCTAVE FOR CHRISTIAN UNITY

~

Today, for the first time, the Church steps officially as it were into the new year. We're offered purpose again and the aim is unity. The ideal that 'they may be one' might well be as theologically distant as it ever was but the relatively small number of practising Christians still left in Britain are conscious of a unity of purpose as never before. Christians now have an instinctive feeling that they are being marginalized within society.

Those carefully orchestrated covenants signed in the 1980s during the frenzied days of new-found ecumenism now seem artificial – a fancy window-dressing that fell apart for any number of good reasons.

It has taken the major assault of the 1990s to make Christians realize that Christ is best served when we ignore what cannot be resolved and band together for the moral certainties we all agree He taught. At last the penny has dropped that it is Christianity – not Methodism, nor Anglicanism, nor the Free Churches – that is the target of the secularists. An attack on any one Faith individually is in fact an attack on us all.

Perhaps, like the shortage of vocations, it is Christ's way of teaching us what we should already know – that He is the Way, the Truth and the Life and it is our simple needs, not our narrow ambitions, He is there to supply.

So the Unity Octave means more than it ever did. Buried in the small print of the covenants signed all those years ago was the nub of what we should be striving for now. It was the agreement that we should act jointly in Christ's name whenever a threat presented itself. It is still a promise kept better parochially than at national level, more's the pity.

In this week of unity Christians have the opportunity to give an unchurched society a vision of one Church centred on Christ not divided by Him.

19 January

ST WULFSTAN

The traffic warden had taken post by my car. My heart fell. 'Sorry,' I rushed to explain. 'The service went on longer than I thought.'

'Ten minutes longer,' he retorted, his little black book in his hand by now.

'It was a Unity meeting,' I floundered on, 'and it was hard to gauge how long it would last.'

He pointed to the Methodist church and asked if I belonged to it. I shook my head, explained I was a Catholic, and started to tell him what Unity Week was. He checked me, 'I know all about it.' My heart beat again – here was a Christian traffic warden.

Hope died as he licked his pencil, made a note in the book. Then he paused and asked me what had happened. Well, I explained, there had been a procession, the reading of a covenant signed some years before and we'd sung 'Bind us Together, Lord'. He only looked up when I told him that as a Catholic I didn't often hear good singing in church.

At this point he tore out the form he'd been completing and stuck it on the car in front. If he heard my sigh of relief he didn't show it. Confidence reasserted I babbled on about the rest of the service.

'Did it do you any good?' he queried.

'Well, yes it did,' I confessed. 'It made me realize we Catholics are not alone – their problems are our problems too, everything from broken homes to drugs. Their anxieties are identical, our confusions similar.'

He licked the pencil again, made a swift notation and I swear he had a slight smile as he said, 'I've no confusions. I'm a Catholic. I just follow the rules.'

With that he handed me the ticket wrapped in cellophane. If only he'd been an Anglican.

SS FABIAN AND SEBASTIAN/UNITY OCTAVE

A Catholic, a Moslem and a Jew died and found themselves at Heaven's Gate. Ssh now, this is no joke … I think. Jesus welcomed the Catholic, Mohammed the Moslem, Moses the Jew. The three arrivals – as habit dictated – kept a respectable distance from each other, conscious of their differences over the centuries.

'Please,' asked the Catholic of Jesus, 'will I get to see the Father?' Jesus nodded.

'Is Allah within?' queried the Moslem.

Mohammed smiled, 'Yes.'

The Jew looked directly at Moses. 'And Jehovah?'

The great beard shook as if disguising a chuckle and Moses proffered his staff.

In silence the newcomers each followed his guide. They passed through a soundless, terrifying panorama of history as it had happened. Jews massacred Assyrians, crusaders butchered Jews, Moslems lay waste Spanish cities. So much fury, anger, destruction, cruelty.

For a while each man thought he stood not in Paradise but in Hell. Eventually the grotesque visions ceased. They found themselves on a verdant plateau of indescribable beauty. And, ahead of them now, Jesus, Mohammed and Moses sat together beneath a tree so coolly green and inviting that the new arrivals ran towards it.

'What kept you?' Jesus asked. They stood dumbstruck, unable to express the horrors they had just witnessed.

'Come,' invited Jesus, extending His hand to the Jew. 'Now you are all ready to see the Father.'

So they progressed into Paradise – Jesus leading the Moslem, Moses the Christian and Mohammed the Jew.

Only in Heaven – or so it seems – will the Father's will be done, that they may be one.

21 January

St Agnes

If not the first then Agnes is certainly the most prominent of the young virgin martyrs of the first century who chose death before dishonour. There were many more, right up to the twentieth century and Maria Goretti who made the same choice. Chastity − a woman's chastity, that is − was a treasure held beyond price not just by Christians but by all faiths.

By the 1990s it had been debased − no longer valued but valueless. The denigration began only in the 1960s when it became fashionable for convent-trained girls to deride the ethos of purity in which they had been trained, rushing blindly into what had become a sexual revolution. What had been held inviolate for millennia became overnight the tedious relic of what was seen as a domineering education. Women's Lib had much to answer for. But even without that movement the notion of liberated sex would have decayed the ancient principles of morality.

For the major faiths the abandonment of traditional purity was shattering. Perhaps even more so for Catholics − no sluggards in this new race towards promiscuity − who had been reared in the consciousness of the purity of Our Lady. Little wonder that the closing decades of the last century saw an incredible rise in the rate of lapsation.

Some lay the blame with an obvious target − the almost universal use of artificial contraception. Others criticized the Church's response to this in the encyclical Humanae Vitae. In Britain, Cardinal Heenan, overwhelmed by the reaction to the encyclical, tried to stem the flood of departures with the offer of a 'conscience clause'. His compromise came too late to save entire generations leaving the Church and was a matter of scandal for the traditionalists.

Young Agnes, pierced by a sword, rather than lose her virtue would have received scant respect from her peers in the twentieth century.

22 January

St Vincent of Saragossa

M uch is made of martyrdom within the Catholic Church. Yet the fact is that apart from what Catholics have done to Catholics – and that was pretty horrific – there have only been three major persecutions.

There was an intermittent one pursued by the Romans during the first few centuries after Christ, then the Protestant persecutions of Catholics in the sixteenth century and the English attacks upon the Irish over many centuries.

St Vincent is one of those saints remembered but scantily for the manner of his death – after suffering on the rack he was roasted on a gridiron. This was in 304 during a persecution randomly begun by the Emperor Diocletian.

These Roman attacks on Christians were spasmodic affairs. Even Nero's was short-lived and something of a sideshow, however bloody. When things went wrong for the emperors the increasingly large number of influential Christians provided a handy community to blame. Christians were, after all, a secretive bunch and unlikely to bite back to any effect.

The post-Reformation persecutions – particularly in England – were similar. They had the advantage of being politically expedient and a source of income for the Crown at the same time. As in all things, the English were nothing if not pragmatic.

Of all the persecutions the ones in Ireland were not only more vicious than the rest but were the most ignorant, the most cloddish. The thoughtless wounds delivered there were never to be forgiven nor forgotten.

Catholics venerate their martyrs in much the same way as a regiment will honour its heroes. Similar too is the association made with spilling blood. It's a notion alien to many of the Eastern faiths who find us both crass and ignorant. Yet Catholic pride in martyrs palls before the Holocaust and the holocausts that went before. And who, we must ask, perpetrated those slaughters?

23 January

St Emerentiana

~

L ike you, perhaps, I'd never heard of Emerentiana. Duty bound, I looked her up in *The Oxford Dictionary of Saints*. Just another of those fourth-century virgin/martyrs done to death whilst praying at St Agnes' tomb. No doubt, somewhat crossly just at this moment, she is someone's Guardian Angel.

In a frenzy of spring-cleaning some years ago, the Vatican department concerned with hagiography – saints to you and I – knocked any number of holy heads on the haloes. Philomena, I seem to recall, was given her marching orders and St Christopher was another. Naturally Catholics took little notice of this pious butchery. I certainly didn't – the same St Christopher has sat on the dashboard of every car I've driven since 1948 and there he will stay. I'd no more take a journey to Timbuctoo or the village shop without him.

You see, Catholics are devoted to their saints. Not all, by any means, but the one or two they acquired in childhood and have grown familiar with ever since.

As we're still within the Unity Octave let me acknowledge that our devotions in this manner are often a puzzlement to non-Catholics, and at worst a scandal that perpetuates division. Most at contention, alas, is the Catholic reverence for Our Blessed Lady seen by many outside Catholicism as an attempt to short-circuit God. In the same way they might also regard our prayers to saints once human and therefore fallible as a sort of blasphemy.

Hopefully, in the days ahead of us, we'll explore how Catholic familiarity with saints in no way diminishes the way in which we regard God. The saints, we believe, will intercede with God – not because He doesn't know of our trials but because we don't like to bother Him. It's as simple – and as complex – as that.

St Francis de Sales

'He who watches out for his pennies and farthings, will be still more careful regarding crowns and pounds' said St Francis de Sales. It's little wonder that this seventeenth-century bishop and writer became in time the patron of all hacks – from the lowliest reporter to the most renowned author. Another aphorism to come from him was 'More flies are attracted by a spoonful of honey than by a whole barrelful of vinegar'. A literary figure himself, he appreciated and inspired in others a respect for the power of the pen.

Yet Rome has a poor reputation for suffering mildly the integrity of thinkers. The Index – or to give it the censorious title it so well deserved, the Index Librorum Prohibitorum – was the method used for 400 years, until 1966, to discipline writers in a highly selective manner.

For instance, neither de Sade nor Rabelais ever found their way into the Index. So we're left wondering why pornography, soft or hard, escaped whilst others were pilloried. Boccaccio and Galileo were indexed until they recanted. Kant, Rousseau, Spinoza – thinkers – and Hugo, Balzac and Bacon – authors – remained forbidden reading for Catholics until 1966.

Look closer and you'll find that some 5000 books were condemned not because of their potential danger to our innocence but because they were seen as a threat to the status quo of the Roman Establishment.

The Church, it seemed, was prepared to wield the big stick of censorship only when its authority was endangered. It was content to remain mute when pornography decayed the very soul.

Only latterly, by the by, did that most despised caste of hack, the sub-editor, understand that Francis was their patron too. 'Be brief,' he admonished, 'when you cannot be good.'

CONVERSION OF ST PAUL

A neat Feast to close the week dedicated to ecumenism. Neat, because without Paul we'd be neither Catholics, nor Anglicans, nor Free Church. Probably we'd be largely pagan, or members of yet another Jewish splinter group – the Nazarenes.

Paul knew a good proposition when he saw it, even if it took a bump on the head along the Damascus Road to drive it home. Paul – publicist, intellectual, opportunist – was everything the 11 apostles Christ left behind were not. In his own words, he was all things to all men. And that was a point of view wholly alien to the fisherman Peter and company. Only Judas had a touch of Paul's insight but chose to use it inopportunely.

Paul, surely, was the shrewdest choice Jesus made even if it came posthumously. After the Crucifixion, even after the Resurrection, perhaps even after Pentecost, there must have been a sense of huge loss amongst the disciples. Christ had given no hint that He had left behind a powerful timebomb ticking in the person of Saul of Tarsus. He was so unlikely a character to detonate the cannons of Christianity. Yet, was he any more unlikely than Matthew the tax collector or John the dreamer?

Why was Paul not amongst the original Twelve? It's an intriguing question. Until, that is, you realize the apostles' need later for just such a catalyst outside their immediate community.

The difference, so glaring, between the Petrine and the Pauline influences within the Church are as sharply marked today as they were then. Peter today could never be anything but a Catholic. Paul could never be anything else but a Christian. In recent years we had a living example – Basil Hume was Peter to Derek Worlock's Paul. As it had 2000 years before, the mixture gelled. Christ is surely the God of surprises.

26 January

St Timothy

T oday's Feast sees Christians return to their own pews in good conscience that they have done their bit for unity for this year. Appropriately the child of a mixed marriage – his father Gentile, his mother Jewish – Timothy was well educated and swiftly talent-spotted by Paul. Because of this choice we can infer that Timothy was intelligent, sharp-witted, malleable – and almost certainly patient. Courageous too – not just because of where he ventured but because he did so with Paul who was not always the easiest of companions.

On the whole, Catholicism is not a solitary Faith. Ignore for a moment our inability to welcome strangers to our church, our obvious difficulty with the tactile quality of the Sign of Peace, and you'll find that at heart we are a gregarious folk. Almost tribally so.

In evidence of this I offer a host of societies still flourishing and wholly based upon strong comradeship – the St Vincent de Paul Society, the Union of Catholic Mothers, the Knights of St Columba, the Catenians.

I admit that these groupings have echoes of a past sectarianism, harking back to those days when to be Catholic was to be 'different'. And how we gloried in the difference. The organizations we formed at the start of the twentieth century were more bastions than social venues. They were a way of ensuring that Catholic lads could meet good Catholic girls; that charity would be dispersed as Christ would have wanted; that wine would be taken in Catholic custom.

Society, you feel, will inevitably marginalize these societies. Sadly so, for Catholic companionship has a merry ring.

27 January

St Angela Merici

———⌒———

Angela, somehow the name you'd expect the Superior – she baulked at the title Foundress – of the Ursulines to bear. Sharp, not given to frills, descriptive, defined – just like the excellent education offered by Ursuline Sisters since the sixteenth century.

Originally the members of the Order were not required to wear habits nor take vows. Rome didn't much like the idea – then, as now, it likes to know that the periphery answers to the hub.

In 1955 the 20 provinces of Ursulines – from places as disparate as Barbados and Manchuria, England and Hungary – numbered 6724 Sisters in 246 houses. Although still to be found in eight dioceses in England and Wales I'd not hazard – nor embarrass them – with a guess at present membership.

For a time in the 1960s the English Church attempted to disguise the haemorrhage it was suffering from deserting priests and nuns. All too soon it became apparent that the wound could no longer be hidden nor staunched. Even so, for a decade or so, all emphasis was laid on the dearth of priestly vocations. Not until the late 1980s was the savage toll on women religious fully acknowledged. Only one women's Order worldwide was not only holding its own but vastly increasing – the Missionaries of Charity, benefiting from a Foundress not only alive but already tipped for sainthood.

One by agonizing one the schools the nuns had run, the hospitals they had manned, were either closed or handed over to the laity or the local authority. It was a loss that society – knowingly or subconsciously – has yet to come to terms with. It was as if Our Lady's very mantle had been removed from the nation. And the nation was the poorer for it.

28 January

St Thomas Aquinas

Jesus, master artist, painted on the broad canvas of humanity. Yet even this was miniscule compared to His creation of the universe. That portrait was executed in detail so precise that we can never hope to examine more than just a speck of it. When it came to humanity He used broad, simple strokes and tints we would all recognize. Almost as if He was leaving the nitty-gritty of His sketch for us to finish.

One of the people who took on this task was Thomas Aquinas, Dominican friar, Doctor of the Church. Although not yet 50 when he died, he had completed five volumes of *Summa Theologica* – the blueprint for all Christian apologetic.

Few Catholics will have read the *Summa Theologica* apart from those whose task it has been to study it. It has few, if any, 'soundbites' that can be quoted. Yet much of our belief was etched into time by the artist who followed Christ. Here is the merest touch of the master:

> The Church is catholic, that is, universal: a) first with regard to place … The Church has three parts, one on earth, a second in heaven, a third in purgatory: b) the Church is universal with regard to all conditions of human beings; nobody is rejected, whether they be masters or slaves, men or women … c) it is universal in time, and those are wrong who allow it a limited span of time, for it began with Abel and will last even to the end of the world.
>
> Exposition of the Apostles' Creed

In the fourth century, Augustine, that first great Doctor of the Church, had said: 'We exist because God is good.' Almost a thousand years later Aquinas built on this: 'Every being that is not God, is God's creature. Now every creature of God is good and God is the greatest good. Therefore every being is good.'

At this point, a thousand thousand seminary students have muttered, 'QED'. And turned, gratefully, to their study of the broad canvas of the Gospels.

28

29 January

ST GILDAS

Gildas was a monk in South Wales. Something of a historian he was less than kind to his Anglo-Saxon neighbours. Hurry on some 1400 years to 1883 and you would have heard Pope Leo XIII saying: 'The first law of history is not to dare to utter falsehood. The second, not to fear to speak the truth.' At the time he was opening the treasure of the Vatican archives to the public – the first time such immeasurable knowledge had been made available outside a select band of churchmen.

In one sense all religion is history. And history, unlike theology, is an exact science given that the evidence has not been falsified. And the history Catholics live with is all in the Gospels. So we were angry, back in 1985, when the Bishop of Durham spoke of the Resurrection, so carefully documented, as being 'a conjuring trick with bones'.

What immediately irritated ordinary Catholics was their conviction that Jesus Christ was a very simple man. Well, not that exactly. Rather, He left us a very simple message. And we know instinctively that it takes a clever man to make things simple. Now Professor Jenkins was a clever man too. He spent a great deal of his working life teaching theology – and there's nothing simple about that. Come to think of it, Jesus would have been a poor theologian. He made everything so easy to understand. Even death. Even the hardest thing of all about death – the notion of resurrection.

Jesus' own death was bloody, final and brutal. It was as if He looked forward to the time when some clever-clogs would come along and claim He hadn't died at all. Which is just what happened. Not just in our own lifetimes but even a short time after His death.

Our Faith stands or falls upon the veracity of the history given us in the four Gospels. Our own eternity lies in the truth of the Resurrection. Little wonder we were so cross with Dr Jenkins.

C hrist is never far away. In Ward 5 – four men lying each side of it – it was so quiet that even the soft thump of a plastic urine bottle jerked old men's eyes open. The friend I was visiting dropped it as he struggled to hide it under the bed when he saw me. I felt anguished for the embarrassment in his eyes as the yellow tide crept across the floor.

In moments a young auxiliary was on her knees. Whish, whosh, wipe, she went busily, all the while singing 'Promise Me You Will Leave Me Never'. Old eyes around the ward closed down, the drama done. The nurse patted my friend's pillow. 'There now, love, don't worry. They're a daft shape, aren't they?' They smiled privately at each other, and she bustled away.

I felt honoured. For a split second I'd been privileged to see humanity at close quarters. For this microcosm of compassion I felt indebted. It was, as St Peter had said a long time before on a different occasion, good to be there.

That morning's papers had returned to the vexed question of euthanasia. How can we possibly know, I wondered, when God is ready to write 'finis' to a life? How can we ever be sure that a life is purposeless when it can still inspire such virtue?

My friend relaxed, his hands slowly unclenching. He is – I almost insulted him by writing 'was' – an engineer. People somewhere were that very moment driving over roads he had designed; bridges he had helped build.

When the trays came round I knew it was time to be off. The pretty auxiliary cried out: 'Grub's up!' Tired eyes opened. They showed that curiosity that forever separates humankind from beast. And reflects the soul that is only God's to take. In His own time.

St John Bosco

J̲ohn Bosco loved children. He took the poorest of the poor – as he had been himself – and transformed their childhood from squalor to joy. And, just as importantly, trained them in life skills. Catholic priests, debarred from physical fatherhood, tend to be good with children. One in particular comes to mind. He was grand with kiddies. When he bounced into a classroom of tots – he seldom walked – little hearts beat with joy. On the way to the rostrum he'd pick up a couple of mites, one under each arm, and seat them on the teacher's desk. 'Now, Joanne, and you Tommy, take the class – I'm tired and want a snooze.'

It was a strange way to start an RE class. But it worked. By the end of the period 20 young minds would have grasped clearly that God made them, that He loved them and would be forever at their sides.

He made First Confession a wonderful encounter with Jesus; at First Communion there was a present for every child, a loving kiss for the girls and a wild whirl for the boys. A child falling down during break would have this priest at hand to kiss the bruise better; a tot left alone in the playground would be swept into Father's arms and soon surrounded by classmates as Father told them one of his stories. From then on their eyes would always search for the one alone, the Christ who was their neighbour.

He was a joyous priest, bubbling with a sense of fun, great with children yet understanding their parents' problems too. So why were tears so near his eyes when I met him? Why do the children in Class 1 RE lesson now sit dully bored when he tells them of Jesus? Why do they wonder how it is that their priest no longer loves them, has no time for whirleyjigs, nor hugs, nor fun?

A single comment did it. A thoughtless, cruel, rancid, ignorant remark made by a stranger watching him in the playground. You can guess the comment. I cannot forgive it. Ever. It has robbed so many little children of so much, forever.

1 February

ST BRIGID OF IRELAND

A dieu then, January. And thank God for it. How the elderly hate you – you and your equally grasping associate, November. In other months we can slip almost furtively towards God, surprised perhaps, apprehensive even. But we don't leave in the rasping enmity of those two killer months. Now the anxiety of January has passed the Church's elderly can get down to the task God still has for them – availability. Just being there.

The Church in her wisdom never writes off the old as purposeless. No one is ever that. However handicapped, however poorly, the elderly have their tasks and therefore a reason for living. They can make a gift of their prayers for the young too preoccupied to pray themselves. They can advise with the hindsight given them by a lifetime's experience. But above all else, they can listen. They can be attentive ears for those careering about in a hectic world that hasn't the ability to be still and know that He is there.

This power of the old – the very privilege of being old – has diminished as the value of the extended family has been ignored. Age has come to be seen as a disease rather than the family asset it is. The aged have slipped from their natural role as counsellors to the status of encumbrance. In the age of every convenience the family too often decides its elderly are inconvenient.

To exile grandparents is not only cruel insensitivity, it is foolishness. Worse, it is a crime. It is robbing children of the patient heart always ready to beat with theirs; it is thieving the elderly of the purpose which is their right – to serve God until death.

The home that evicts grandma forfeits its right to be a home. It becomes a house – a place of transience, lacking stability, rich in everything but what really matters – love.

CANDLEMAS DAY

T oday is the result of our debt to Mosaic Law. It recalls the Purification of Our Blessed Lady and the Presentation of Jesus in the Temple. This Law required mothers to make a sin-offering 40 days after giving birth. The same Law pronounced women unclean for seven days after the birth of a male child and excluded them from the sanctuary for 33 days after the birth.

Until comparatively recently the Catholic Church required that women be 'churched' after childbirth – a rite derived from the Mosaic Law. Political correctness – and some rather odd notions about this Blessing – has led to churching being abandoned by all except the more traditional.

Instead, today, we will bless candles and carry them in procession to signify Christ as the light to the Gentiles and in remembrance of His presentation in the Temple. Scotland takes a blander view of today – Candlemas is the time to pay rents.

The candle plays a vital part in liturgy and the life of the Catholic. It is obligatory at our baptism, just as it is essential at our departure. In between, it lights our altars and heads our processions.

The candle is the token we place before our statues so that when we leave the church a part of us remains behind to remind God that we called. Originally used practically by the Christians in the catacombs and later at pre-dawn Masses, the candle has come to symbolize enlightenment, its clear flame in the dark the purity of Christ's message.

For both Jew and Catholic the candle is indispensable. Perhaps an acknowledgment that however much we attempt to confuse the love of God the candle's flame draws us back to His ultimate simplicity and our utter ignorance of His nature.

3 February

ST BLAISE

The Church is nothing if not orderly. Everyone and everything has its place. And the same goes for the saints. Today most churches will hold the Blessing of the Throat through the intercession of St Blaise. He inherited this special devotion not just because he was a doctor but because he was able to save a boy who was choking on a fishbone.

Today, then, priests will lay crossed candles against the throats of those who present themselves with throat infections and invoke St Blaise to assist in their cure. As at Lourdes, they may not find apparent cure but their Faith will bring them comfort. So often the miracle we seek is not physical at all – rather it is the solace found in discovering God's will for us.

Catholics have specialist saints for most diseases of the body and for those of the mind too. St Dympna, for example, will intercede for the mentally sick whilst St Rita is at hand for women unhappily married. St George – he was after all a soldier – will assist those with genital diseases; Apollonia is at hand if you have toothache and James the Great has become associated with rheumatism.

I can understand sceptics who deride these customs. But, like all sceptics, they fail to look deeper than they should. If they did, they would realize that all suffering is a highly personal experience. Pain cannot be shared, however compassionate the carer. Yet somehow the agony and the fear must be revealed. It is at this stage that a saint is able to offer the comfort a grieving body requires. Good psychology or good theology – it matters little to the sufferer.

Neither should the value of the blessing involved be forgotten. A blessing going from priest to sufferer conveys both love and grace, implies understanding of need and imparts a brush of love with a concerned God.

4 February

St Gilbert of Sempringham

In many countries the Christian name will reveal the bearer's religion. In Ireland, say, you'll not meet a Catholic Norman nor a Protestant Thérèse. Nor, oddly, a Catholic Gilbert. Yet St Gilbert was a major cleric of the eleventh century, founding his own Order, the Gilbertines, and some 13 monasteries. Both Order and monasteries vanished with the Reformation.

Other things are vanishing – amongst them that peculiar shorthand by which we recognized fellow Catholics. Some marks of identification were obvious – fish on Fridays, smudged brows on Ash Wednesday, the Sign of the Cross when passing a church which was the home of the Blessed Sacrament. Others were less apparent – inclination of the head when the name Jesus was mentioned, the deference to a passing priest or nun.

Most Catholic homes still betray their owners' Faith. There will be a statue of Our Lady, the Sacred Heart badge above the door, perhaps a holy water font and almost certainly a little plastic Madonna from Lourdes which, when prompted, will rattle 'Ave Maria'.

Yet, above all our pettier pieties, it is the Crucifix that is always dominant. Mostly it is visible at our waking, honoured before our sleeping and there at our departure. It is the central focus of our private lives; subconsciously or consciously it hovers there throughout our working lives. In our churches it shares centrality with the living Christ in the tabernacle. It is seldom out of sight and only reluctantly out of mind.

Sadly it was a priest whom I once heard coin the phrase 'petty pieties'. The expression hurt me then as it does now. There can be no piety that is ever petty, just as there can be no God who is ever anything but understanding.

St Agatha

L ike most of those of my generation I had an Aunt Agatha. She would have been appalled to read of the torments inflicted upon her namesake. And I'll spare you the details too except to say she is the patron for diseases of the breast.

Yet the fact remains that all our saints were probably at some time or other someone's aunt or uncle. For saints are us, should we be given the grace or the opportunity to make sacrifices for God beyond the usual call on our devotion.

The doctrine on Purgatory owes much to the soul's obligation to be purged before appearing before God. The same doctrine implies that those who leave Purgatory for Heaven are in fact saints. So Aunties Maud, Agatha and Ada are now, please God, amongst the elect together with Uncles Tom, Sam and Joe. Haloes and harps may have been far from their minds in life but at some point after death they have surely become viable possibilities.

Sanctity somehow becomes easier to cope with when you appreciate that the old man selling papers on the corner, the lady busking from her barrow, will one day be saints – right there alongside the big guns of Christianity with exactly the same privileges of looking upon God.

The sufferings of saints were not unlike many of the sufferings our contemporaries are obliged to accept. The key to sanctity must therefore lie in the manner of such acceptance. We acknowledge the truth of this when we grieve someone's death with the words 'They surely had their Purgatory in this life'.

God, we are told and know by instinct, is just. It follows that the many for whom this life has been burdensome will find swift transit to Him when they die. Jesus promised as much – not once but often. And the promise culminated in the Sermon on the Mount.

6 February

SS PAUL MIKI AND COMPANIONS

S ome 50 years after St Francis Xavier took the Faith to Japan that country produced its first martyrs. It says much for Japanese tolerance that the interval was so long and was only prompted by the boasting of a Spanish seaman which incensed the ruler's sense of dignity. Paul Miki and his companions – they numbered 26 and included several Europeans – were the first to be martyred for their Faith in the Far East although hundreds were to follow them in the seventeenth century.

Despite our claim to be the universal Church, most Catholics are curiously parochial when it comes to recognizing martyrs. But then the Church as a whole is only really coming to terms with the reality that Jesus was not a good-looking Florentine noble but a tough country boy out of Galilee – not the place to look for either refinement or good manners.

Over the years to come European Catholics will have to come to terms with the realization that missionary activity no longer operates West to East. All indications are that if we are to have priests and nuns then we will have to hope that Africa and the Far East will supply them.

And when that happens, as it will, we will also find ourselves following Nkola I in the guise of Peter the Pope. We have to anticipate too that Nkola will have entirely different priorities from his predecessors. They will be pragmatic rather than esoteric. Nkola will look to see the starving fed, the land fairly distributed. He will be less concerned with cosmetic theology than he will be anxious to encourage social justice. When Nkola comes – as he must – he will teach Western Catholics much about racism for he will be black – just as Christ was Middle-Eastern.

Nkola I will transform the ethos of Catholicism. Overnight the lesson will be driven home at last that Christ did not die for white Anglo-Saxons but for humankind itself.

7 February

St Richard

O n this date, back in 1979, Archbishop Derek Worlock wrote to his people in Liverpool and gave the first intimation of the National Pastoral Congress he was to organize in 1980. He started by telling them what they knew:

> It is well known that many nominal Christians in England and Wales have stopped going regularly to Church. Yet, although they drift away from worship and Church membership, young and old alike are often fascinated by the person of Jesus Christ and His teaching. Many still read the Gospel; many still pray. Some say they are not rejecting Jesus Christ but only the Churches and other so-called Christians. Even in a generation superficially faithless, Christ has the power to move hearts and to draw people to Him. He offers them still a way to follow, a truth to hold on to and a life that is unending.

We didn't know it then, but the keywords of that Congress were there written – the Way, the Truth and the Life became the core of all that was discussed in Liverpool from 2 May to 5 May 1980.

For Derek Worlock the Congress was the expostulation of all he had gleaned from Vatican II. Attended by over 2000 people – many of them young, observers from many Faiths – it touched crescendo for Catholic Britain but was reduced to a whisper by the time it had been examined in Rome where it was largely ignored. Rome saw the resolutions in the same way as it saw liberation theology – as a threat rather than as a signpost.

Even so, the resolutions ignored, the National Pastoral Congress of 1980 would prove to be a blueprint for the Catholic Church. And it should not be forgotten that the architect was Derek Worlock, a bishop convinced that the quality of the Christian was infinitely more important than the Church's numerical strength. On that ruling you could say that the jury is still out.

8 February

———— ☙ ————

A round this time of the year is the first of the 'special' Sundays that crept into the liturgical calendar around the 1970s. Education Sunday has a twofold purpose – to raise awareness of Catholic education and to help pay for it. And it doesn't come cheaply. Schools probably represent every diocese's biggest bill and it has to be met by a falling Mass attendance. Paradoxically, those asked to foot the bill are largely elderly parishioners with no direct interest in their local school.

An unfair burden, you might think, when the parents benefiting are not at Mass yet appreciate Catholic education so much that they very often connive to ensure their children receive it.

What matters, though, is the quality of this education. And here you'll discover the most divisive debate Catholics conduct amongst themselves. For a start, few dioceses teach from the same syllabus. And each syllabus varies immensely in its Catholic content. In adjoining areas one group of children will, in effect, be taught comparative religion whilst the other will receive traditional instruction in the Catholic Faith. And there's the rub: a friction so abrasive it has been pitiful to watch.

In the last analysis, practising Catholic parents have a right to see their children leave school fully informed on the beliefs of their Faith. They anticipate that 12 years or so within a Catholic ethos will prepare their children to live their Faith. It has not been happening. Catholic children have emerged with scant Catholic knowledge, no greater than their apprehension of the beliefs of a variety of other Faiths.

Education Sunday – Catholicism's hot potato. Yet St Paul says in the reading for that day: '. . . the gospel will save you only if you keep believing exactly what I preached to you – believing anything else will not lead to anything.'

9 February

ST APOLLONIA

~

Today's saint is the dentists' patron. As my tooth – I do have others – is aching I'll leave it at that. But not without a little prayer to her for relief. The truth is, I need to say more about Catholic education.

First a truism – it begins in the home. A good Catholic home has visual reminders of the Faith; there are night prayers said together and perhaps a decade of the Rosary. Being a Catholic is not a part-time job – it's a perpetual awareness of Jesus' presence in the home.

At primary school a partnership should commence – between child, parents, teachers, parish priest and God. Leave out just one and the process starts to crumble. Our present difficulties stem from the absence of one or both of the parents from the equation. Even so, most primaries manage to send on children who have received two Sacraments, if not three, and are familiar with the love of Jesus.

At secondary school the object of RE should be to bolster this love with deeper knowledge of Jesus Christ. And this within the context and the teaching of the Catholic Church. The young adult should also be familiarized with the beliefs of other Faiths – to understand something is to respect it. Yet, all of this with the premise that the Catholic Church is One, Holy, Catholic and Apostolic. If this truth sounds arrogant then the teacher is at fault. But it remains the truth for those educated in a Catholic school.

Sadly, more and more secondary pupils, confused by a huge menu of Faiths, have gone on to college without religious conviction of any kind, let alone Catholic. With parents long lapsed, the parish connection broken after primary school, these young adults after 12 years of Catholic education are lost to the Church. But not, happily, lost to God, who will assuredly find them.

By the way, the toothache has gone. Think what you will. But in faith, please.

St Scholastica

The sister of St Benedict, Scholastica was the first Benedictine nun. A more recent Benedictine nun who was my friend met the most appalling calamities with a quiet smile, saying confidently, 'I'll have to have a word with the Boss.' Those close to her knew just which boss she meant – and it was not the Mother Superior. It was God.

There are times – Catholics recognize them instinctively – when a job is too big for any saint, too outrageous even for Our Blessed Lady. At such moments the plea is urgent, direct: 'God help me!'

I suspect formal prayer is less familiar to Catholics than it is to Jews or Moslems. There is the Rosary, but that can become something of a mantra; there is the Memorare, but that is directed to Our Lady. There is the Lord's Prayer, but that is more formal than urgency demands.

That leaves Catholics with what were called ejaculations. And in this style of prayer the Irish are particular experts. 'Jesus, Mary and Joseph' can express anything from astonishment to deep grief. But it is also a remedy for immediate aid. 'Lord Jesus, help me' is straightforward and unambiguous. 'Christ help me' is desperate, whilst 'God help me' can be panic-stricken or plainly despairing.

My Benedictine friend would insist that any prayer, in any form, that was a message straight from the heart, would in all surety be heard by the Boss. We have His own word for this – not just once, but many times. Yet His promise requires something from us – our faith in He who made the promise. Faith and familiarity are the underlying strengths of Catholicism: faith that He is listening, familiarity with His telephone number.

The Catechism had it right – 'the raising up of the heart and mind to God'. Your heart, your mind, your words, your prayer, anytime, anywhere. The Boss is listening.

11 February

OUR LADY OF LOURDES

Today those who will later in the year travel to Lourdes start their pilgrimage with a Mass to commemorate Our Lady of Lourdes. Lucky you, if you've never been to that French town. It means that you've never been desperate for hope; never sought to explore the periphery of Faith; never urgently needed reassurance.

There's the argument – and it's valid – that we don't need to trek hundreds of miles to encounter Our Lady. But that undervalues the worth of pilgrimage, and denigrates the purpose of penance.

So why the journey when Our Lady is only a prayer away? Why Lourdes, where there is so much tatty commercialism? Because it is there where it happened, where the promise was made and the invitation issued.

But sophisticated folk like us don't venture to Lourdes for physical miracles, do we? We don't go knowing that tumours will melt away, backs mend, kidneys function once again. Not us, it's fashionable nowadays to go for ease of mind, to calm trepidation. Miracles? They're for others, perhaps – not for us.

But isn't that as wrong, this tepidity of faith, as it would be to blame God for witholding a cure? The journey to Lourdes must always be made in anticipation of the impossible. Then, if no cure is there, then we know for sure God's plan for us and, strengthened, we follow it.

Many good pilgrims – of all faiths or none – journey to Lourdes in perfect health simply because it is where we know Our Lady appeared. An equal number go to help others along the journey. And there are erstwhile Thomasses who want to see how the inspiration found there is created.

One thing is sure about this pilgrimage – it is purposeful. It is never without a miracle for all who go. It's a place to be solitary amongst the multitude or gregarious within a small group. Today at Mass we'll tell Our Lady we're on our way, we'll anticipate the joy of meeting with her.

12 February

ST ETHILWALD

T his monk and eighth-century Bishop of Lindisfarne would
not have been plagued about this time of year with the mass
of statistics which appear showing the numerical strength or
weakness of the Church. He would be spared too the pontificating
that follows on the causes of lapsation.

The truth is that Catholics don't lapse over big reasons but for
little ones. I came pretty close to lapsing when I was seven. In those
days the queues for confession were long and wearisome, particularly for a small child. I had just reached the head of mine when an
adult brushed past me, stealing my turn. Sixty-plus years on and I
can still recall my hurt, indignation, anger and sense of injustice at
what happened in God's own home. At seven my Faith was in the
balance just as positively as it would be later when I encountered
cruel death.

Catholics don't renounce their Mass for the perceived gross injus-
tices of God or His Church. Their departure – silent, almost furtive
– is usually the actual thoughtlessness of their fellows.

Speak with the lapsed and you'll seldom find denial of great
creeds, of God's existence, the Pope's infallibility. But you will trace
down a cruel brush with hypocrisy, a boorish priest, an encounter
with a lack of human charity.

Poor God. So often we serve Him badly in the one single order
He gave us – to love one another. Christian love is little different
from espoused love. It requires patience, understanding, generosity
and compassion.

Some say that 'compassion' was a Vatican II buzz word that has
been done to death. Even the charities talk of being affected by
'compassion fatigue'. Compassion burns at the very core of
Christianity. The only hope of all those who have lapsed is that they
will be warmed by God's compassion as reflected by those of us still
practising.

D epression is often called a black dog – an insult to a cheerful Labrador of fond memory. But a black dog trotted by my side as I drove to witness a Solemn Profession at the Welsh convent of the Poor Clares of Ty Mam Duw. In a corner of the small chapel I found a place for myself and the dog who refused to be left outside.

We were early. There was time to admire fresh pine, polished to perfection, the delicate wrought iron lattice enclosing the Sisters and keeping us out. My bottom numbed, as bottoms will; the dog growled. That oasis of peace was no place for the likes of us who knew that outside only disaster loomed. And no bones at all. I asked black dog what we were doing there. He just grunted, laid heavily on my shoulder. We both knew we'd be better off in the world, trying to cope with our anxieties.

Then a bell rang. There was the softest of swishes as brown habited Sisters took their places, unseen by us. But we could sense their beaming, fresh-scrubbed faces as their song became a roar.

A Sister read simply from the Song of Songs: 'I adjure you, if you find my beloved, tell him I am faint with love.' Black dog and I knew this was no idle quest. She meant it. We cowered.

Dear Mother queried the candidate: 'You have put your hand to the plough and from this day forward there can be no looking back. Foxes have holes and the birds of the air their nests but the Son of Man, your Spouse, had nowhere to lay His head. Are you prepared to follow Him completely until the end?'

Sister Cherubina Clare of Holy Mary, face beaming, said boldly: 'I am, with the grace of God.'

Black dog slept. My heart throbbed. Unbidden, my eyes watered. I told myself this was no place for clandestine encounter with emotional confusion. I held back the tears until, later, I pulled into a wooded lane. Nothing, of course, had changed. Dogs cannot change colour, nor people avert disaster. Yet how good it had been to find joyous certainty in a little Welsh convent.

SS CYRIL AND METHODIUS

T hree unlikely saints share this Feast day. Cyril the monk and Methodius the bishop, both of them selected as patrons for Europe. And then Valentine – doctor of medicine, martyr and the patron of lovers. Sadly you'll not find Valentine mentioned in your liturgical calendar. In 1969 he was downgraded, debased perhaps because of his association with frivolous romance. Such a pity. Whilst not denying that Europe can do with all the saintly intercession it can get I think that lovers deserve the same consideration.

Brothers, Cyril and Methodius were highfliers in their day which was about the middle of the ninth century. Cyril produced the Cyrillic alphabet, whilst his brother was one of the early enthusiasts for a vernacular liturgy.

Poor deposed Valentine gained his reputation because his Feast fell on the day, 14 February, when tradition had it the birds of the air chose to mate. Another theft, if you put it that way, from pagan days. But then the early Christians were smart enough to link liturgy loosely with the old heathen rites. They understood the value of inculturization even as more recent Christians forget it.

Fortunately Christmas fell historically at the right time – in the midst of winter when folk's hearts needed something cheering. With Christmas fixed it was not difficult to place Easter and its hope of new life in the spring. And the Church would make much of the harvest festival because that was the time the pagans celebrated nature's bounty.

Nature was God's clock long before Judaism or the arrival of Jesus. St Paul pointed out that what pagans had celebrated by instinct they could now celebrate by reason. Hence my regret that Valentine, successor of so many gods of love, should be cast aside. With him went countless millennia of human race memory.

R onnie Knox, doyen of Catholic apologists, defined a paradox as 'a statement of the obvious so as to make it sound
untrue.' He could well have had in mind the impossible and
glorious list we have come to call the Beatitudes. They conclude –
using Knox's own translation – 'Then Jesus, the Advocate, the Judge
we must in turn face, ends: "Judge nobody, and you will not be
judged; condemn nobody, and you will not be condemned; forgive,
and you will be forgiven . . . the measure you award to others is the
measure that will be awarded to you."'

These are the golden rules – gold because they are both rare and
of inestimable value. At His seemingly simplest, Jesus is at His most
paradoxical in the Beatitudes. You can almost see the bemused faces
of the peasant farmers as He tells them: 'Blessed are you who are
poor; the Kingdom of God is yours.' You can see the wrinkles form
as He goes on: 'Blessed are you who are hungry now; you will have
your fill.'

'It's always pie tomorrow', some must have muttered as they
slipped away to face the reality of finding cash to pay the Roman
taxes. And through the centuries there are those who have seen the
Beatitudes as contemptuous sops to the downtrodden poor.

Hopefully we will know better. We will sense the twinkle in
Jesus' eyes as He heaps paradox upon paradox until finally the message sinks home – our position in this life is of relatively little
importance. What matters is the life to come and whether, by our
actions, we have deserved the riches promised.

Jesus was not the one to leave His listeners baffled. Having whet-
ted the curiosity, He is direct enough: 'Now I say to you who are listening to me, love your enemies, do good to those who hate you,
and pray for those who treat you insultingly.'

I once heard a priest smilingly reassure his people that the
Beatitudes were glorious hyperbole. That's not a risk I'd take.

SS JULIANA AND BENEDICT JOSEPH LABRE

This St Benedict – pardon the expression – was a bum. He tried his hand at being a monk but no community wanted him, so he took to the road. The world saw him as a vagrant. He knew he was a pilgrim.

His life was curiously similar to a man of our own times – John Bradburne, a Third Order Franciscan whom the Poor Clares are supporting for canonization.

Born in England in 1921, John served with the Gurkhas in Malaya and Burma during the Second World War. Mystic, poet, a man with a huge ability to make friends, he tried his vocation after the war with both the Benedictines and then the Carthusians. But like St Benedict Labre his eccentricity made him unable to conform to community life.

He turned pilgrim travelling mostly on foot through England, Europe and finally the Holy Land. Deciding he would be happy as a hermit he went to 'seek a cave' in Zimbabwe. Instead he stumbled upon a settlement for lepers at Mutemwa. For the next 17 years he lived with and cared for his 80 leprosy patients.

He was found shot dead in a ditch during one of the many incidents that happened from time to time in Zimbabwe. During his funeral a pool of blood gathered beneath his coffin. Curious, his mourners opened his coffin. But there was no sign of bleeding. It was seen, though, that John was not dressed in the Franciscan habit as he had wished. The habit was found and John was buried in it.

It is all too easy to read glibly of the hermits, vagabonds and eccentrics who found canonization centuries before and to forget that our own age and the ages to come will continue to produce holy men and women of every kind. Sanctity is not unique to an age or a tradition – it is pursued forever by the most unlikely amongst us.

17 February

SEVEN HOLY FOUNDERS OF
THE SERVITE ORDER

Servites find God in people. I remembered that when I bumped into God at Tesco. I'm always glad when this happens; the surprise is akin to finding a rose in a gravel pit. He had been inspecting the fish and before I could ask him whether it was as fresh as Peter's had been he looked at me and smiled. You could say, if you must, that he wasn't God at all – just an old man like myself, wearied by a thousand worries. But then, you didn't see his eyes. I did. And God was in them.

Having found Him once that morning I went on to search Him out. For a moment I thought I'd spotted him in WH Smith but when I saw the eyes I knew I'd been deluded by a gentle voice. Most children, naturally enough, reflect His presence. But that's cheating – there has to be a rose in a rose garden.

It's a dangerous game, this searching for God. Forget the rules and you end up a pantheist believing nature is the only reality – that God *is* the wind or the breaking waves or the shimmering trees. The trick is to be aware that they, like us, are no more than His creation.

It does begin to worry me when, in the course of this hunt for God, there are increasingly more moments when I find Him more readily on the mountaintop than in the pew. Times when the oaken benches are barricades – stubborn, solid, unyielding. Then I recall the cash-hungry priest who confided to me that what really mattered were bums on pews.

Chesterton pointed out that the safest place to hide a body was on a battlefield. Sometimes I worry that we haven't made the same conclusion – that the easiest place to hide God is in His church.

Thank God, then, for the little red lamp before the sanctuary that indicates He is always at home in the tabernacle.

18 February

FRA ANGELICO

P ope John Paul II, looking at Fra Angelico's paintings in the Vatican, remarked: 'Why do we need miracles? These are his miracles.' Nevertheless the Dominican priest and artist provided the other miracles required for his canonization which took place in 1982, 527 years after his death.

The timespan indicates how tough it is to make it to the top as a saint of the Catholic Church. Admittedly, if you founded an Order or even belonged to one, your ascent will be speeded considerably. Not only do Orders have the time and the skills required to promote causes, they have the money too. Sanctity does not come cheaply.

There are several stages on the road to canonization. First, the cause has to be introduced. More simply, a great deal of first-rate public relations has to be created to make the potential saint's name known to those who matter within the Congregation of Rites. There follows a great deal of correspondence between Rome and the diocese concerned. Then hopefully the process of beatification can begin. A postulator is named to defend the cause, together with a batch of lawyers and procurators. There is then a tribunal and the numbers involved rapidly rise to include theologians, consultors, prelate officials, cardinals and, of course, the official best known to the public – the Promoter General of the Faith, better known as the 'Devil's Advocate'.

Add to this sea of bureaucracy the proven demonstration of two miracles and you begin to understand why it is that even Mother Teresa may have some little time to wait.

It's truly said that the Catholic Church thinks not in years but in centuries. How delightful, then, to think that one second after her death Mother Teresa was handed her halo by a beaming St Peter.

19 February

They called it Merry England, although there are the spoilers today who would insist it wasn't. I prefer to think there was a joyous England once and it was created around the parish and the multitude of saints' days which gave everyone a frequent holiday – or holy day.

At the hub of all life was the church – a place to be merry in, be it a christening, a wedding or a festival. In death too you were within the shadow of its walls – safe, snug, never to be forgotten.

The parish was a close community, inclusive of all human nature. Eccentricities were tolerated, vices understood, virtues recognized, evil swiftly detected. Priest or lord of the manor offered arbitration, and dispensed care or compassion as required.

Idyllic it probably wasn't but then neither was Eden in the end. Husbands and wives had grown together from childhood so did not come to marriage as strangers. Perhaps ambition was curtailed when every one had their station. But even that was not immutable and could be bettered with the passing of each generation.

It was the time of the Old Religion. The awe of the people centred on God; the joy of the people expressed itself in the frequent celebrations of Our Lady. The villainy of the masters far from the village seldom intruded, an uncaring lord would in course of time be succeeded by a better.

This, then, was what we exchanged for the factories and the mills, for the endless terraces of mean houses blind to neighbours. It was – that 'Merry England' – a Catholic England. It demonstrated for a little while what can be achieved when folk live in harmony of Faith, in a genuine belief that at the centre of all things there stands Jesus. And, by His side, His mother.

It is the task of every parish to recapture that old sense of community.

St Wulfric of Haselbury

A nimal rights supporters will be pleased that Wulfric, a keen hunter over the Somerset hills, gave it all up when he chose to become a hermit. It is certain that he would have left the field even sooner if the eleventh century had boasted a Catholic Animal Welfare Society as it does today.

Catholics are great joiners. There are well over 150 societies for them to join nationally and probably more at diocesan level. Many of these are religious or charitable as you might expect. The surprise comes when you spot the large number of professional Catholic societies that not only exist but thrive.

The reason is historical, harking back to our ghetto days: the need doctors, nurses and lawyers, for example, had to meet and discuss the new moralities society was forcing upon them. Then Vatican II threw up other groups determined to preserve what they could of the old Church and its liturgies.

More latterly, organizations have sprung up to assist the casualties of the growing divorce rate (Catholics divorce with exactly the same frequency as non-Catholics), the trickle of priests leaving the priesthood to marry and the problem endemic to every parish – the unmarried mother.

Music draws Catholics together. So does history. So does the need to find a Catholic partner. And, paradoxically, there are societies for those in mixed marriages providing a chance for them to share mutual difficulties.

Sometimes I sit in my pew and look around me at the immense variety of folk God draws to Himself each Sunday. I'm astonished – and joyful – that before Him we all find the same miraculous unity of belief.

St Peter Damian

T his Damian was no leper but a polished eleventh-century cardinal diplomat; he is a reminder that there is not one Catholic
Church but two – the spiritual Church and the official
Church. They each need each other yet often enough down the years
they have been in contention. So much so that Pope Adrian VI commented: 'We all, prelates and clergy, have gone astray from the right
way and for long there is none that has done good. No, not one.'

As a diplomat, Damian was paving the way for a long line of successors. Men of suave understanding, but above all, men of considerable power. Trainees are selected soon after ordination, usually
recommended by their bishops. Their instruction in the Vatican is
lengthy, painstaking. At the end of it they will be posted abroad as
assistants to a nuncio, a papal legate assigned to a major state to represent the interests of the Holy See.

They are more than mere ambassadors even though they share
the same privileges. Their duty is both diplomatic and spiritual; their
interest is not just in the secular affairs of the state but in the spiritual life of the Catholics there.

Some bishops in the host state will see the nuncio as a Curia spy,
others will use him as a conduit for access to Vatican government.
His task is to be impartial: let the local church get on with its business but report back to Rome just what is happening. Ordinary
Catholics will only be aware of his presence when high-ranking
bishops are to be appointed, for it is the nuncio who forwards to
Rome the final list of three names suitable for the vacancy. And,
with the list, no doubt his own suggestion.

Fortunately we pew Catholics see little of the Church's official
face. All too often, when we have to, we end just a little scandalized
and tainted by the encounter. This is nothing new, it was thus down
the centuries until the whole business blew up in the conflagration
that's termed the Reformation. Today there's still reformation within
the Church. But gentler. And love, not power, is the springboard.

22 February

———— ❧ ————

When we pray for the unemployed, I wish Paul Potts's vehemence could be read among the bidding prayers. The verse impressed me in 1948. And nothing has changed. God knows where Paul is now but this is what he wrote:

> I'm like spittle from the mouth of truth
> I am a nuisance, sure I irritate;
> I make you feel ashamed
> I bring gooseflesh to your face
> I overwhelm, I tire you out, I make you hesitate
> If you are one to take advantage or make a dime
> From Joe's stupidity or Mary's crime.
> But listen people anywhere punching time;
> If you're walking to the moon
> I've got clean sox for you.
>> 'Poetry gets a haircut' from *Instead of a Sonnet*

The Church does its job best when it tells it like it is; when it is an irritant; when it makes even politicians feel ashamed – no light task.

In my own lifetime the Church, to her credit, has done just this – through worker-priests in France, through brave clergy in South America and South Africa, through our own priests here in Britain who have joined the unemployed on their marches.

There is no frustration so great as that of powerlessness. It is what finally decays the long-term unemployed, it is what stifles their families' efforts to struggle out of the mud that holds them down.

The last 50 years haven't been easy for the Church – trying to find the balance between what is Caesar's and what is God's. But, succeed or fail, she tried. And for that, many thanks.

23 February

ST POLYCARP

Funny how we build up pictures in our imagination only to have them destroyed by fact. Polycarp was not the sweet damosel saint of my mind's eye but was in fact a student of St John who put the Gnostics in their place. But not for long.

Throughout the Church's history there have been – and are – Gnostics. Almost every heresy betrays a trace of them. They are the ones who cannot accept that Christ founded the Church to be His decisive teaching authority.

Cardinal Basil Hume had contemporary Gnosticism in mind when he pointed out that as a Catholic you cannot pick or choose what to believe – it is a menu you accept in its entirety or not at all.

Beneath the compassionate role the Church has found herself in recent years, there is a strip of steel, a discipline, Catholics attempt to warp at their peril. Even St Augustine was aware of this yoke, anguishing in his *Confessions*: 'Therefore did You break my bones with the rod of Your discipline.'

Latter-day Gnostics plead that discipline must be tempered with mercy – just as if God, who drew up the rules in the first place, had not ensured there was a place within them for mercy. They say that contemporary society means that age-old moralities must be exchanged for contemporary customs.

Catholics tend not to be confused by the clamour of varying dissident voices. They lend an ear here, a sympathy there. Above all, they are aware of their own imperfection when attempting to follow a Faith that counsels perfection. But in the end they know they are lucky. In the end they have only one course open to them – their clear duty is to follow Peter. They will do so as perfectly or as imperfectly as they are able. But they'll do it with some relief that there is, after all, only one road.

24 February

Shrove Tuesday*
St Matthias the Apostle

T he last day of Shrovetide, the last opportunity to be shriven before Lent begins tomorrow. Feast or confess – the choice is up to you. The reality is that pancakes will come to mind more swiftly than repentance.

Despite being graced with five names, reconciliation is the Sacrament most endangered at the start of a new millennium. Call it the Sacrament of conversion, or penance, or forgiveness, or reconciliation or just plain confession and the end result will be the same – we are not receiving it the way we once did.

The Saturday night queues, once so much a feature of Catholic life, will be found more readily at the supermarket than in the church. So what happened? How did we come to ignore Christ's very own promise to His apostles – 'Whatever you bind on earth shall be bound in heaven, and whatever you loose on earth shall be loosed in heaven.' No room for doubt there. And the One giving the promise is God.

The glaring cause for the lack of queues – as it was for the flurry of lapsation in the 1960s – is Humanae Vitae, the encyclical that forbade artificial contraception. Some who found the edict intolerable left. Others came to a deal with their consciences and shopped around for a priest – and there were many – who would grant absolution. The resulting compromise was not just uncomfortable – it was unCatholic.

Next there came the exodus of the priests themselves. Penitents were reluctant to open their hearts before men who themselves might well be doing something else tomorrow. Add to this the growing custom of giving general absolution at christenings and marriages and the trek away from the dark confines of the 'little box' was just about complete.

Yet the numbers receiving Holy Communion have vastly increased. Now there's a paradox for the Church to get to grips with.

* If this movable feast does not fall today then see note on p. xiii.

25 February

ASH WEDNESDAY★
ST ETHELBERT OF KENT

―――――――∽―――――――

The ashes we receive today are perhaps the last remnants of good old Catholic triumphalism. After all, we've lost most of our neatly externalized signs of piety. To disdain meat on Friday is to be numbered amongst the socially correct; to remain mute and sitting at a Protestant friend's wedding is not to be encouraged; a Catholic's divorce is just a sadness anyone can share with us.

When Pope John Paul II was still laying down the baselines of his philosophy back in the 1970s he pointed out – proving what an accurate prophet he was to be – that there was a more dangerous crime than sin. It was the murder of a person's sense of sin. Today that is the most widespread of all homicides.

Perhaps after all we should not undervalue what external marks of Faith we still have. A touch of ash is no poor thing if, for an instant, it revives in the supermarket queue a flicker of devotion now lost. Similarly, a touch of pride in a banner or in history can't hurt if it resources a little courage at the right moment.

Whether these aids are flags or ashes doesn't matter a jot providing they produce enthusiasm rather than boredom. The most significant emblem we still have, after all, is the Cross.

Today's ashes were once a peculiar mark of distinction for only the most renowned of public penitents. Then, it seems, their friends felt sorry for their singular penance. They donned ashes too and stood alongside them so that the penitent would not be so obvious. A touching case of liturgy being inspired by a display of humility and affection. But then, as we found after Vatican II, liturgy is not ingrained in granite – it is an expression of the People of God.

★ If this movable feast does not fall today then see note on p. xiii.

26 February

My friend Martin leapt into Lent with all the enthusiasm of a masochist at the Inquisition Ball. I would dread the question I knew was coming: 'And what are you doing for Lent?' It was no good hedging. No point in implying horrendous rigours, breathtaking denials. Martin wanted facts, not surmises. That I knew full well he would complete Lent two stone lighter, heavily jaundiced about the eyes and narrow-cheeked didn't encourage me.

I often wondered how he could find anything further to do by way of penance. He was a daily communicant; each and every night found him cycling the terraced streets of Birmingham visiting on behalf of the SVP; he ran the Boy Scouts and served at every morning Mass. But each Lent he found a novel way of mortifying the little flesh he had left.

My half-hearted murmur to the effect that I'd thought of giving up whisky (the mental reservation being that I'd drink beer instead) or cigarettes (my pipe was cheaper) didn't dim that piercing eye one iota. Loath to injure his faith in me even further I'd say with certitude that I intended to read the right books. A crafty move this, for I knew his passion for theology.

But any hope I had of getting away with reading Morris West evaporated when he'd produce a pocket copy of Augustine's *Confessions* or *The Imitation of Christ*. With Martin there was no escape, no easy way of passing the next 40 days in any style of mental comfort.

Martin was the last of a dying breed – the ascetic layperson. The old Catholicism was littered with the like of Martin; the new Catholicism is very much more gregarious. The same Lenten sacrifices are still made but in company with others rather than trudging the solitary road of the spiritual vagabond. One thing though is certain – if Martin is not now amongst the elect, the rest of us can give up.

27 February

ST GABRIEL POSSENTI

A n unusual saint to kick off Lent, St Gabriel Possenti had a nickname before coming to Christ via the Passionists. He was called 'Il Damerino', the ladies' man. As a monk he still enjoyed laughter. But not for long – he died of tuberculosis in 1862 at the age of 24. Canonization followed in 1920 when he was named Patron of Youth.

So perhaps it's not so unusual to place him at this point in Lent. For Lent has become as never before a special time for young people. Nowadays they pull out the stops and do what the young do so well – they raise money. They'll run and skip, fast and save – this in startling contrast to the days of my own youth when our penances now seem so self-centred, selfish even.

Yet (and isn't there always a 'yet' in human conduct?) fun and games, competitiveness in fundraising, the gimmicks involved, don't all these lose something of the true essence of Lent? It was never intended to be one long Red Nose Day. It was, is, a remembrance of 40 isolated days in which we come face to face with ourselves, with the idea of our own mortality.

Christ didn't go into the desert to prove how tough He was – the hardship was only incidental. He went there to sort out His purpose, to reach the rock we all have to find for ourselves.

Lent, if you so choose, can be a flavour of monasticism, a hint of asceticism. But always a period of thought. A time to heal old wounds, resolve pointless quarrels. All part of a process of lightening the load so many carry unnecessarily.

Let's face it – sometimes the only stranger in our lives is ourself. Like Dorian Gray we have a picture in the attic that we seldom dare look upon. Lent is the time to trundle up there and see how great a contrast there is between what we should be and what we have become. And such is the mercy of God that we are given the chance to add the odd brushstroke or two.

28 February

ST OSWALD OF WORCESTER

The cruellest admission parents can make to a child is that they love him but don't like him. God, I reckon, must be in a similar position many times with us. Without undue humility most of us would admit that by God's standards we are far from pleasing. The purpose of Lent is to change this.

It's the time to shake hands with yourself, examining the eyes carefully, weighing it all up – is this the sort of person you'd want to meet? There's nothing introvert in taking 40 days off to discover if you like yourself. Christ put it succinctly – why look for a splinter in the other man's eye when you've a log in your own?

It's as desirable for parents to like their child as to love it. After all, loving is a natural function. Not loving is unnatural. But liking – that doesn't come naturally. Liking arrives after long experience. It's a personal decision not foisted on us by nature. It depends upon a variety of observations made in many circumstances.

It's as well, then, that Jesus only asked us to love one another. Even that can be difficult. But think how much harder it would have been had He insisted upon us liking everyone. That's part of God's wisdom – He never asks us to do more than we are able.

Think how shattering an encounter it would be if, at Heaven's Gate, we encountered love without liking, pity without compassion, understanding without sympathy. Truth is, we'd realize immediately we stood in Purgatory; we'd know at once how much leeway we had to make before crossing the Gates.

Forty days, then, to see if you can bring yourself to like the face in the mirror. Not too long, nor too short. As it was for Christ, so for you – if you really mean to do it.

A leap year offers us the rare chance to enjoy a day that really does not exist. It is, in a sense, the gift of time itself, a sort of absolution for enduring all those days for which we must give account. So, here it is, this weird anomaly dangled before us to use as we will.

It's a day bereft of saints to honour, demanding no obligation on our part, asking only that we etch our personality on its hours and minutes. It's almost a responsibility except that it implies liberality rather than duty – which would explain why the strange custom freeing women to propose to men originated.

This sense of freedom applies more to Catholics than to others. For they operate under a discipline, the Daily Missal, which regulates their days with benevolent paternalism.

Perhaps today is the occasion to think about time. And time, as theologian and scientist for once agree, is a man-made convenience. An old Catholic legend tells the tale of a father who died shortly before dawn. His son begged the priest to celebrate Mass for the repose of his father's soul. And this the priest did, even as the sun rose. Well satisfied, after the Mass, the son dozed after the sleepless night. But in his dream his father – gaunt, agonised – appeared to him. 'Son,' he pleaded, 'why did you take so long to pray for my release from this place?'

Our Lord hinted so many times that we could have no conception of either eternity or the place we will spend it. He warned us that there were many aspects of His Kingdom that would be beyond our conception.

We live in an age when every query must have an answer. If it's not instantly available then scientists promise us it will be in the future. But today, living as it were on borrowed time, we should find it easier coming to terms with the mysteries Jesus touched upon but did not expound knowing how finite our grasp will always be on the things that really matter.

1 March

ST DAVID

⟶

'Having exhausted all these ways of tempting Him, the Devil left Him.' The scene in today's Gospel appeals to us – beaten, no doubt morose, a poor loser, the Devil slinks away. But, the writer reminds us, only for the time being. Dafydd of Wales – from which we get Taffy – had no doubts when it came to the reality of the Evil One.

A Welsh priest reminded me of this once as my hand stretched for the holy water font as I left his church. 'You only take the water going in,' he rebuked me, 'when you might have the Devil on your shoulder. It's to be hoped you haven't met him in here.'

I've always been grateful for his advice. It means one less obstacle in the Catholic rush from church which is by no means simple. There's the genuflection. So few do it nowadays – just a nod in the direction of the altar. You stand a real risk of injury if you attempt it against the tide. Then that little table at the door, crammed with goodies. Cards for every Catholic occasion from birth to death, plastic saints, the struggling Catholic press – put together with such determined integrity, only largely to be ignored.

Then there's sure to be someone with a plate. In a flash you have to dig for silver to assist a priest in China, a child in Rwanda or the single mum down the street. And, if it's that sort of parish, there's the priest's hand to shake. Dangerous stuff, believe me, leaving a Catholic church – we evacuate as if the Devil himself was on our tails.

Which brings us back to the holy water. And by the time several hundred grubby fingers have probed the font it's as well it's holy. But the water is as essential to the Catholic regimen as candles. Like candles, it illuminates in us a sense of the simplicity of God's care. Light and water, like faith, the mix that's peculiarly Catholic.

2 March

ST CHAD

That bit of me not Scouse is Brummie. And at the heart of Birmingham – now isolated on its own island – stands St Chad's Cathedral. Four large bones of the Midlands' saint are beneath the altar. An awesome thought when you look at the fantasy of modernity that surrounds the cathedral on all sides.

There's a marked difference in the style of Catholicism in our major English cities – Liverpool, Manchester and Birmingham; a difference that depends upon when the Irish came and how they were received. They poured into Liverpool and Manchester in the nineteenth century – impoverished, bewildered, mostly countryfolk for whom the cities provided a cultural shock. The priests and the churches they built so rapidly were their only point of familiarity. They did what the poor have always done – they bred, they laboured, they gravitated to the jobs the natives spurned. They accepted the only authority they trusted – the Church.

The result in Liverpool for many years was a city riven by sectarianism. In Manchester, Catholics achieved a Mafia-style dominance. In Birmingham, though, it was altogether different. There the Irish did not arrive in significant numbers until 1939 when they were rapidly recruited for the factories producing arms. Then, after the war, the city needed redevelopment. The Irish who made their way there at that time were entirely a new breed – professionals, people with skills to offer to a market greedy for them. In truth, in Birmingham, the Irish never had it so good.

The Church in these cities reflects all of this. North-west Catholicism still has much of its early tribalism. But Catholics in Birmingham live a gentler Faith for it is something that has never set them apart, nor endangered their livelihood. It's almost as if Liverpool and Birmingham were Catholic lungs but set 100 miles apart. The difference says much for martyrdom, real or imagined, but little for the universality of a Church that cannot comfortably bridge so short a ride down the motorway.

3 March

ST CUNEGUND AND ST NON

At Belmont Abbey – a mile or two from Hereford – there's a chapel dedicated to St Benedict. More than once I've travelled many miles just to absorb its silence. For silent it is – three walls of great stone and one, looking out to the altar, of glass. Close the door and you are as close to hermitage as many of us are likely to come.

I discovered the chapel as a boy. It was there I took a boy's many anxieties. There I prayed urgently, sometimes desperately, for my parents back in the Blitz, for success in the exams I knew I couldn't pass, for a place in the first XV, for . . . the list was endless. As eternal as youth seemed to be then.

Over the years that followed – perhaps four or five times, no more – I recalled St Benedict's Chapel and scurried there convinced that just one hour would be enough to quell whatever turmoil was current.

On the chapel's altar stands a statue of Benedict. He carries his book of Rules, and has one finger to his lips. Silence, he demands, and the words rush to mind – be still and know that I am here.

Everyone, at some time or other, needs such a place. It may not be as obvious as a chapel, or as grand as a cathedral. It can be in a wood, atop a mountain, by the seashore. But it is somewhere – a haven for bruised souls.

For all its often boisterous liturgy the Church has always understood this need to be solitary, calm, open to God. Hermits, visionaries, anchorites abound, even today. Too often it seems to be the privilege of the Religious, although they pay generously for it. But it is open to all of us to open our ears to silence, to speak not with the tongue but with the heart. So often, as described in Francis Thompson's poem 'The Hound of Heaven', we flee God when all we have to do is be still and wait for Him.

4 March

St Adrian of May, St Casimir

W here does poor Moggie go when the last tin of Whiskas has been downed? Whilst theologians have winced at the notion of pets in Heaven there's a determined phalanx, from St Francis onwards, who claim there would be no Paradise without their devotion. Pope wrote:

> He asks no angel's wings, no seraph's fire,
> But thinks, admitted to that equal sky,
> His faithful dog shall bear him company.
> 'An Essay on Man'

The sad fact is that animals tend to fare badly in Catholic countries. Donkeys suffer in Ireland, bulls in Spain. Only the frigid English, it seems, defend the beast's right to share in the hereafter.

So notable a Doctor of the Church as Thomas Aquinas gave the matter more than passing interest. And, in reality, even he seemed unable to come to a positive decision. He made several admissions: animals have souls because they can recognize, desire and understand objects placed before them. He also admitted that not only do animals have the ability to memorize, but they have the imagination to call their memories to mind. But in the last analysis Aquinas opines that, whilst animals can be wise, caring even, they possess no free will and therefore cannot enjoy the fruits of free will – Heaven.

St Ciaran of Saighir

For the life of me, I cannot think why we never credit Jesus with a sense of humour. He was a Jew – a race endowed with sardonic wit, with an appreciation of a good chuckle. Without full knowledge of the Jewish love of irony Jesus would never have pierced the armour of a Jewish audience. Our armour is similar. Sunday after Sunday we sit solemnly through passages intended by Jesus to make us laugh first and think afterwards.

Imagine you are sitting on a low wall in the village square in Cana. It's pleasantly warm, the locals are in the café sipping, Jesus stands by the well in the centre of the square. There's a hush, He starts to speak. You listen.

'One day,' He starts, 'a Pharisee and a tax collector went into the temple to pray.'

A titter runs through His audience. A ripple of smiles as they steal glances at the Pharisee leaning against a tree. And some look at the tax collector chewing on bread and olives. Jesus follows their gaze and smiles.

'The Pharisee stood there and said this prayer,' Jesus goes on. 'I thank you, God, that I'm not like this tax collector.'

As He says this, Jesus mimics slightly the thin voice of the Pharisee and draws Himself up to His full height. There's another murmur of soft chuckles as folk look at each other and wink knowingly. And when Jesus gets to the bit about the collector lowering his eyes and praying, 'Be merciful to me, a sinner', the crowd bursts out laughing. But Jesus, smiling too, raises his arms for silence and the punchline: 'The man who exalts himself will be humbled, the man who humbles himself will be exalted.'

You join the discreet clapping. It can be no more. For the Pharisee is still the Pharisee and the collector will be knocking on your door this afternoon. But you hurry home to tell your wife: 'This Jesus tells a good yarn.'

6 March

WOMEN'S DAY OF PRAYER

〜

A prayer before I start today: dear Lord, don't let me be patronizing. There is Man and there is Woman. Together they are Mankind. If that's chauvinism, I'm one of those who recognize the superiority of women, their ability to put together a world we men so often destroy, their vastly superior contribution to the Catholic Church today and in the past. Don't, dear Lord, let me offend what I still see as the Gentler Sex.

Women move busily today between the churches to pray together, sing together, talk together. A theme will have been chosen to be followed nationwide. And they will follow it conscientiously, prayerfully, even humbly – because it was a man, not a woman, who coined the phrase 'the hand that rocks the cradle rules the world'.

Catholic men, particularly, know this. They have grown up with the knowledge that it is a woman who kisses the hurt better, a woman who rules the home, a woman who ensures they get to Mass, a woman who organizes the life of the parish, a woman who, ultimately, will hold the man's heart in her hands.

A Catholic congregation is predominantly female. Even at the altar now it is probably a girl who serves Mass. Holy Communion is as likely to be ministered by a woman as by a man. Most parochial activities will be organized by women. It is to women, rather than men, that the Church looks for practical evangelization.

For the life of me I never understood the full blast of feminism. Why would women have to fight – and fight dirty, at that – for something they have always enjoyed, men's servitude? And feminism within the Church itself – how absurd. Good Catholic men are brought up to recognize Our Lady in their mothers, and Mary, the wife of Nazareth, in their wives. Please God they will always do just that.

7 March

SS Perpetua and Felicity

These two young women were martyred in remarkable circumstances in Carthage, less than 200 years after Christ's death. Less remarkable, but no less heroic, was Maggie Griffin who would tell you – should you have the temerity to ask – she was 'as old as her teeth and a bit more'.

Certainly she was as old as the pillar she sat behind at all Masses. She remembered the church being built, remembers going door to door every Friday night to beg pennies for its bricks. Remembers that when there were enough pennies the bishop sent them a bulky Irish priest who bullied, bribed and cajoled a team of sweating labourers to give their Saturday afternoons free in return for all the beer they could down that night.

Finally, late in the 1930s, the bishop was invited to open the new church. The navvies, spick and span in new blue suits and shining boots, formed the Guard of Honour whilst Maggie, in her blue Legion of Mary sash, strewed rose petals before the high priest.

A year or two later she would marry one of the navvies, curtailing his visits to the local pub, restricting him to beer and snooker in the CYMS club. He was happy with the new lifestyle until, in 1942, he died somewhere near Tobruk.

When the priest's housekeeper was killed in the Blitz Maggie moved into the presbytery as a matter of course. The bulky Irish priest was long gone – to build other churches, schools. In his place was a silent man from Connemara who blushed whenever Maggie put his bacon and cabbage before him.

Some insisted that the priest's housekeeper was a barrier. Perhaps some were. But Maggie was always a sieve. The timewasters, busybodies, scroungers with mothers dying in Cork – they were all deflected. The despairing, the frightened, the homeless all found themselves in Father's study, their very arrival there a recommendation.

How much poorer our parishes are now, without their Maggie Griffins.

ST JOHN OF GOD

J ohn of God was an oddity. But, as we're discovering, saints usually are. Out of tune with everything we recognize as normal – a decent family, home, job. Not for them a weekly excursion to Mass to thank God for what we have and encourage Him to give us more.

John started life as a mercenary soldier, tough as old boots. Then, somewhere along the line, he turned his home in Granada into a hospital for down-and-outs, thus founding the Brothers Hospitallers. He died rescuing a drowning man. He was 55 – an age when we are preparing to top up our pensions.

Christianity has never been a safe business. Follow it as Christ preached it and you'll never enjoy that retirement cottage in the country. The ones who follow Christ as He wished it done are all adventurers – prepared to bet on His promise that to enjoy Heaven we must hazard all now.

But, God help us, most of us aspiring to follow Him are not gamblers. We're plain stick-in-the-mud folk preoccupied with our children and the next sale of wallpaper at Do-it-All. If we have a religion at all it's because our parents, God bless them, dug us a rut and we simply followed it.

We hope, most of us, that if the time ever comes again to be counted we have the stuff of martyrs still within us. We hope, but we can never be sure. As it is, we daily watch the slow pin-prick crucifixion of Christ on television and in the papers we read. And we do nothing. If we can't act on His behalf in the little things, who is to say what we'll do when the chips are down?

Yet, ordinary as we are, we have the temerity to hope that somehow we'll slip unnoticed through Heaven's Gate. Most of us pray that when that time comes Peter the Guardian will be looking the other way. Or, as the Irish put it, may you be dead half an hour before the Devil knows it.

9 March

St Frances of Rome

~

Those who work for themselves know that the hardest boss is yourself. With this boss there's no watching clocks, planning holidays, working with an eye to a bonus.

When we come to die, like it or not, we're all self-employed. A brooch you could once find at Lourdes was inscribed: 'The last hour is your own'. And so it is. Whether own boss or time-puncher, you are then your own boss. And answerable.

In one of those old prayerbooks we all have stashed away I read, as bold as you like, 'Death, Judgment, Hell or Heaven forever'. No sub-clause as a get-out. No slight hope of error. No 'gentle Jesus' or kindly Our Lady on the touchline to help. Just those two last things and the consequences.

You have to wonder about that 'old' Church. Was it right? Is our future black and white and not drawn in the soothing pastels we use today? If so, what hope for us?

A little scared – a whole lot, in fact – I looked for the alternative. Life always has one, doesn't it? And I came up with a revelation. The old prayerbook didn't tell us who judged us. Perhaps it is not God at all, perhaps it is ourselves who are the final judge and jury.

In that last hour we face God, true. But He says nothing, not a single word. He betrays no prejudice, no indication of His total knowledge of us. Simply, He waits for us to justify or condemn ourselves. For our part, in such a presence, we cannot escape the truth. There can be no evasion, no omission. In our hearts, no hiding places. We will reveal ourselves to Him and in the process will have judged ourselves. Simplicity itself. What we have to desire is that the severity we show ourselves will be matched by His pity. See how wily I am. An old prayerbook frightens the pants off me and the first thing I do is run for cover. I just hope it is there when I need it.

St John Ogilvie, SJ

John Ogilvie was one of that long succession of Jesuit priests tortured and then done to death because he could not renounce the dictates of his conscience. Like many martyrs before him he had not the least wish to die; he certainly had no love of the pain of torture. He stated quite clearly that he had every respect for his king, James I, but found himself unable to agree with the King's spiritual supremacy over the Pope.

Catholics tend to forget that those who died for the Faith were just as much terrified of being hung, drawn and then quartered as we would be ourselves. Whether in an Edinburgh cell – as John was – or in a Gestapo prison, as so many others were, the stench of fear would be little different.

The only astonishing thing about cruel deaths like these is that it is human beings – even well-intentioned ones sometimes – who inflict the agony. Just as we ask ourselves whether we could accept a martyr's pain so perhaps we should also ask the corollary – could we inflict the pain? Someone did. Someone not unlike us – a Scot, an Englishman, a German. Probably not doing it because they enjoyed it, but just because they were instructed to do so.

The executed and the executioner have more in common than would at first appear. Both are prepared to undergo an act repugnant to them. And both act out of a sense of self-protection – the former to save his soul, the latter to save his skin.

Glibly we might assert the first is heroism and the second cowardice. But then, we're prejudiced. We're not likely to be called upon to die horribly, nor required to inflict horrendous death. All we know for certain is that in war soldiers, all soldiers, are capable of a bestiality alien to their natures in times of peace. And, whoops, here's the paradox – the soldier's ability to kill is termed heroism; his inability to do so could well bring charges of cowardice. What a mixed-up world we live in.

11 March

ST AENGUS

Lord, how simple You made it. A man and a woman, attracted by the spark of love in each other, marry and mate. They are not the only creatures in nature to have one mate for life. They then have children. Or perhaps they cannot. If this is so, You fill their hearts with generosity and longing so that they can offer their home to a baby without one.

So simple. But just look at the tangle we have made of the plan. First, we cannot resist improving on what we see as Your deficiencies – we play around with the process of fertilization until, God-like ourselves, we claim to do what only You can do. Clapping ourselves on the back, rushing to publish our papers, we say we can go one better than You.

Want an intelligent child? No problem. Want a boy child? It can be assured. Want a healthy child? Our scrutiny and our test tubes will eliminate doubt – or the embryo.

Then we go further. We do what You would never dare to do – we create life where no life was intended. And, should there be failure, there's always the laboratory sink. When all this fails we have arranged matters so that couples longing for children cannot adopt them. They are no longer available – for we have passed laws to abort babies at any time, in any circumstances.

Dear Lord, You gave us simplicity. A natural, beautiful process to renew our race. We have stood by, apart from some brave folk, and watched the simplest of moralities crucified. But then, Lord, You know something of this Yourself, don't You?

Only one virtue has arisen from this current abuse on life as created by You, Lord. It is that Your children – Jew, Catholic or Moslem – have found a second cause in common they all hold sacred. The first is Your existence, Lord, and the second is the protection of the unborn child. It could be enough, Lord, in time to achieve the impossible and draw us all together in Your cause.

12 March

ST ALPHEGE

Little is known of this tenth-century bishop of Winchester - other than that they nicknamed him Baldie. But ten centuries on he had a namesake, another Benedictine, Father Alphege. He was the headmaster of Belmont Abbey when I was a boy there. They say you never forget a good teacher so I'd like to pay tribute to this one who died all too young.

Father Alphege – I can only think of him as Alf – taught English; especially he taught the love of literature. His study was a tiny room but at night he would cram in a dozen or so of us and we'd talk poetry, the classics, but most of all we'd talk the power inherent in words – their use and their misuse. Towards midnight a bottle would be opened, cider, wine, sherry – whatever he had to hand. And when midnight was long since gone we'd be despatched to our dormitory.

Next morning, around 6.30, if you were serving his Mass, you'd creep up to his room in the monastery and batter on the door. And you'd awaken the whole floor until at last he emerged. He said the swiftest Mass I have ever known. I would still be mumbling the Confiteor when he had arrived at the Consecration.

It was our delight – for then the boys ate with the monks – on more than one occasion to see him prostrate before the Abbot's table throughout supper: his penance for unpunctuality.

Around him he moulded a school of boys – no more than 200 – in a manner wholly Benedictine. It was a community, true, but a community of individuals. There was no impersonal stamp on the boys he trained, no ruthless subjugation of personality. His rules were obeyed but they were like Benedict's – neither onerous nor lax.

Later he was to be Abbot for a short time. Then – the story is somewhat blurred here – he went as chaplain to a convent. The truth, one monk confided, is that he was burned out. I would have said used out. And I couldn't pay a teacher a better compliment.

13 March

Family Fast Day

I t's full title is the Catholic Fund for Overseas Development. Too much a mouthful, you'll agree. So it became Cafod. It was the brainchild – like so many organizations of the Church in England – of Derek Worlock, who was to be Archbishop of Liverpool.

Twice a year, one Friday in Lent and another much later, Catholics are asked to fast and to donate the cash saved to Cafod. So next Sunday we'll find the green envelopes waiting for our gifts to the Third World.

Originally fasting wasn't a practice that had an altruistic aim in mind. It was inherited from the Jewish Day of Atonement, kept on the tenth day of the seventh month, and was a mortification of the flesh imposed by God on the Israelites. Moses and Elias, we know, fasted for 40 days and so would Jesus. And so too did we long ago. The Moslem Ramadan of today echoes the severity of the Christian fast centuries ago.

Cafod's Family Fast Day is a gentle reminder that not so long ago, in my lifetime certainly, Fridays of Lent were strict exercises in avoirdupois. Two to three ounces of food were permitted at breakfast time, eight to ten ounces at supper time. And the most particular Catholic families would carefully weigh what was placed on the table.

Some exceptions were permitted – labourers, the poor, the sick, those over 59 years of age were excused. Come Good Friday, though, and it would be a brave Catholic who took even the minimal 'collation.'

In schools today children will have 'rich man, poor man' meals: a reminder that whilst we might fast, just a little, others starve, frequently. I like the new way of doing things. St Francis de Sales spotted the difference when he wrote: 'We do not become perfect by the multiplication of exercises, penances and austerities, but rather by the purity of love with which we do them.'

A t the start, the middle and the end of Lent there's the Cross. It was once a reality – two lengths of wood, rough stuff, unplaned, attached one to the other by hefty nails. It was utilitarian, hastily hacked to a point at the base so it could be stuck firmly into the ground. The splinters scarcely mattered – the Man due to hang on it would die anyway.

Give or take a century or so the Cross had become a symbol. It would have been as roughshod as the original – a couple of twigs tied together. Something that, like the fish, would indicate the Christian.

As the centuries rolled on, Christians were men and women of status. The Cross changed accordingly. Smoothed, polished, made of the finest wood, it would be garnished with gems until finally a figure appeared upon it. A figure sculpted from gold or silver. The grander the church, the finer the crucifix.

In its new guise as symbol the Cross was bright red on the crusader's shirt as he used it to disguise his plunder. Then, from being a symbol, it slipped into the role of alibi for men canny enough to recognize its power. Much the same happened with David's Star and the Crescent of Islam which, like the Cross, had begun as reminders of God's presence.

Only latterly has the Cross reappeared as plain wood. It was a significant stride for Catholics when even popes put aside the richly decorated crucifixes for bare wood or simple iron. It was one of the richest legacies of Vatican II and yet went unremarked. But not by the bishops there who took the new simplicities home with them.

It took centuries but it seemed the Cross had once again come into its own. Yet, a further hazard remains. In our glib, slick age the Cross could become a logo – another disguise no less dangerous than the ornate symbols of the past. When we kiss it – as we will on Good Friday – we must understand what it is we adore: the Man on the wood of the Cross.

15 March

St Longinus, St Clement-Mary Hofbauer

I n the days when such things concerned us more, we would ask friends to name the New Testament character who most intrigued them. The centurion was always my choice, with Judas coming a close second. Perhaps yours would be today's saint, Longinus, the soldier who pierced Jesus with his spear. Both he and his spear became the stuff of legend. But there was nothing legendary about the centurion who politely stopped Jesus making the journey to heal his servant with the great words of faith: 'Domine, non sum dignus ut intres sub tectum meum', then adding, 'Sed tantum dic verbo, et sanabitur anima mea.'

It is the only part of the Mass that I still feel constrained to mutter to myself in Latin. For I owe that centurion a lot. Not just my sanity but my Faith too. The importance of the centurion is, first, its utter authenticity. It rings solid, true. It happened. The centurion is as real to me as any old soldier who has 'swung the lamp' during the long nights of confidences. Then there's the soldier's integrity – he won't let a Jew defile himself by entering his home. He could command it, but he doesn't. And last there is his faith. Discerning faith somehow touched with the memories of the campaigns he has fought, his vast experience of men and how they react in battle.

Then the centurion inspires immense curiosity. What did happen to him afterwards, after he found his old servant was cured? Would he, the intelligent man he was, have followed the Nazarene's progress with more than curiosity? A man of his character surely would have done. If so, would Jesus' execution have appalled him, or would he just have felt passing pity for another religious man who had stepped out of line? More intriguing still, would he have spoken to Longinus and, if legend is true, would Longinus in time have convinced him of Jesus' claim as King of the Jews? Sometimes we long that the Gospels had been twice their length.

16 March

St Finan Lobur St Abraham Kidunaia

It was the ordinariness that frightened him most about Hell. He had been prepared for fire, reptiles, encounters with the more horrific of history's characters. All this he had expected. But now he stood on a shale beach whilst reluctant grey waves lapped the stones. And that was it. Hell.

He watched the slow waves; they neither advanced nor retreated. They just broke sullenly at the same point that they had since he arrived. Neither had the pale apology for a sun shifted. It still just touched the far misty horizon, neither rising nor setting.

Since dying and finding himself on the beach he had trudged miles. Or so it seemed. For he always came back to this same spot. Or were all places in Hell the same? He was rapidly coming to that conclusion.

Endlessly he walked and walked. But always the sun was in the same place, the tide at the same point. 'There has to be more to Hell than this,' he raged out loud. 'There has to be fury, anger, the clash of wills. There has to be fear, a headlong flight from a devil's fury, pain, suffering.'

He paused, attempting to analyse what he felt – looking out on that placid sea. 'There has to be … something. Some sort of activity.'

One hundred thousand years on and still he stood there - on that forlorn beach, watching that same immobile sun. In Hell.

Well, what did you expect? Hell, Catholics know, is the absence of God. More it need not be. No inferno, no hot coals, no demons other than the ones we create for ourselves. At the end of the millennium the Vatican was busily recreating the thinking on the Devil and Hell that had been current for centuries. They need not have bothered. Just as we cannot envisage the joy that is Heaven, so we can only guess what vacuity Hell might be. Lent's not so bad a time to think about this.

St Patrick, Patron of Ireland

It ought to be easy, this day to celebrate St Patrick. It ought to be a happy romp in wit and laughter tinged with whimsy. Yet it cannot be done. Not in honesty, not without dulling the ache Ireland has become in England's heart. Not without ignoring the sword England has plunged into Ireland's soul so many times.

Superficially, the slaughter of the past 40 years on Patrick's Isle has been carried out by Catholics or Protestants – an outrageous libel which shames both Churches and degrades all they hold dear. It denigrates too the 99% of people on the island of Ireland who would welcome peace after centuries of wrongs.

There must be a special vale of sorrows in Heaven where tears are wept for the wrongs done in the name of religion. Nigeria, Rwanda, Yugoslavia, Ireland: all places – and there are many more – where God is flouted on the banners but denied in the heart.

Even so, Christians must ever hope. Perhaps in St Patrick's own prayer, the Breastplate:

> Christ with me
> Christ before me
> Christ behind me
> Christ below me
> Christ above me
> Christ within me.
> Christ at my right hand
> Christ at my left hand
> Christ in every ear that hears me
> Christ in every eye that sees me
> Christ in every mouth that speaks of me
> Christ in every heart that thinks of me.

Happy St Patrick's Day.

18 March

St Cyril of Jerusalem

Many strange men have been called to make Jerusalem their home. A Franciscan, Fr Eugene Hoad, was one of them. Amongst the jobs he attracted there was the chaplaincy to the Palestine Police. Every Catholic joining the Force in the 1940s would be taken by him on a tour of the holy places. I was one of these Catholics.

It was an incredible tour of demythologizing and ended by the shores of the Sea of Galilee. On the shore there he asked our little group to turn away and look only when he called. After a few minutes he did so. To our astonishment he was standing on water more than 100 yards out. To our greater astonishment he then walked towards us over the small waves until finally he stood before us grinning.

He was a big man, rumoured to carry two .45s under his brown habit. I reckoned St Peter must have looked much the same. He sat us down in a circle.

'I just walked on the waters – yes?'

We all nodded.

'When Jesus did the same it was recorded as a miracle - yes?'

Again, we nodded.

He grinned again. 'And so it probably was – when He did it – but when I did it I just walked out on a ledge of rock hidden by the water. No miracle.'

He paused. 'Whether He knew of the same ledge I've no idea. What I do know is that miracles are things men can mess around with, try to explain away. Just like I've given your Faith a jolt just now - yes?'

In unison, we confessed he had.

He roared, 'Then it's pretty poor Faith you have, lads, to be jolted by a little trick like that. You'll need stronger Faith than that if you're going to march with Christ to the end.'

I read somewhere, late in the 1990s, that Father Eugene had died. In Jerusalem, of course – a city that has enticed so many holy men and clasped them close to her.

19 March

SOLEMNITY OF ST JOSEPH

I t's the hands – a craftsman's hands. Dry, strong, decisive. No doubt scarred too. Think of St Joseph, as we do today, and you can't ignore those hands. It was no accident that the carpenter was the one chosen to lead Jesus throughout His childhood. A good joiner is hard to find today. It was probably no different in Nazareth.

Joseph's position in the community would have been one of dignity. His skill ensured him status. In fact, there are writers who suggest Joseph would have been a businessman of some note, employing a small staff.

Whatever his stature in Nazareth, it was due to the endurance of his humility that he went virtually unacknowledged until the Middle Ages and, even then, he was cast as the funny man in the mystery plays. It took Teresa of Avila to find him a serious role as the intermediary for a holy and happy death. And, very much later, those hands were recognized when he became ennobled as St Joseph the Worker.

His anonymity is symbolic of those lost years of Jesus, covered so dismissively by the short comment that He grew in grace. But then, there are so many omissions in the Gospels that tantalize us.

We know so much of the prophets, from their boils to their fiery temperaments. Yet all we know of the adolescent Jesus has to be deduced from studying contemporary social conditions. But, if the son is truly father to the man, we can make some accurate guesses. Particularly about Joseph. And the emerging picture is one we can readily accept – that of a patient, caring craftsman whose hands are already sculpted to lead us gently through death with the minimum of fear and in the comfort of expectation. He is the layperson's saint. One of us.

20 March

ST CUTHBERT

Cuthbert – saint of the North – was all you'd expect from a saint of the South. Refined, erudite, charming, companionable. All the attributes we look for in our parish priests.

The condition of the Catholic parish priest has altered immeasurably in just a few decades. From being paterfamilias to a bevy of young curates, father in spirit to a thousand or more Massgoers, he's now more likely to be a harassed old man in his 50s living a life not just spartan but solitary. He will be overworked, expected to be master of many skills that are nothing to do with theology, and something of a drudge in an organization seriously undermanned.

That's the truth of it. But his parishioners tend still to frame him on a canvas at least 30 years out of date. He is 'Father' still. Father who will sit patiently for hours in a confessional without visitors; Father who will baptize our babies, marry us and finally bury us. Father who will be criticized for not visiting us, yet the last time he did we forgot to turn off *Coronation Street*. Father who is continually asking us for money – for charities, missions, the roof, our schools. We scarcely note that he never asks for himself.

He may live alone nowadays without assistant or housekeeper but he is still the sink into which we flow our tragedies. Seldom do we stop to ask where he directs his own. At death he must find the right words; for the jobless, the right connections; for the single mother, a working knowledge of the DHSS; for the convert, a map of the Church; for the married and engaged, wisdom beyond his years.

Besides all this, he no longer has tenure of his parish. At a moment's notice he can be transplanted. He has the rigours of the Religious without their privileges of community. Yet, despite all this, he has one undeniable advantage. To those amongst whom he moves he is still 'Father', our Father. A title unique in all its implications.

21 March

St Benedict St Enda

Imagine, if you will, a Europe brutalized by wave upon wave of savage tribes, swooping without order or compassion, where they would, when they would. You might even say, cynically, nothing has changed. But, yes, it has. And the change started with the man who founded monasteries at Subiaco and Monte Cassino in the sixth century. His name was Benedict. And he liked order.

He was orderly himself, and calm. And this is what he reflected in the Rule he composed for those who would live in his abbeys. It was what the civilized world was looking for too. People were weary of bloodletting, of being dispossessed on a regular basis, of being bullied at a time when order had broken down and there seemed to be little to replace it.

Benedict's Rule asked neither too much nor too little. The abbot was to be a wise man, a discreet man. His authority would be open to counsel from others and it would be for a limited time only when he would return to being a monk amongst others. Monastic life would be lived in moderation and with a sense of charity.

As the monasteries flourished so too was the Rule taken to the people living around them. Not just Benedictines, as they came to be called, followed Benedict's Rule. Other Orders, such as the Carthusians, Cistercians and the like, borrowed from the Rule when they were being formed.

Much more importantly, the Rule began to influence the actions of secular leaders, lowly and mighty. It became a philosophy that simple people could understand and put into practice. And when the Benedictines started schools and hospitals within the communities that grew up around their monasteries, Benedict's Rule began to saturate into every level of Christian life.

If this great feast falls in Lent, today's monks will have dispensation to celebrate. It is the way Benedict, compassionate always to our needs, would have wanted it. He had, after all, a unique grasp of the manner in which common sense could itself be Godly.

22 March

LAETARE SUNDAY, 4TH SUNDAY OF LENT

The Gospel is that of the Prodigal Son, the theme is rejoicing. Midway through Lent, today once had the nickname 'Refreshment Sunday'. The altar would be strewn with flowers and, frankly, most would take a day off from Lent's rigour.

About this time too my friend Martin would casually pose the question: 'How's Lent going?' Three charged words. And I didn't have the courage to tell him that things are different now. But they are. Apart from the efforts of the youngsters the hardest part of Lent is convincing your conscience that sackcloth is no longer the style of the season.

Perhaps the change came when we first said sagely: 'It's not what you give up that matters, it's what you take on.' Great. True, well intentioned. But, cunning as we were, that's where the new philosophy remained – well-intentioned codswallop. We were happy to abandon the past but omitted to replace it.

The Church lost a great deal when it temporized with the hardships of Lent. But then the Church was faced with a considerable problem. Should she keep the stern rules, thus losing even more who felt them to be archaic? Or relax the rules, thus presenting a Church palatable for an age more concerned by hypocrisy than regimented piety?

There was a commendable justification at hand, and it was heard more and more frequently. The Church is not a stolid institution stuck ingloriously in the mud. The Church is a pilgrim Church, forever moving forward, subject to change, responding to the changes a contemporary society requires.

The matter is not resolved. Perhaps, pilgrim that she is, the Church will never resolve this dilemma. In the meantime, she's lucky – she's founded on a rock.

23 March

St Gwinear, Patron of Cornwall

There's an army instruction about taking up a defensive position: 'You must be able to advance or retreat.' Common sense really.

There's a similarity. The Church is an army whose leader is Christ. But defensive, no. The Church doesn't take up defensive positions. Protective ones, perhaps. The Church's first role is to advance. Not attack, mark you. It is, as we've all learned, a pilgrim Church – moving towards a goal placed by God and known only to Him.

We have no idea where that goal is. It may be beyond the very next horizon, or far beyond a billion horizons. We've no conception when it will be reached. All we know with surety is that God set His Church a destination and even showed us the path along which we might reach it.

If, therefore, we believe in both the existence of the goal and the path, we have to admit that mobility is the next thing required of us. That movement will take us through an ever-changing landscape – this is no unchanging Hell we are in. Not just the surroundings will change. We will change, just as every journey in some way alters us. Only our human nature cannot change. That is immutable.

The word 'traditionalist' used in connection with Catholics is neither accurate nor welcome. It is a slur when used by some, an alibi when used by others. A Catholic can only be a Catholic – a member of a Church rightly claiming to be one in its teaching, holy through its people and apostolic in its leadership. Those who seek to muddy clear definitions are mischievious. Or worse.

Those who seek to anchor the Church in the past are as foolhardy as those wantonly denying the clear promise Christ made to His pilgrim Church. It is foolish and naive to think that the centuries will not, and should not, change the form of this Church. But it would be lacking in faith not to believe that Peter is forever there to guard the matter.

24 March

ST DUNCHAD ST HILDELITH
ST MACARTAN

~

Time to lighten up a little, I reckon. Unfortunately today's stern saints are not the ones to help us. So I'll have to turn to my barber. Traditionally the trade is supposed to breed garrulous men but my barber is a taciturn fellow, strictly limited to 'short or long?' and 'that will be four fifty'.

Recently it was different. He had been bitten on the raw by something an Anglican bishop had said. Not only had he doubted the veracity of the Resurrection – old hat stuff by now – but he had gone on to say that he saw no valid reason why youngsters should not enjoy trial 'marriages' and felt it was good for them to get sex out of the way before they embarked on love.

My barber was so indignant I feared for what he had left of my beard. 'They're supposed to be men of God, aren't they?'– snip, snap – 'and here they are giving the kids all the wrong ideas'– snap, snip – 'I don't know what the . . . . . Church is coming to – that I don't.'

In between his attacks, I managed one query: 'What Church do you belong to?' I asked.

He shook his head vehemently. 'C of E, I suppose, if I was pushed to say. I go to funerals, weddings and the like. But it's not necessary to be there, is it, to know that what that vicar said was wrong? He knows the rules. He ignores them. No wonder the country is in a mess.'

He flourished the scissors a last time, tore off the towel and shouted, 'Next!'

Walking home, I realized it was wrong to call Britain Godless. You cannot write off 2000 years of tradition overnight. There is, after all, such a thing as a race memory. And it made it all the more urgent that so-called nominal Christians should not be scandalized. Talking in measured soundbites, the Bishop had done just that. It wasn't fair of him – not to the memory of Dunchad in Iona, Hildelith in Barking or dour Macartan over in Clogher. Nor to my barber in Bootle.

25 March

SOLEMNITY OF THE ANNUNCIATION OF THE LORD

~

Nine months before Christmas and Our Lady learns of her pregnancy from an angel. Today's Gospel, as written by Luke, is the sure fire spark for titters in the Lower VI of the convent school. Later, the titters will have become loving faith or disdainful denial of an incident beautifully told by the evangelist.

We are asked to accept so much that is incredible. The appearance of an angel to a young Jewish virgin, the almost brash way in which she is told her condition, the gentleness of Mary's reply: 'I am the handmaid of the Lord, let what you have said be done to me.'

Again, almost as if Luke anticipated scepticism, there is added another incident, almost like a throwaway – that the elderly Elizabeth, up to then barren, was already six months pregnant. The incredible is immediately succeeded by the impossible in what appears a balancing act of spiritual powers.

It is yet another incident that proves you must either accept all that the Gospels say or none of it. Like Faith itself, your credulity must be as open to your mind as it is to your heart. Try to tinker with what the evangelists wrote, believe this bit, deny that, and you'll never escape your confusion.

Ireland is the only country left now that publicly rings the Angelus bells each day at noon and six o'clock on radio and television. The opponents of this little act of remembrance have been strident but haven't yet, thank God, silenced this wonderful memory of the very first Christian prayer:

> I am the handmaid of the Lord,
> Be it done to me according to thy will.
> And the Word was made Flesh.

And thankfully still dwells amongst us – today and all days.

St William of Norwich

Twelve-year-old William was a tanner's apprentice allegedly kidnapped by Jews, tortured and then crucified. A spurious tale which no doubt, in 1144, gave those who owed Jews money the opportunity to kill them and renege on their debts. If that isn't true of Norwich then it was most certainly true elsewhere in Britain as in Europe.

It wasn't that anti-Semitism was widespread – which it was – it was that Christians were taught – indoctrinated – that the Jews murdered Jesus. That simple, that horrendous in the consequences down the centuries.

Because of their inherited guilt the Jews were hard put to find any career other than usury. Roads to chivalry and public honour were closed to them. Laws governing estate and condition were strictly enforced. True, they might practise medicine, dabble in science. But these were anyway suspect arts, magical at best, devilish at worst.

So they lent money, a service frowned upon by good Christians yet essential, as now, to promote commerce. Often enough, when the debt became too great, the borrower would simply institute a brief persecution and his debt was cleared.

The crusaders carved a bloody trail through the European Jewish communities to finance their wars. In the ensuing centuries all the great countries of Europe found the Jews handy scapegoats – in much the same way, paradoxically, as the Romans had used the Christians.

It was to culminate – we hope and pray never to be repeated – in the greatest holocaust of all time when Nazi genocide, aided by Christians in several European countries, simply attempted to annihilate an entire race.

It is only in living memory – and recent at that – that the Catholic Church erased the traces of anti-Semitism from its liturgy and made formal apology to the race which gave birth to Jesus.

27 March

ST RUPERT

It was a sight so rare that every eye followed the family that wended its way into Mass. Father, mother with babe in arms, and six children ranging in age from 4 to 14. That they were the same family was evident – faces, hair, deportment even, mirrored the parents. Strange, I pondered, that even in a Catholic church their appearance should be so much a rarity as to merit curiosity.

It's true to say that all of us there took a shared pride as they quietly filled one entire bench. This man, this woman, neither in any way harassed nor woebegone, had challenged the social correctness of their age and produced children, a family, in direct contrast to others who had opted for a Jaguar, a detached house and holidays in central Spain.

The ones in the know, the sociologists, tell us that by 2020 each family will consist of 1.75 children. Even allowing for the unfortunate .75 of a child, the forecast is chilling. It foreshadows the time when legislation will limit the size of family permitted, just as legislation presently encourages the disposal of children unlikely to measure up to society's assessment of what a human being should be like.

The family we watched was neither smart nor dowdy. Some clothes were clearly hand-me-downs, the pram in the porch was a vintage vehicle on which much love had been bestowed. At Holy Communion the organization of the family became apparent, a manoeuvre to be admired. Ma and Pa first with oldest girl taking charge of the two little ones. Then some chopping and changing so that all received Communion and the little ones a blessing.

You knew instinctively that this would be the pattern throughout this family's life – there would always be one member there to assist another. The little group was already its own community, had its own rules, duties. But in the last analysis it was only bound by one thread, and that was love. Was it my imagination, or did those with 1.75 children look somewhat sorrowfully at each other?

28 March

St Arild

⟨~⟩

The historian Leland says of this Gloucestershire lass that 'one Muncius a tiraunt cut off hir heade becawse she would not consent to lye withe hym.' Now her relics lie in Gloucester Cathedral.

Nothing, then, is new. Muncius is alive and well, operating in just the same manner throughout the world. Everything changes except human nature and human desire. All of us know that a Muncius gene lurks somewhere deep down in us. He may be well buried now and forgotten but that gene, which the Church calls Original Sin, is not. It's been there ever since Eve's apple – or, if you prefer *2001: A Space Odyssey*, ever since humans found they could kill with a dinosaur bone.

Since Abraham we've come to recognize this fault that so often fractures the human race. Since Jesus we've known what to do about it. As ever, knowing something is just not enough.

The doctrine of Original Sin pre-dates the New Testament; it was a bone of contention in ancient Judaism. St Paul tackled the onerous problem that a good God would create a soul in sin, and after him Augustine and the great Doctors – right up to Cardinal Newman.

Most Catholics are not involved in these niceties of theology. Their guide has been the Sacrament of Penance and a tutored conscience. But confession has fallen away and consciences are not as sharp a guide as they once were. Consciences have not just been blunted by an increasingly secular world; they have even been dulled by a new uncertainty about the old certainties.

The problem faced by the Church in this new millennium is not so much the devastation of Faith but its erosion through the constant nibbling at all that makes it unique. It's as if an artist sneaked into the Louvre and changed the mouth on the *Mona Lisa*. The face of Christ – and of His Church – can be altered in the same way.

The most powerful man I ever met in my line of business took me to the Savoy – my first and last visit – and when I asked him a question he would doodle on the menu before answering me. Later I was told it was one of his little tricks. Or perhaps he'd read today's Gospel, the one which tells more about Him than most other incidents, the one in which He challenges the man without sin to take up a stone to kill the woman accused of adultery.

Twice, as they try tricky questions on Him, the Gospel tells how Jesus bends down and writes in the dust with a finger, saying nothing. As beguiling as any thriller writer, John doesn't tell us what Jesus wrote or why. Plenty have taken guesses, but that's all they are and will ever be.

Was He playing for time, defusing a difficult situation? Or was He almost mischievously distracting them from their anger? We'll never know. But then there are so many things we will never know in this life. If we did then we'd have forfeited this great gift of free will which has been given us for either our salvation or damnation. Francis Thompson has given us in 'The Hound of Heaven' the most vivid picture ever of the anguished terror this free will can become:

> I fled Him, down the nights and down the days;
> I fled Him, down the arches of the years;
> I fled Him, down the labyrinthine ways
> Of my own mind; and in the mist of tears
> I hid from Him, and under running laughter.

There are some who deride Catholicism for diminishing the act of free will. They reckon the Faith blinkers its lovers, sets them between the traces and gives them an unswerving corridor down which to race to Heaven. Free will, they say, doesn't come into it – just blind inertia. Just how far removed from the truth can any observer stand? A warning then – if you're standing outside this Church waiting to come in, watch it, friend, this is no easy ride.

St Johan Climacus
St Leonard Murialdo

Washing up today – a little treat that comes my way from time to time – I tried to remember how we used to do it before liquid soap. I couldn't. Hooked by now, I was soon babbling the altar boy's responses at the start of Mass . . . ad Deum qui laetificat juventutem meum. In no time at all I was romping through the Confiteor and Gloria too. Far from the frothing sink.

Messing about with memory banks is a hazardous occupation for older Catholics, just as is living in the past. Trigger memory and you come up with odd generalizations.

Were our priests holier, more attentive to their people? No – more self-contained in their communal presbyteries and enough of them there to visit. Were people better because they went to Mass? No – many were scared stiff of the consequences if they did otherwise. Did this make people holier than today? No – more of them were ignorant of His love.

Yes, generalizations. But the kernel of truth is there. Like labourers working on a tight contract, we Catholics have to be careful which boulders we hump into the future. Many are not worth the effort, others are essential.

The arguments we have amongst ourselves are because some will load themselves with the rubble that is no longer bricks. The wise ones are marking the artefacts they know will be of value in the future. And if we sound like the labourers working on the Tower of Babel then that is what we have become.

Pope John Paul II played honest foreman in this demolition cum construction. He identified what must be carried from the past - dissociating the Church from what was a mess of nostalgia and making clear which stones still remained at the foundation.

In the meantime, just be glad of the Fairy Liquid as you scrape away at the plates of memory.

31 March

G od loves a trier, I muttered as I filled in my lottery ticket. 'It could be you' is a slogan that could have been invented for Catholics. God help us, we're inveterate gamblers – whether it's 50p on the Bingo or half the Irish priest population at Cheltenham's Gold Cup, we're forever jousting at fortune.

I have to admit that so far as the lottery is concerned I've been reduced to spiritual blackmail. At first I always informed Heaven – and whoever is the patron saint of gamblers – that 10% would go to Jospice, our local hospice. After a week or so of inactivity I felt compelled to raise the anti. A quarter would be for Jospice, I informed Heaven. Surely an offer they couldn't refuse. After a year or so the offer stands at 60:40, in Jospice's favour. Alas, Heaven isn't biting.

So what's wrong up there? Don't they want to help Jospice? Perhaps there's an alternative answer. Perhaps Heaven reckons it wouldn't be good for me to be a millionaire, or for Jospice to receive so much that all the good folk who presently help there would sit on their hands and relax, thereby losing a great deal of virtue. Only Heaven knows. And Heaven isn't talking.

Much of the prayer that goes up to Heaven is a bit like mine – a challenge rather than a plea. As pray-ers we tend to be unsophisticated. Despite the pious homilies on the virtue of prayer we are essentially primitives at the task, more at home in a Turkish bazaar than in a church. We offer God what He already has in exchange for what we think He has forgotten to give us.

In the end the best prayer is probably the one we cry out in times of crisis. No intended blackmail then – just desperation and the faith that He will hear us. As for how He answers, well, that's something different and best kept for another day.

1 April

St Gilbert of Caithness
St Hugh of Grenoble

D ryden, one of the princes of the Enlightenment, offered a
cynical thought on politicians but apposite for this 1 April:

> Fools change in England, and new fools arise;
> For, though the immortal species never dies,
> Yet every year new maggots make new flies.
> 'Absalom and Achitophel'

Those flies could so easily be us. For, as we grow older, two traps lie
in wait. We tend either to forgive too readily or else we forgive too
reluctantly. Either way, the danger is that we become lazy fools.

Forgiveness is a tricky effort on our parts. Given too lightly, it
infers that what's forgiven was unimportant anyway. Witheld, it can
decay someone's very soul.

But assuming we manage to forgive correctly, does it infer that
we then have to forget? The answer emphasizes the gulf there is
between the Old Testament and the New, between Judaism and
Catholicism.

In anticipation of the new millennium, Pope John Paul II made
apology to the Jewish people for the many wrongs inflicted upon
them by Christians down the centuries, from the crusades to the
Holocaust. Whilst some said that the apology was not sufficiently
abject, most of us hoped for forgiveness. It was not wholly forthcoming. Only in part. The gesture backfired, for the Christian had
hoped that the Jew could forget. And that would have been to deny
the difference between the two philosophies.

Reduced to the absurd – when Aunt Maud forgives Uncle Tom it
will in no way ease their future relationship unless she also forgets his
offence. It is Uncle Tom who will never forget. As Cardinal Newman
put it: 'No true penitent forgets or forgives himself; an unforgiving
spirit towards himself is the very price of God forgiving him.'

St Francis of Paola
St Mary of Egypt

S t Mary was a prostitute who paid for her pilgrimage to the Holy Land by selling herself to the sailors on the boat that took her. After some sort of Damascus Road experience she took three loaves, and took herself off to the desert about the River Jordan. She never left it.

Her tale reflects our Catholic understanding that the journey to Faith is less important than the fact that you find it. The greater the original sinner, the greater the eventual saint. And so many Catholics have made truly remarkable sinners.

The deathbed repentance is no fable for Catholics. It is the very stuff of the legends we were taught as children. That old soak of a sailor dying in the brothel's squalor yet managing to squeak at the very end, 'Sorry, Jesus', is no myth for most of us. We know that all that is required for salvation is repentance. The trick lies in knowing whether or not we'll be given the grace at the end to call for it.

Our favourite personal prayer is the 'Hail Mary', closing as it does with this very hope: 'pray for us sinners, now and at the hour of our death.' No vain hope this, nor forlorn. We just know that after so many pleas Our Lady will be there to ease the moment when we most need her.

You may think this Faith facile. Yet it is as true for the erudite as it always has been for the simple. Another word for it is confidence – and both the learned and the ignorant know the value of confidence. In fact, the simple know its meaning better than the learned. Which is why the Catholic Church – when its arms are wide open – has so often been the refuge not just of the sinners but of the masses too. A good death, in the last analysis, is all the Catholic wants.

St Richard of Chichester

S trange but true, that a model bishop of the thirteenth century should have written the words for one of our modern hymns. St Richard wrote this prayer which is now sung regularly: 'O most merciful redeemer, friend and brother, may I know thee more clearly, love thee more dearly, and follow thee more nearly, day by day.'

Kindly words, gentle enough to remind us that Lent is running apace now. Holy Week is waiting in the wings with its distinct acts of triumph, betrayal and agony. So make the most of calm whilst you can.

With a bit of luck you'll have bumped into God recently. He may even have walked part of the way with you. But how would you know? Does He grab our coat-tails? Does He trip us up?

Yes, in a sense, He does that sometimes. We call it sickness, sorrow, grief. We don't always realize it's God trying to tell us He's with us. Sometimes, if we won't stop the express racing, He has to put a rail across the lines. If we seriously want to encounter Him we'll stop. The alternative is to crash on. Even then, He'll be there, holding our heads to His chest, taking our hands, stilling that useless urgency that sent us crashing.

Lent can serve many purposes. It can help cure an addiction, reveal a strength we thought we no longer possessed, heal a broken friendship, encourage us in charity. But if it doesn't at some point bring us into encounter with Our Lord in the desert then it is not complete.

There's still time. You'll like the desert, once you've been there. For a start, it's empty – except for Him. It is silent – only His voice. It is vast – He is, after all, Lord of the universe. It's a place to lose yourself, a place to find yourself, if you'll just listen. To Him.

4 April

ST AMBROSE   ST ISIDORE

Two great intellectuals of the first-century Church are celebrated today: Isidore was in fact nicknamed 'schoolmaster', whilst Ambrose was ranked with Augustine and Jerome as Doctor of the Church.

Obsessed as we are with simple tales of loaves and fishes, water into wine, don't we sometimes miss the greatest miracle of all? The distance between Rome and Jerusalem, even in the first century, was not excessive. But the intellectual mileage between the centre of the known world and the arid province of Palestine was huge. Yet, within 500 years, the dialogue at the heart of educated civilization all centred on the teachings of a country lad from Nazareth. It is mind-shattering how many great intellectuals of that period espoused the cause of a remote Jewish rabbi who died a felon's death. Would that the last 500 years had thrown up the giant minds that fabricated the first stirrings of Christianity.

But the miracle doesn't end there. Jesus, after all, left as His legacy a simple Faith. Whatever the arguments that rage about the Gospels they are clearly accurate, lacking any pretention, free of the clutter that can gather about precepts when great brains gather. The miracle is that that simplicity went untouched. Give or take a few mistranslations it has come down to us intact and wholly comprehensible.

Sure, the great Doctors parleyed and quibbled, as is the wont of such men. But the essence of what that gentle rabbi said and did remained sacrosanct. The great men were wise men after all. They played about with matters of authority, of organization, and later of power. But, miracle of miracles, the Man Jesus came through to us for what He truly was.

We are Catholics and not simply evangelic because we see purpose in enshrining the Gospels within the strong walls of authority. We look to that authority to preserve the essential purity of Jesus' words and actions.

5 April

Palm Sunday of the Passion of Our Lord★

It starts. Re-enactment of the week that changed the world. Listen:
'Tell me, Leah, tell me what you see – a curse on this blindness.'
'To be honest, Jacob, not a lot. Just the Galilean riding an ass.'

'But is it the same man, Leah – the one we went to see on the mountain that day?'

'Yes, I'd know those eyes anywhere. He's the same.'

'What's all that din, Leah? I can hear a funny rustling noise above the children's babble.'

'It's the kiddies, Jacob – they're pulling leaves from the trees and throwing them in front of the ass.'

'Ugh, a nasty Roman idea. All wrong for one of ours. The priests should be there with incense and plumes. Are they there, Leah?'

'Can't see any. But you'd not expect them to be, would you, with Pilate's spies all around.'

'What are the people shouting? I can't make it out.'

'It's the children, Jacob. Shouting . . . I can't make it out.'

'Is that all, Leah, just children? No grown-ups here?'

'Their parents are there all right, but hanging back in case there's trouble, I'd guess.'

'Oh, Leah, you're useless. What arms have they got? How many outriders? How large is his army?'

'I can only say as I see, Jacob – don't be crotchety. There are no armed men – just a bunch of farmers, they look like.'

'So much for all that gossip, Leah. A new leader to prod the priests and drive out the Romans. And not so much as a sling between them. Phooey – take me home, Leah.'

She led him to their home above the city road. Like all blind men he was anxious to touch the familiar again. Out there in the open he was vulnerable. He was disappointed. His image of a new leader didn't include a donkey.

★ If this movable feast does not fall today then see note on p. xiii.

6 April

MONDAY IN HOLY WEEK★

I t had been a difficult birth. But Rachel didn't mind – just so long as she could present her husband with a son. All mothers, it seems, long for a son as first-born. Fathers tend not to mind. Unless, of course, they are powerful men with assets to pass on.

The neighbours were concerned for Rachel. It was a small village where everyone knew everyone else. And Rachel's husband was a respected man there. When landlords raised rents he was the first to challenge them. If a family was in need it was Rachel's man who went door to door asking for food or money for them. He was, plainly, a good man. So it should have come as no surprise when Rachel's son was born that the little community celebrated. Her husband was more than a little embarrassed by the shower of good wishes and small gifts that arrived at his door.

The women came first, of course, to hold the child, pet and kiss it and, surreptiously, make sure it had all it should have. There was no doubt – a fine, healthy bouncing boy. A credit to her.

In the inn her husband found it hard to buy a round as was the custom. So many who had reason to be thankful to him insisted on treating the new father.

One of them asked: 'What do you want for him, old friend?'

He hesitated, sipped his wine, then said cautiously, 'That he be his own man.' Then he added, 'And in being his own man that he should care for the feelings of others and follow Him who is the Lord of us all.' The men clapped him on the back – he had spoken as they knew he would. Then they all went to his house for a peek at the baby.

'What name will you give the boy?' asked one of them as he tweaked the baby's toes.

Mrs Iscariot smiled over the baby at her husband. 'We thought Judas,' she smiled.

★ If this movable feast does not fall today then see note on p. xiii.

7 April

TUESDAY IN HOLY WEEK★

Typical of the Man that, after a triumphal entry into Jerusalem, he should stay a day or so with a leper at Bethany. Typical too that one of the things he did there was to ensure that a simple, ordinary person would never be forgotten. It was not that Jesus just had good manners, it was that everyone He met counted with Him.

It was during this stay that the woman – there have been lots of guesses as to whom she was – anointed His head with costly ointment to the indignation of those with Him. Amongst them, presumably, Judas. Was this the straw that broke this camel's back you must wonder.

Jesus leaps to the woman's defence. 'You have the poor amongst you always,' He reacts to the charge that she had wasted money which could have been given away. 'I am not always amongst you.'

Then He says those wonderful words which must have thrilled her as much as they baffled others: 'I promise you, in whatever part of the world this gospel is preached, the story of what she has done shall be told in its place, to preserve her memory.'

What a promise! So similar to the one he made to the centurion and would make later to the good thief. Formidable promises all – and to such simple people.

We're told that, just after this, Judas went off to do the deal for the 30 pieces of coin. All so logical. How often are men's good deeds misinterpreted? And so often by good men themselves who are too blinkered in their virtue to recognize that generosity is so much more than what you do with your cash, it's what you do with your heart.

So, on the Tuesday of Holy Week, we're back to that word, that oh-so-Catholic word, 'little.' A little act on the threshold of the world's greatest event has the promise of Jesus it will never be forgotten.

★ If this movable feast does not fall today then see note on p. xiii.

8 April

WEDNESDAY IN HOLY WEEK*,
SPY WEDNESDAY

O ne word jars in the Mass. The word is 'betrayed.' Yet it has to be there. Insensitive, ugly, frightening as it is — it has to have its place in the Eucharist because to leave it out would be an omission. And there are sins of omission as well as sins of commission.

Christians are given not a partial story but the whole sequence of events in their daily Mass. Nothing is omitted — from the Creed to the Consecration every Mass delivers the story of Jesus in its entirety.

Spy Wednesday is the archaic description of today's place within Holy Week although in parts of Ireland the expression is still heard. It's the day, of course, that Judas must have gone — afire with indignation after the matter of the ointment? — to denounce Jesus, not just for His acceptance of the ointment but, much more importantly, because Judas himself felt betrayed that the Man from Galilee was clearly not interested in revolution of the kind envisaged by him.

Hesitate before you condemn Judas. There are few of us for whom betrayal has not been our sin too. In fact, it's just possible that Judas' motive was purer than our own. Each time wife or husband lust secretly for another, they betray the other. Each time a teacher favours one pupil rather than another, the act is betrayal. Think about it — almost every sin we commit has its origins in betrayal.

'To thine own self be true' was Polonius's advice to Laertes in *Hamlet*. But the truth is we can seldom be true to ourselves, without at some time betraying all we hold dear.

Betrayer is the hardest accusation we can make. Today we make it against Judas. Tomorrow Our Lord could make it against us.

---

* If this movable feast does not fall today then see note on p. xiii.

9 April

MAUNDY THURSDAY OF HOLY WEEK*

T oday's emphasis is on the priesthood, the day when the
Eucharist was instituted by Christ at the Last Supper. But for
the bishop of a diocese it is something else – a revelation of
the extent to which his priests respect or love him.

From every parish they are invited to join him in the cathedral
for the blessing of the holy oils which will be used throughout the
coming Church year. Whatever the size of the diocese their massed
presence is always awesome. Equally expressive is their absence if, for
some reason or another, the bishop is currently held in low regard.

It is the one day of the year when the shepherds comprise the
flock, with the chief shepherd treating them to lunch afterwards.
Unlike Religious, secular priests have little opportunity to feel the
strength of their unity. Increasingly their lives are lonely. At one time,
monthly deanery meetings – where priests from six or seven
parishes could gather – supplied the comradeship all men needed
doing the same job. Nowadays ages are too disparate for these meetings to offer the same comfort.

So they'll make the most of today – similar years from different
seminaries will group together; the talk will go on well into the
afternoon. When men have to spend so much time disciplining their
tongues it's good to have the chance to let it all hang out.

Today, too, the Pope's annual letter to his priests will be published
– all too often a highly spiritual missive concocted by a Vatican
Office when all these men really want is a pat on the back and reassurance.

Tales told – and priests tell good tales even though they tend to
be brittle – it's back to us, their people. For, when all is said and
done, we are their family.

* If this movable feast does not fall today then see note on p. xiii.

GOOD FRIDAY*

My people, what have I done to you?
How have I offended you? Answer me!

The question posed time after time in the Reproaches at today's service that brings together all but the most obdurate Catholics. It's a day so awesome that from mid morning until late afternoon the heart dares scarcely breathe. Yet the cause prompting this grief occurred 2000 years ago. Incredible. Astonishing that we feel so numb with sorrow so long after the event.

The struggle to keep Good Friday sacrosanct as a Christian memorial has largely failed. The most we can do amongst a people now largely unchurched is to take the Cross to them as they surge to the markets for their weekend shopping.

Perhaps this is the way Christ wants it – His followers away from the churches and into the streets, there with the people, no whit different from the disinterested crowds who must have watched Him carry His Cross towards Golgotha.

The morning is the time for evangelization; the afternoon time for the convinced to kiss the foot of the Cross. We scarcely notice this is one of the few remaining days of fast and abstinence. As at all moments of mourning, food is far from our thoughts. There is just this strange vacuum in time that absorbs us, empties us of every thought other than that at 3.00 in this afternoon Jesus will cry out, 'It is accomplished', because:

> We had all gone astray like sheep,
> each taking his own way,
> and the Lord burdened him
> with the sins of us all.

* If this movable feast does not fall today then see note on p. xiii.

11 April

HOLY SATURDAY*

T**hose** who counsel the bereaved will tell you that their hardest task is often to convince those left that it is not wrong to feel relief – deep, satisfying relief that it is all over.

It is the same relief we feel, guiltily, today. Christ is dead. No more shame, no more suffering, no more apprehension. An end to long hours anticipating anguish, sharing the pain of someone we love. For it's not easy to companion the one you love as they die. However sweetly death may come, in whatever guise, you live each moment with them in trepidation of what is inevitable. Then, as they breathe their last, you instinctively breathe your first conscious breath for a long time.

Death is a cleansing. The end of the agony for one, the start of a different life for another. It takes only one major leap of faith on the part of the bereaved – that a good God waits with open hands for the one who has left. Left like this, it is right to feel bereft, angry even. Until faith steps in to point out that where the other has gone you will surely follow, in God's good time.

Holy Saturday sees the balance swing back from despair to relief; from annihilation to hope. The cool of the tomb after the fetid heat of yesterday reminds us that the worst is done. What is to come, we have no idea. But, for certain, the suffering is passed.

Your only choice is whether to attend the Easter Vigil tonight and be present for the Mass of Resurrection or to lay your head gratefully down in tranquillity knowing that tomorrow brings the the answer to every question we have ever asked ourselves.

Meantime, you know with certainty that the one you love sleeps only briefly in the death which, as Man, He had to pass through. In death, as in life, He shared every human experience with us.

---

* If this movable feast does not fall today then see note on p. xiii.

12 April

EASTER SUNDAY★

H appy Easter! It's as trite as describing the Sistine Chapel ceiling as a pretty mural, the Livingstone Falls as a nice waterfall, Attila the Hun as a wayward lad. Happy Easter indeed!

I love bunnies, guzzle Easter eggs, can grow only daffodils. But, excuse my indignation – Happy Easter? *Astounding Easter!* Astonishing Easter! Incredulous Easter! All that ever was, all that ever will, all that matters, all that concerns us – it happened today. And never, ever, let them tell you differently.

Christ died. The evidence is irrefutable – you know it so well. The torture, the spear in His side, the nails in wrists or palms, the three hours in the heat of the day upon a cross. The evidence of those there, our knowledge of the efficiency of a Roman execution squad. Have no doubts. Christ died.

Christ was buried. All witnesses will have seen something different, as at any event. But all witnesses will agree on one salient point: in this case, Christ's burial. The man who gave his own tomb was there, friendly disciples and family were there, less friendly soldiers and priests were there. Christ, dead, was buried. Of that you can be sure.

Christ rose. But first things first – today the tomb was visited and found empty. Body stolen? 'Conjuring tricks with bones'? Soldiers sleeping on sentry duty? An apostle's plot? We've had the lot down the centuries and worse even today.

No – Christ Jesus died and Christ Jesus rose from the dead. The days to come prove that beyond any doubt whatsoever. It's as well they do. For without the bodily Resurrection of Jesus we have nothing, will never have anything. Deny it only if you want to be forever a pebble on the shores of Hell.

★ If this movable feast does not fall today then see note on p. xiii.

———————— ✑ ————————

However do we scramble down from the sublimity of yesterday to the dusty plains that are our ordinary lives? For a moment, perhaps, we share the confused bafflement Christ's followers must have felt on that first Easter Monday. 'Where do we go from here?' they must have queried bemusedly.

The rumours of the Resurrection would have been flying amongst the disciples, sparking an impossible hope that perhaps, after all, there was cause for hope. It was a perilous period – from now until Pentecost – for all those who had held Jesus precious.

In a real sense that peril still exists for us, despite our huge advantage of being familiar with the Gospel stories of Jesus' appearances over the next days. For there were many yesterday who celebrated with Him His Resurrection who will not give Him much thought between now and Christmas.

'High days and holy days' was the way we once described the Catholic whose Mass attendance was minimal. Nowadays, such is our enforced humility, we are grateful for even such sparse devotion amongst many we love.

So our cry at the start of the third millennium is no different from that of the disciples on the first day of the first – 'Where do we go to from here?'

As ever, there's only one direction – forward. But it will be a lonely, fruitless journey if we make it alone. Somehow we have to ensure the companionship of those 'high days and holy days' Catholics. It's as if today, the Easter drama done, we start off on a perpetual road to Emmaus taking with us those we love in the hope that on the journey we will all be joined by Christ.

As it was before, the road to Emmaus involves more than a sense of direction. It is both a teaching and a learning experience – for us and for those accompanying us. But luckily, like that first Easter Monday, the Teacher remains the same.

14 April

CARADOC OF WALES

~

C aradoc was a harpist who lost his job as a result of losing a greyhound. Yes, a long story but it ended happily with him being buried at St David's Cathedral, revered, but never canonized. The Welsh – like the Irish – enjoy saints with a good tale to tell.

Their relics, of course, play an important part in Catholic life. Not an aspect of piety, I confess, with which I have great sympathy. But I do have a tale about one relic.

At one time I lived in a desolate place. (I'm being very cautious about names here.) My good friend was a priest who was custodian of the area's most precious relic, a skull. One blustery night – well, it would have to be, wouldn't it? – he called with an ornate box. Within was the skull. Would I care for it over the next week? He was called away far and urgently. I agreed and he left.

Such a week I never want to live again. My home was remote, insecure. The responsibility weighed more heavily each night. In the end I hid the skull under the bed. Where else? In due course the priest came back, relieved me of the treasure and the next I saw of it was on television when a cardinal prostrated himself before the casket.

All over England, small and large, portions of saints are revered and held inviolate. All altars used to have a relic buried beneath them. It is our ancient belief that to touch or be blessed by a relic is beneficial.

Thank God the custom is not an article of Faith, merely an act of Faith. On a bookshelf in front of me I have, framed in silver, the tongue of St Catherine, a bequest of my saintly grandfather, God rest him. In the centre nestles a long-dead maggot. To be honest, there are relics of my Faith I am happier without.

15 April

PATERNUS OF WALES

C atholics have come a long way in Britain since 13 April 1829, when the Roman Catholic Relief Bill was finally passed giving them emancipation. It had been a long tussle. Three Prime Ministers were largely involved – Pitt resigned when the House refused it, Grenville stuck his heels in and objected to it, then Wellington supported it.

Through the Bill Catholics were able to take their seats in Parliament, they were enabled to vote. All offices of state became available to them except Regent, Lord Chancellor and Lord Lieutenant of Ireland. An oath was still required of Catholic MPs – they had to deny the Pope's power to interfere in domestic matters in Britain and they had to recognize a Protestant succession on the Throne. Needless to say, the monarch could not be a Catholic.

It took another 30 years – in 1850 – for the re-establishment of the Catholic hierarchy. Yet, 100 years later, in 1950, there were almost twice as many practising Catholics in Britain as there were members of the Church of England – four million as opposed to two million.

In a succession of wars Catholics had more than proved their heroism and their loyalty to the Crown. In the professions – especially in medicine – their presence was formidable. In the world of letters and art they were equally well represented. In short, a religion proscribed and ostracized for two centuries had sprung back to centre-stage. And in the last 50 years of the twentieth century Catholicism was not just reinstated, it had become fashionable, perhaps reaching a peak – who knows? – when the death of the Benedictine Cardinal Basil Hume became a focus for national mourning.

At the turn of the millennium it really did look as if the Church was well placed to take the high ground in matters of public morality. Time will now tell.

16 April

ST BERNADETTE   ST MAGNUS

T hat God of surprises at work again. Whilst Our Lady chooses an ailing, illiterate peasant, Bernadette, to be her voice on earth, God selects a pirate, Magnus, to be His. You just can't tell what will happen next in Heaven, it seems.

The Times was the first newspaper of note to report the strange event:

> A girl named Savy of Lourdes gave out at the beginning of the year that the Holy Virgin had several times appeared to her in a grotto near the town; and as on the 4th March she intimated that another visit might be expected, some of the local authorities and a great crowd of spectators accompanied her. But no virgin appeared, though the girl remained some time in the grotto in a state of ecstasy, and her lips moved as if in conversation.
>
> Some persons believed the visitations real and made offerings in the grotto, others treated it as a piece of imposture. The prefect at the department appears to be of the latter opinion as he has just given orders that the offerings in the grotto shall be removed by the police; that the persons who pretend to see visions shall be sent to the hospital in Tarbes and be subject to medical treatment and that those who spread the 'absurd tales' of heavenly visitation shall be prosecuted for spreading false news.
>
> May 21, 1858

The reporter only got the name wrong. The girl was named Bernadette. Bernadette Soubirous, a teenager living with her impoverished family in an abandoned police cell.

God of surprises indeed. Since that report appeared pilgrims have made their way to the out-of-the-way Pyrennean hamlet now a town of substance. At the rate of three million a year they flow to the spot where Our Lady told the young Bernadette, 'I am the Immaculate Conception.' They go – and they believe.

17 April

St Donan

———∼———

Confession holds a certain mystique for non-Catholics but their criticism is usually the same – that the priest knows nothing of married life. . .

Father, I love my husband dearly but I hate the sex side of things. I don't mind if he gets that elsewhere so long as he comes back to us. Is this a sin?

Forgive me, Father, but I get so angry with my wife. When I want to make love she pretends to be asleep. It's ruining our marriage. What do I do and is my anger a sin?

I may have Aids – I don't know. And I don't want to know. Surely it's not a sin to sleep with my wife if I don't know for sure?

Then, say confession's critics, what does a priest know about real life when his life is so insulated. . .

It was the crack, Father, I'd never have done it if it wasn't for the drugs. That's no sin, is it, Father?

I love my daughter, well, you know, Father, I love her more than I should. But it isn't like a sin, not for either of us.

Father, I'm taking cash from the till. But it's because they don't pay me properly. That's only justice, isn't it?

There's a misconception that priests enjoy hearing confessions their people make to God in their presence. Nothing is further from the truth. For many priests the confessional is a penance to be endured. The fact they are witness to a sinner prostrating a soul to God must be little recompense for hours spent in the fetid atmosphere of shame.

Trained as they are, young priests may not originally know how deeply humans can sin. But it is a job quickly learned – either that, or it can suffocate them. But never say they don't know about life.

18 April

ST LASERIAN   ST APOLLONIUS

One hundred and fifty years after Christ's death Apollonius, a Roman senator, testified before the Senate that as death was inevitable it followed that the only part of man to have value was his soul. They beheaded him. But the seed was sown.

Two thousand years on, the debate still goes on. If the brain still puzzles surgeons, how much more are we baffled by the mystery of the soul? All we can say for certain is that unlike the dicky ticker or the aching joints, we can only judge its health by our reaction to moral challenges.

Poets would have it that we can see the soul reflected in eyes; others say it is in laughter or in tears. It uses the body as a vehicle, and when that vehicle stops, the soul departs it. Untrammelled then by physical infirmity it can fly free – where and how, we will, as Apollonius told the Senate, discover upon death.

In truth, we haven't travelled far since Apollonius's reasoned statement to the Roman Senate. St Teresa of Avila had her own image:

> I began to think of the soul as if it were a castle made of a single diamond or very clear crystal, in which there are many rooms, just as in heaven there are many mansions.

Thomas Aquinas was naturally more clinical:

> The mind is a subsisting form, and is consequently immortal. Aristotle agrees that the mind is divine and perpetual. Note that word 'mind.' He saw the soul as an organism surpassing the range of the body.

St Ambrose had a straightforward distinction that appeals:

> The soul is the user, the body for use; hence the one is master, the other servant.

In the end, it's up to us to know our own souls. And, having found them, we must be able to live – and die – with them.

————— ✑ —————

Today was the clincher. Not enough for Thomas that so many he knew and trusted had seen the risen Jesus. He was just like us: 'Yeah, but . . .'

And because of pragmatic Thomas who believed only what his eyes saw or his fingers touched we all now look up at the Consecration of the Mass and can say: 'My Lord and my God.' Five short words only but they distinguish the Catholic from a member of any other Faith. In echoing Thomas' act of faith we acknowledge the actual physical presence of Jesus on the altar at that moment. Together with our belief in the bodily Resurrection of Jesus this act of Faith is a full summary of what we believe.

That's why there's no room for the dilettante, the equivocating, the 'yeah, buts' in Catholicism. By all means have your own opinion on girl altar servers, Mass in the vernacular, even women priests – *but*, on these two articles of Faith, you're in or you're out.

Throughout life there's much on which we must compromise. Not to do so would infer that we're always right. And that, we are not. Whilst there can be no compromise with sin, most of what is creative for the good of religion and the human race is often enough the subject for debate. And, as Catholics, we know the debate has one chairman with the casting vote – or the last word. We accept that, even as we compromise.

Pilate asked 'What is truth?' and we've been struggling to find an answer to his question ever since. But, thanks to poor, bewildered Thomas we need never pose the question about the only truth that matters. Thomas did so very adequately.

St Caedwalla
St Agnes of Montepulciano

Time for the school league tables, time for anguish or triumph. Yet there should be neither. For the good Catholic school there can be only criterion – that it's a caring Christian community enjoying a common sense of purpose. A bonus, of course, if the children excel in all subjects. But only that – a bonus. Something extra to that which is essential.

A good Catholic school provides what no league table can annotate. It's composed of children, of varying and various abilities, who live together in love, justice and security. Then this whole rich mixture is bound by the Faith they hold in common.

Make no mistake about it – the Catholic Church in this country has beggared itself for the sake of its schools. So much so that perhaps the time has come for them to have their own league table.

Perhaps we should publish how many primary pupils continue to practise their Faith after moving on; how many find the seed in their school of a religious vocation; how many return to their parish church when there's no longer an obligation. In a sense the Catholic directories provide these answers. They list Catholic marriages and baptisms, Mass attendances, those offering themselves for religious life. These are the figures of a league more vital to Catholic parents than any other.

The good Catholic parent – the realistic one – asks simply that the primary school produces good Catholics and instinctively knows the rest will follow.

If we are not concerned first and foremost with the Catholicity of our schools then perhaps the time has come to think twice about the cash we pour into them and divert it to the poor in fact from the poor in spirit.

21 April

St Anselm

It's not likely that Anselm, Italian-born Archbishop of Canterbury, terror of the early Norman kings, could ever be described as a 'one-liner'. But from time to time he produced what today would be called soundbites.

Nothing is more certain than death, nothing more uncertain than its hour.

I do not seek to understand that I may believe, but I believe in order to understand. For this also I believe – that unless I believe, I should not understand.

To sin is nothing else than not to render to God His due.

What Anselm gave us was the proof of God's existence via reason:

For everything that is, exists through something or through nothing. But nothing exists through nothing. For it is altogether inconceivable that anything should not exist by virtue of something.

Whatever is, then, does not exist except through something. Since this is true, either there is one Being, or there are more than one, through Which all things that are exist. . . Since truth altogether excludes the supposition that there are more beings than one, through which all things exist, that Being through Which all exist must be one. . . There is, then, some one Being Which exists in the greatest and highest degree of all. . .

You will need to read that not once, nor even twice, but many times. Having done so, you might empathize with Anselm's dying words:

I shall gladly obey His call; yet I would also feel grateful if He would grant me a little longer time with you, and if I could be permitted to solve a question on the origin of the soul.

The time wasn't granted. Perhaps He thought Anselm had said it all.

22 April

THEODORE OF SYKEON

Theodore crops up here because tomorrow is the Feast of St George and Theodore spent much of his spartan life encouraging others in devotion to the soldier's saint.

His biography in *The Oxford Dictionary of Saints* is astonishingly detailed for a hermit/bishop of the first century. His mother and sisters were both prostitutes who kept an inn; his father was in a circus as an acrobatic camel rider. The future saint's life was no less colourful.

Much more colourful, in fact, than the man I sat next to in the train the other day coming home from town. Yet, I suspect that he too − if not already − will be a saint. He had, you see, the first requirement − he was patient. And he cared.

They sat there, his wife and two little girls, bubbling over with the excitement of the day's shopping. I could tell it was the hundreth or more time one little girl had started her talk with her Daddy with 'why?'.

'Daddy, why does the train go slowly here?' He explained. 'Daddy, why are the people in the train so old?' He whispered. 'Daddy, why is that man there picking his nose?' He blanched. 'Daddy, why does that man look like Santa Claus?' He turned anxiously towards me, saw my smile, and was grateful.

'You'd be sorry if she didn't ask why,' I murmured to ease his embarrassment.

He thought this over for a while and then nodded. 'Yes − because then she will have grown up and left us,' he commented wisely.

It was my stop. Otherwise I'd have told him that with such parents the little girl would never stop asking why. Only the questions would change. And the Father who answered them.

23 April

St George of England

S t George is almost as much myth as was the chivalry that was
once supposed to surround the business of arms. It died with
the invention of the crossbow – as demoniacal a weapon in its
day as the atom bomb today. The only difference is that the Church
of then denounced the bow with far more vigour than our Church
of today decried the atom bomb.

But chivalry was so much more than heroic antics with lance and
sword. It was the code by which men lived and were judged. It was
the secular background where the treasures of the Church could be
safely laid. It had only a short reign – perhaps no more than 200
years. But what a golden age that must have been when social and
religious obligations were wholly intertwined in harmony.

A time when women were respected; the poor defended; the
right upheld; and a man's courage could win him a place in the
higher ranks. If this was paternalism, then what better form of society have we found since?

Chivalry depended wholly upon a man or woman having a sense
of honour. Honour, in its turn, devolved upon a one-to-one relationship. Just as surely as the crossbow's long-distance bolt annihilated single combat, so the move away from chivalry marked the
start of segregating people into anonymous groupings until we no
longer had individuals but the deprived, the handicapped, the black,
the inarticulate, the powerless. Categorized and oh, so very neat. So
neat that should we ever come face to face with a black, handicapped, unemployed single parent we are personally embarrassed by
the encounter.

Because, somehow, somewhere, we lost the capacity chivalry gave
us to meet the challenge head-on. We replaced the responsibility of
individual chivalry with impersonal structures that would distance us
safely from the need to exercise honour face to face.

St Egbert St Fidelis St Wilfrid

Spring – but don't ask me why – always seems such a Catholic season. Perhaps it is hope – God knows we Catholics have that. Perhaps the strength newly gathered from the Easter miracle. Who knows? All I know is that the oldest Catholic Society of men in Lancashire, the Broughton Catholic Men's Charitable Society meets about this time each year. They meet and sing a long song together that hearkens back to the Penal days. It's certainly socially incorrect but, my God, it's rousing. Here's a verse:

For what concerned a man's belief there needed no great search,
They knew but one high road to heav'n, and that was through the Church,
A Church that priz'd the humble man and held him full as dear,
As those of high and noble blood with all their costly gear.

(*Chorus*)
And thus they passed a happy time, as everyone may know,
When our old Catholic Fathers lived a long time ago.

They knelt beneath the self-same roof and said the self-same prayer,
And all alike, both rich and poor, could meet as brothers there,
For ev'ry place was free to all of high or low degree,
They felt at home as children do, around their mother's knee.

(*Chorus*)
Full well the homeless wand'rer he had not long to wait,
If he could but contrive to reach the nearest convent gate;
The trav'ler worn, was welcomed there with kindly Christian glee,
And cheerful monks performed the rites of hospitality.

(*Chorus*)   'The Broughton Song'

It's unlikely that anywhere in England you'll find the like of these Lancashire anachronisms who not only revere the Old Faith but for the most part put it into practice. No wonder, when the Church faltered elsewhere in England it always flourished in the hills of Lancashire. And still does.

25 April

St Mark the Evangelist

I t is the winter of AD 64. You are a Christian in Rome and all about you the great city is burning. The flames, the devastation, last well into the next year and the Romans, ever a fretful folk, are calling for someone to blame. It is you, the Christian, on whom the fury falls.

Accusation and counter-accusation follow until everyone is, as Emperor Nero hoped, utterly confused. Even your own peace of mind is ruffled. Until a document begins to circulate amongst your little group, a document that brings huge incentive to your Faith, enables you to put up with what is to come in a short, nasty persecution.

It is John Mark's Gospel, the first to have been written giving, as the frontispiece says: 'The Gospel of Jesus Christ the Son of God.' Those early Christians found this news vitally inspiring because they would have known that Mary, Mark's mother, was one of those who gave the first disciples shelter and hospitality when things were rough in Jerusalem.

There is no doubt that Mark was familiar with Paul and Barnabas as well as being known to Peter. And it is supposed that Mark was describing himself in his account of the arrest of Jesus: 'There was a young man there following him, who was wearing only a linen shirt on his bare body; and he, when they laid hold of him, left the shirt in their hands and ran away from them naked.'

It's certainly not the type of detail anyone other than the one closely involved would have given. Which, of course, gives a particular validity to all that Mark – eyewitness to the most moving capture in the history of the world – had to write.

Mark, unlike the other evangelists, had little literary talent but a huge insight into Jesus and His times. Tantalized, we can only try to guess how great an effect his straightforward account of Jesus' life had upon those who so readily died for the Jew crucified in so far a country.

116

26 April

ST CLETUS

They were saying in church: 'Another fine mess the Church is in.' A bishop or a priest, I forget which, had gone off with a pretty woman to the delight of the media, which followed their every move with journalistic cupidity.

'A fine mess,' they continued to mutter for the weeks of the extensive coverage of the elopement. But they'd got it wrong. It was not the Church in the mess, nor the Church that made the mess, despite the screams of those who renewed their demand for a non-celibate clergy. It was an individual in the mess or the throes of delight, however you judge it.

Whilst it's true to say that the Church isn't a building, nor an institution, nor a bureaucracy, nor even the Pope, it is people, so you have to admit that people sometimes make an unholy mess of things. What we do as a people Church is usually good; sometimes what the individual in the Church does is bad.

What will be sad for the Catholic Church is when the departure of one of its priests no longer makes news – that will be the time for real worry. Faced with the demands the Church makes upon its priests the real wonder, the hard news, is that so many have stayed the course. Our surprise should be for them – not for the incredibly small number who find the sacrifices demanded of them too great.

Luckily we have reached a stage in general charity when the departing priest is no longer the victim of bitterness. Much as we regret his departure mostly we are conscious of what he has done. If there is awkwardness, it is because he will be forever a man apart in our eyes. In the course of time – and given the number of married Anglican ministers entering the priesthood – it could be that the priest who left will be invited to return. Unless there really are those prepared to throw the first stone, they will be welcomed.

27 April

St Machalus St Zita

Ever since Peter's outburst at Pentecost the Church has actively sought converts through evangelization. As ecumenism gathered pace in the 1970s so the steady stream of converts began to dry up. Then, 20 years on, upon the ordination of women in the Anglican Church, the flow of converts renewed. Yet this was 'issue' conversion, and a single issue at that. It was now up to the welcoming Church to show its new members that we had much more to offer than the absence of a female priesthood.

There are many, within the Church and without it, who think the choice of Catholicism is an intellectual step. In part, yes. But essentially embracing the Catholic Faith is a love affair, an act of the heart before it is an act of the mind.

Some converts would deny this vehemently, disappointed as they have been by our 'coldness' at Mass. And they have a point. We are not gregarious either in church or outside it. We have been reared, so many of us, with the notion that the Mass is Christ-centred and so absorbed are we in that idea that we tend to ignore our neighbour.

For the cradle Catholic, Faith begins in the womb as the mother prays to that other mother, Our Lady, and kneels before the altar in hope. It's the start of a relationship that will last throughout life, however much the one lover offends the Other who only too readily forgives the worst infidelities.

My heart goes out to those converts – and they are many – who entered the Church through the vision of their new Lover at Benediction.

Obviously you can enter the Catholic Church through intellectual exercise. But at some point soon thereafter your mind must step aside to permit the heart to take you that last step towards Him.

28 April

St Louis de Montfort
St Peter Chanel

Father Baylor was a Montfort Father. He appeared one day in my office. And I have never been able to forget him. He was skeletal yet exuded strength. His handshake was a vice. Into his face was burned 50 years of African sun and rain. Outside it was bitter, yet he wore a thin anorak, darned check shirt and baggy khaki pants. 'I'm from the Valley of Death, Zomba, in Malawi,' he said simply, 'and my people are starving. The rains failed.'

I have never encountered such whipped steel in any man before or since. And never shall. Fr Baylor – I never knew his Christian name – had been 50 years in Malawi, mostly in mountainous jungle. English came hard to him. He was part engineer, part mechanic, part farmer – he was wholly priest and wholly man. He died, as he had wanted, not so long ago in Malawi where he is buried in Zomba.

He was a missionary, one of thousands all over the world who anonymously give entire lifetimes to the communities in which they are placed.

All too often they are the forgotten army of the Church. Yet they are the best of the Church – men and women who abdicate family, friends and country for some arid strip of desert, some infested shanty, to care for the forgotten ones and the beloved of God.

Some return home for a break every five years or so. But many cannot – or will not – pay the fare. Then, for most, the remote spot where they are becomes home and their country sees them no more. When they grow old some Orders will recall them to retirement. It's a call they dread. But, men and women under orders as they are, they return. Then sit a while, a year or two, in awkward deprivation of all they held dear, until they die. Forgotten to the last, Christ's forgotten army. But not forgotten by Him.

St Catherine of Siena

T he dominance of women in the history of the Church only mirrors the importance they played in Christ's life. Neither was their role ever secondary but always complementary. That's the way it was then and the way it has always been ever since.

Catherine of Siena is a case in point. A fourteenth-century Dominican, she never learned to write yet the treatises she dictated saw her respected as a spiritual leader of her age. It was largely at her urging that the exiled papacy, in the person of Gregory XI, returned to its proper place in Rome.

When she grew weary, as she must have, of Gregory's vacillations over the move from Avignon, Catherine must have looked at the bust of 'Pope Joan' in Siena's Cathedral with more than a passing interest.

'Pope Joan' probably never existed, yet at Catherine's time her legend was all too familiar. The story goes that some time around the ninth to tenth centuries a woman disguised herself as a man sufficiently enough to become a cardinal. The tale is graphic. It tells how, after being elected pope, she gave birth to a child whilst mounting her horse. Legend separates at this point and you can choose between her dying then and there or being stoned to death by an angry Roman mob.

Folklore it certainly is but, for a time in the Middle Ages, just like some athletes today, popes upon election had to undergo a physical examination.

One thing is certain – Catherine would have made a better pope than Gregory XI or even his successor, Urban VI. Whilst this may be music to the ears of those who campaign for women priests it's also highly unlikely that Catherine, the Dominican through and through, would ever have supported their cause.

30 April

St Pius V

⟶

W hat we know of the Battle of Lepanto, the last sharp crusade, we largely know from G.K. Chesterton's raging poem, 'Lepanto.' You remember – the Turks are on the warpath and must be stopped:

> And the Pope has cast his arms abroad for agony and loss,
> And called the kings of Christendom for swords about the Cross.
> The cold queen of England is looking in the glass;
> The shadow of the Valois is yawning at the Mass;
> From evening isles fantastical rings faint the Spanish gun,
> And the Lord upon the Golden Horn is laughing in the sun.

Such was Europe's apathy in response to Pope Pius V's plea to stop the heathen in his tracks. Don John of Austria brought about the Turkish defeat and saved the entire Mediterranean coast from Moslem domination.

It was the Dominican Pope's last major effort to suppress heresy. And it was as ruthlessly carried out as were his steps to strengthen the Inquisition and control the activities of the Jews.

The six years of his papacy in the mid sixteenth century saw his excommunication of Elizabeth I and the consequent persecution of Catholics in England. Diplomat he was not. But reformer, yes. And at that stage of the papacy he was what the Office called for.

He was a tough chap but he practised what he preached. Always wearing the hairshirt of the penitent he accomplished in just a few years the near impossible task of Christianizing both Rome and the Vatican, cleansing the immorality rife in both.

Perhaps, as was said, he was the man for the time. Perhaps, as he insisted, the severity of the Inquisition was necessary for the preservation of the Faith. At such a distance in time we cannot be sure. But I hope he's not the first saint I encounter.

1 May

St Joseph the Worker

'God's good and Paddy's working', they used to say. The inference, of course, was that God is only good when Paddy has work. And if you're jobless, powerless and on Social Security you can see the point of the distinction.

The Catholic National Pastoral Congress of 1980 spent a lot of time discussing work and its effect on the human condition, and the lack of work and its effect on the human soul. Trouble was, the ones discussing it were largely well-to-do, middle-class and articulate – the best their parishes could find to send and represent them. True, there were the obligatory jobless and a few people from ethnic minorities, but they too tended to be activists, experienced in asserting the rights of the under-privileged and the racial minorities.

To his credit, Derek Worlock, convenor of the Congress, was fully aware of the danger of calling the middle class spokespersons for the hopeless, incoherent huddle the poor really are. But there was little he could do to rectify the inevitable. The poor are so often poor because of the very reasons they could never be delegates to a highly cerebral gathering.

Good suggestions were made at the Congress, notably that the Church should take the initiative in creating work. Every parish should look for the unemployed in its midst, then do what it could to create work, even unpaid, to give the jobless a sense of purpose, a solidarity with those about them.

Today we'll have prayers for human work. Ten to one it will be the employed praying for the jobless. For when Paddy isn't in a job then he tends to blame God and give Him the cold shoulder. You can't blame Paddy for that. Nor God. Just an increasingly technological society that so soon will have no use for Joseph's hands.

2 May

ST ATHANASIUS

I t wasn't all loving and light for those early Christians. Once the first hundred years had passed Christianity seemed destined to denigrate into a violent talking shop. Well, what could you really expect, tossing together Romans and Greeks, Turks and Jews, the whole polyglot admixture that the known world was at that time?

It was not the teaching of Jesus that separated them – that they had largely accepted even if they quibbled still over some of the small print. No, it was definition of what was an emerging theology which had to satisfy men of so many different cultures.

Arius, for an example, was a Libyan acting as a priest in Egypt when he denied Jesus' relationship to God the Father and so launched one of the many first fumblings called heresy. His was named after him – Arianism.

Athanasius was another resident of Alexandria, as was Arius, and the two clashed at a Council called Nicea in 325. Athanasius triumphed on that occasion and so we have the Nicean Creed which today is the basis of all we believe.

It is easy to be scandalized by the many heresies of these early years. Yet, often enough, it was simply a question of people striving for a truth. As Catholics we have to believe that the solutions found in good faith were inspired by the Holy Spirit and thus became an integral part of our Faith.

Over the centuries these truths hardened into doctrine and dogma so that today opposition to these truths, heresy, is a grievous sin. And grievous sin is much rarer than we think. So heresy is not a word to be lightly bandied about – a temptation for some Catholics flying to the defence of what they hold dear. For we are – and thank God for it – a fiery breed still when we sense assault on what we see as truth.

3 May

WORLD DAY OF PRAYER
FOR VOCATIONS

———— ❧ ————

The vocations crisis hits hardest in the Western world where the alternatives for a man or woman of tender feeling are immense. The caring can study social science and become social workers. The compassionate have the probation service. The healers are desperately sought by medical services. The thoughtful can teach philosophy whilst those with a sense of justice can work for one of many charities.

In the past all these characteristics met in a vocation for the priesthood or the religious life. But today is the age of specialists, and specialist care workers have the great advantage that they can live decently and raise a family whilst following their calling. The priest and the Sister cannot.

Christ's challenge to the rich young man who would follow Him is even more spartan than it was then: Sell all you possess and follow Me.

Follow You where and towards what? the young man must ask. And the answer is not all that reassuring. A decrepit house aside a crumbling church? Lonely nights and days spent shuffling the paper that dominates the lives of the poor? Sharing the wondrous vision encouraged in the seminary with the apathetic whose wonder lies increasingly in a new model car and a fortnight on the Costa Blanca?

Of course all parishes are not like this. Nor are all convents increasingly homes for aged nuns in search of young housekeepers. But some vocations will lead to these scenarios. Not forever, perhaps not even for long. But they are possibilities those who decide for Christ must face.

One thing is sure. If there is a vocations crisis who are we to deny that it is Christ's way of saying that the laity has a vocation too.

4 May

FEAST OF THE BLESSED MARTYRS
OF ENGLAND AND WALES

C all in at the English College in Rome and ask to see their most prized treasures – portraits of those young men who set out on their one-way journeys to England over the years from 1535 to 1679.

Over these years more than 200 priests, layfolk – women as well as men – were to suffer a barbaric death, often preceded by torture, rather than deny their Catholic Faith. And these were only the ones beatified – the ones whose sufferings were known to Rome. Many more times that number died or were stripped of their belongings as a result of their adherence to Rome.

A few years back, to facilitate steps towards unity in Britain, there was a move to mute both the martyrs and their achievements. For a time even their own hymn, 'Faith of our Fathers', was deemed a hindrance to better relations between Catholics and Anglicans. It was a foolish act of political correctness that would, if pursued, have hampered rather than speeded the unity process.

For every shire in England, and every county in Wales, holds dear the places where these martyrs lived or died. In York, the bustling, outspoken housewife, Margaret Clitherow, crushed to death by heavy stones for offering priests sanctuary; Nicholas Owen, Oxfordshire joiner turned Jesuit who travelled the country constructing the hiding holes that saved so many of his brothers from discovery; Margaret Ward, the Cheshire skivvy who smuggled in a rope to aid a priest's escape from prison; John Rigby, the servant who stood before the Court's might and refused to deny his Catholicism.

From the 200 martyrs who were elected blessed some 40 were chosen, you might say by random, to be canonized by Pope Paul VI on 25 October 1970. And these 'in spite of dungeon, fire and sword' live still and forever in the annals of Welsh and English Catholicism.

5 May

St Hydroc

M ay is surely the most Catholic of the months. Still imbued with the essence of Easter and with Pentecost yet to come it's the month of hope. It's also Our Lady's very special month – it bears the lightness of her touch, every mark of her encouragement. And, my goodness, how it has inspired the Catholic poet.

> This is the image of the Queen
> Who reigns in bliss above;
> Of her who is the hope of men,
> Whom men and angels love!
> Most holy Mary! at thy feet
> I bend a suppliant knee;
> In this thine own sweet month of May,
> Dear Mother of God I pray,
> Do thou remember me.
>
> E. Caswall, 'Hymn to the Blessed Virgin'

Even the seemingly austere Cardinal Newman wrote in his hymn, 'Green are the Leaves':

> O Mary, pure and beautiful,
> Thou art the Queen of May;
> Our garlands wear about thy hair,
> And they will ne'er decay.

Enjoy then – just as that Mother long ago must have treasured the five-month-old babe she held to her breast, in the jolly month of May.

6 May

St Edbert SS Marian and James

P rayer is a tricky business. If you're good at it, really good, like Marian and James, today's martyrs, you can raise your spirit above the noxious things happening to you and about you. But, for the most part, we're not all that good at it.

When all is said and done, the odds are probably 50/50 whether your desire and God's coincide. Yet most of us continue to be inveterate gamblers and when we are, it is called prayer.

The danger of prayer is that it becomes a needle stuck in some spiritual gramophone. Over and over and over again we bombard Heaven with our own desperate need of the time. Fair enough – Jesus and His saints have told us to do just that. Jesus was particularly positive – ask and you shall receive, He said firmly.

But – and here's the tricky bit – prayer is seldom answered in the way we expect. You can almost hear God chuckling when the thing we prayed for is denied but an entirely new road opens up which we have never even considered. The lesson to be learned is that, yes, God always answers prayer, but not always in the way we anticipate in our blinkered desperation.

When Cardinal Basil Hume was dying he revealed his huge regard for the prayer Jesus gave us, and which we so often gabble without hearing what it says. Say it now. But pause. You'll end surprised by its sheer breadth of content:

> Our Father, who art in Heaven . . . hallowed be Thy Name . . . Thy Kingdom come . . . Thy will be done . . . on earth as it is in Heaven . . . Give us this day our daily bread . . . and forgive us our trespasses . . . as we forgive those who trespass against us . . . lead us not into temptation . . . but deliver us from evil.

Could we really ask more of a prayer? And it's been there, all this time – right under our noses.

7 May

St John of Beverley   St Lindhard

y father, apart from crossing the Irish Sea, never travelled, never took a holiday. It seemed as if his excursion to France in 1914, which lasted all of four years, showed him all that he wanted to see of Europe.

To marry my mother – he was a Presbyterian from Donegal – he had first to take instruction in the Catholic Faith. It took four months longer than was usual because he could not come to terms with a Church that could produce the Inquisition. He never did. In fact, as long as I remember he was what we term lapsed (though our parish priest, who came once a month for a long talk over a glass and a pipe, said he was a lapsed Protestant).

You see, it wasn't just the Inquisition he held against the Church – or more correctly, God – it was the state of his patients. He was a doctor and his practices in Liverpool and then Birmingham were always in poor Irish areas. And poverty sickened him.

Nowadays we don't really know what poverty is. Most think it's when you can't pay the TV licence. Real poverty, the kind he moved amongst every day of his life, stank. The stench was sweat, urine, fear. It was the odour of surrender, hopelessness. And there he tapped foundrymen's chests and tended old women of 35 for their varicose veins, and knew that what they needed he could not give.

He was a learned man with simple tastes. When he died I went to close down his surgery in Small Heath in Birmingham. His call diary was on his desk: Baby Regan 2s 6d. Mary Sullivan 1s 6d. The fees had never been collected. Who would have had 2s 6d in the homes he visited?

When my patient Dad walked slowly up the road to Paradise I hope – and pray too – that the other Physician paid the fees uncollected.

8 May

ST PETER OF TARENTAISE

T he notice outside an Irish cathedral read: 'Perpetual Adoration is temporarily suspended'. Not long after I spotted a poster outside a local church which invited: 'You're without - He's within. Come in.'

Fair enough, I thought, and walked to the door. It was closed. Locked. From being a sanctuary that church had become a castle. And I was outside.

Aggrieved, I walked away wondering what that church possessed which was a fraction so valuable as a soul's desire to be alone for a moment with God. Candlesticks, a few pictures, some pence in the poor-box? What did they matter against the duty of God's visible home to be available at all times? Who are they to suspend, if only temporarily, an urgent need to be alone with God?

In justice, I have to admit that most Catholic churches remain open all day – particularly those in the most deprived areas. It is only as you move outwards towards the prosperous suburbs that Christ is found imprisoned amongst the silver and art which He must begin to despise.

Yes, a drug abuser may enter and snatch whatever may pay for his next fix. And a vagrant may break open any box that rattles. And a moronic vandal may spray the walls with obscenity. And, yes, it will cause anguish, even pain and certainly expense, but nothing so sorrowful as the thought of a God locked away from just one truly questing drug abuser, vagrant or vandal.

The Catholic church is different from others because it is the permanent home of Christ. Before the tabernacle the light burns that signifies He is there physically. More glorious than any Royal Standard above any great palace, the sanctuary lamp gently announces He is home to us. And His door should never be shut.

9 May

───────── ∾ ─────────

There are 5 of them, sitting at desks used by 11-year-olds, cramped, uncomfortable. The heating was turned off at the end of school, they blow on their hands, then open briefcases and take out Biros. They intend to change the face of the world. They are the parish committee on the Third World.

The Chair is Marie, deputy head of the school they are in. Frank, Paul and Enid are teachers too, from the secondary school. Alice is a dinner lady at the local factory. They intend to change the face of the world.

Alice opens with the latest report from Cafod – she is their regional rep. Money is needed desperately for Sierra Leone. Frank makes a note: his school will have a sponsored run which will raise over £100. Paul wants ten volunteers to picket outside a firm which is producing rubber bullets for use in Penang. Mostly the recruits will come from amongst their own friends and immediate family. But they'll be there.

Enid has a particular interest in a group of nuns who operate a leprosy clinic outside Addis Ababa. She has pictures, a long letter from the sisters. She reads it out. For ten minutes the little group isn't huddled in an inner-city classroom – it's in the moist heat of a shanty suburb of the Ethiopean capital, plagued by the flies settling on their sweating faces, smelling the sweet decay of disease.

Next Sunday, they agree, there'll be a collection taken outside the church for the sisters in Africa. It will raise enough to feed the mission for three days.

The Chair closes the meeting after two hours. They'll meet together several times during the next month, each helping the others' ventures, each knowing that what they don't do will not be done.

They are the parish Third World group. And, together, they *will* change the face of the world.

10 May

————— ⌒ —————

Our Lord tells His apostles: 'My little children, I shall not be with you much longer. I give you a new commandment – love one another.'

But how? And always? And where does chastisement come in? Here's a case in point: He scarcely took any notice of me. Tremulously, I'd opened the door to my study having heard noises there. His disinterested glance, lack of any movement, dispelled my fear but left me angry.

'What the heck d'you think you're doing here?' Trite, but what else do you say when you've found a thief in your house?

'Looking for money,' he murmured casually, glancing at me with eyes devoid of any emotion. 'You left the front door open,' he went on, almost in accusation. His predicament was my fault.

Then I realized I knew him by sight – one of a family of four at my own church. He was about 17, his sister younger. I told him what I knew.

He shrugged. 'Are you phoning the Police?'

The question threw me. Once the fear had gone I'd forgotten about that. 'No – but I'll certainly tell your parents.'

He rose from the desk, the same height as myself but not as young in the face as my 70 years. His hands shook.

'Give us twenty,' he demanded bleakly.

So it was drugs. Virtually all such crime in our area springs from that need. If he didn't strike lucky with me he'd go to the next house. An old lady perhaps. I gave him £20. To this day I don't know why. Next Sunday only three of the family were there. He was not. I looked into the father's eyes at the Sign of Peace. I saw there an aching hurt I had never noticed before. There was no need to burden him with my news. Nor the mother – the selfsame weariness was on her face too.

After Communion I asked Jesus, reminded Him, love one another? How?

11 May

ST IGNATIUS OF LACONI

Ignatius was a Capuchin Brother, a questor, one of those who went begging for the enclosed brethren. And, when you're a beggar, you meet with a variety of receptions. Ignatius, like some questors I've met, gave more than he took – in love, affection and his caring way with children.

The Poor Clares, Carmelites and other enclosed Religious have their questors still, and some Orders, like the Little Sisters of the Poor, depend upon begging for the livelihood of those they care for: the Salvationists too – a wonderful army of beggars.

Jerusalem 2000 years ago was no different from the environs of Euston Station today, or the piazza outside Westminster Cathedral. As Jesus warned us: the poor will always be with you. They are. Sometimes selling *The Big Issue*, sometimes just stretching out a hand from the ground. Sometimes touching your heart, sometimes angering you when you feel they could do so much more to better their condition.

It could well be that you are right, that nine out of ten beggars are idle layabouts who earn more than you do simply by doing nothing. But the tenth? Ah – there's the rub, don't you see? The tenth could well be Christ Himself. Or, if not Christ, then most certainly in His image.

So we're left with no alternative. We must give to all, however little, in the assumption that what we give is directly to Christ. The Faith we follow leaves us no alternative. It is the Faith of saints and sinners and we are never able – nor should try – to distinguish between them. That's God's job, not ours.

Charity is a large part of the Catholic's duty – it is one of the few things distinguishing us from the beasts. And charity is love.

12 May

St Pancras St John Stone

All that is known with surety about St Pancras is that for some peculiar reason he gave his name to a railway station. That's not the case with John Stone. He was an Austin friar who, summoned to take Henry VIII's Act of Supremacy, refused saying: 'The Kynge may not be hede of the Chyrche of Ynglonde, but yt must be a sprytuall father adpoynted by God.' Then followed his hanging, drawing and quartering.

Catholics should be proud that Pope John Paul II finally decided the Catholic Church's stance upon capital punishment. In his major utterance upon the sanctity of life he said what the Church had never committed itself to before – that the death penalty had no place in Christian morality.

It was a statement long overdue from a Church which in the past had sought to win people's souls with the threat of death and worse. The sadness is that so many Christian countries and even more non-Christian ones still debase humans by choosing them to be executioners. And worse, there are those who accept the task.

Israel knows something of this predicament. I had been at the trial of Adolf Eichmann and needed fresh air afterwards. I went to a largely German town north of Haifa. Sitting in a café I heard the radio announcement that Eichmann had been executed. To both my bewilderment and my joy the Jews there were mostly aghast at the news that their new State had violated its decision to ban capital punishment. I felt as proud of their reaction as I felt sickened by the thought of yet another death.

For only a mile or two from that town I had witnessed a hanging at Acre Prison when I was just 18. It had been incredibly ordinary. A passive, negligent killing, in total silence, of one man by another. Never again did I ever doubt my opposition to capital punishment. It took another 50 years for a pope to agree with me.

13 May

ST ROBERT BELLARMINE

Bellarmine lived at a particularly sensitive period for European politics. Despite holding high office in the councils of the Vatican – he was, for a time, Professor of Controversial Theology – he had a delicate, if unpopular, view of where secular power ended and Church power began. His advice then was as relevant as it is now:

> God has established in His Church a regime such as that which we have described . . . for in it there is the monarchy of the Holy See, the aristocracy of the bishops, who are true princes and not the mere vicars of the pope, and finally a form of democracy, inasmuch as there is no man in the entire body of the faithful who may not be called to the episcopate if he be judged worthy of that office.

This is a shrewder definition than it may seem at first. For Bellarmine foreshadows the impetus the Second Vatican Council would give in the 1960s to the collegiate power of the bishops. Even today, it is a power that some think has not been fully acknowledged by the Papacy.

In the midst of the rumblings from the reformers Bellarmine put forth a direct statement that permitted no discretion:

> We teach that there is only one Church, and not two, and that the one and true Church is the assembly of men bound together by the profession of the same Christian faith and by the communion of the same sacraments, under the rule of legitimate pastors, and especially of the one vicar of Christ on earth, the Roman pontiff.

But this Doctor of the Church – up there with Augustine and Aquinas – had little of regality in his own life and shunned power, using what rank he held to assist the poor.

14 May

MATTHIAS, APOSTLE, JUDAS' SUCCESSOR

On 14 May 1967, the great and the good gathered in Liverpool for the opening of the Metropolitan Cathedral of Christ the King. Or, as Scousers called it, Paddy's Wigwam. When Archbishop in that city, John Carmel Heenan had looked in horror at the triumphalist plans he had inherited for a cathedral to rival St Peter's. With his usual alacrity – and with great common sense which was his major strength – he scrapped them. Instead, he invited the world's architects to come up with something costing no more than £1m.

Christ the King was the result. There was little room for them at the opening, but the people of Liverpool knew who had really built, as The Beatles put it, 'a cathedral to spare'. They had. And in the *Catholic Pictorial* I told them, and the visitors, how they had done it:

> They did it by touting the streets and the pubs
> and knocking on doors like their own.
> They did it, bless 'em, by giving
> when they had so little to give.
> They did it with dolls and with raffle tickets;
> they did it with pools and with bingo;
> they did it with socials
> and tired old men standing outside churches
> in the wet with a bit of a box in their hands.
> They did it with silver paper
> and tuppenny legacies;
> they did it with cigarette and Green Shield stamps;
> they did it with old newspapers and wedding rings;
> with treasured heirlooms and bits of this and that.
> They did it. And today is their day.

I never have written anything that gives me the same pride I feel in that acknowledgment to the people of Liverpool – bless 'em.

15 May

St Dympna   St Isidore the Farmer

oth today's saints lack any authentic history, but carry a great deal of legend and folklore – rather like our priests. If you've been to a clerical funeral you'll know just how it is.

There will be a handful of layfolk from his first parishes. 'He'd bounce onto the altar, hold out his arms, welcome us. The old Canon didn't like it one bit.' Another would chime in: 'Remember his first baptism? Almost drowned the baby – then said he was teaching it the crawl.' As the ham sandwiches were passed around they'd all nod fondly.

The priests, after the Requiem, will be huddled in their seminary year – his year. 'He had three goes at Philosophy – didn't think he'd make it. But that goal he scored against Ushaw – it was a blinder.' They'll nod. One will whisper, 'I heard the Boss had him up to the house more than once about Humanae Vitae.'

The family he never had – his brother's children and their children – stand apart. 'Poor Mick,' the brother whispers to his wife. 'He must have felt so alone with us all living so far away.'

His son nods. 'Came to stay once with Mary and me. Very reserved, Uncle Mick – couldn't let himself go with the kids at all. He never came again.'

More recent parishioners gather around the blancmange. 'He was a great visitor,' says one, 'and when our Lucy died he just took over – saw us right through it.' Others agree. Out come tales of a life submerged in others, invisible to most, a hand held out here, a heart listening there. All have stories to tell. Singly, they are slight. Put together now, as they never have been in the past, they build into a rich tableau.

For several generations, then, the stories of Father Mick will be told until, in the course of time – like Dympna and Isidore – he will enter parish memory as folklore. It is enough.

16 May

St Brendan St Simon Stock

T he story of keen-eyed Brendan the navigator is as apocryphal as that of Jason and the Argonauts. What they had in common, though, apart from derring-do, was our innate desire to see over the horizon. Whether or not monk Brendan sailed to Greenland or found the West Indies is not so important as the fact that he tried.

The more you immerse yourself in Catholicism the more you are likely to be faced with far horizons of faith. Satisfy yourself that Jesus lived and is adequately recorded and you're plunged into a voyage of discovery as daunting as Brendan's venture into the Atlantic Ocean.

What Jesus said is simple enough to comprehend – after all, He wasn't trying to bemuse artisans and farmers with His learning, He was trying to teach them right from wrong. But take all He said at face value – and you must – then His demands were as excessive as they were bleak. Abandon family, wealth, home; forget about how you're dressed or how you eat; disregard the day-to-day anxieties of living – all for the promise of a Heaven hereafter.

It was a simple set of priorities He gave us, a facile chart that no doubt Brendan and his ilk tried to follow. What complicates it, for us as Catholics, is that it leaves us no scope for deviation. So we call them Counsels of Perfection and plan our own little journey just skirting the oceans and mountains He set in our path yet, hopefully, still arriving at the same destination. It can be termed procrastination – a big word for a little fear that going His way can be just too tough for us.

So Catholicism for most can only ever be a jerky, reluctant tramp towards the horizon He set us. The Church, in its wisdom, knows this and strews the way we must go with a series of rest-stops which have attracted the name Sacraments. The wise – not being heroes – will tarry at them.

17 May

St Paschal Baylon

'**A** JOVIAL monk am I', goes the song. And it could be sung for Paschal Baylon who is remembered for his cheerfulness and a dance he once performed in sheer joy before a statue of Our Lady. Amidst the austerity of the Friars' monastery at Loreto it must have caused quite a stir.

For the religious life connates a high degree of anonymity. Those entering a monastery or a convent do so as individual personalities, perhaps even as eccentrics, but what they have been must then be subordinated to the character of the House they have chosen. As the Carthusians put it: 'Secretum meum mihi' – my secrets are my own.

Most Orders will require three basic commitments – poverty, chastity and obedience. The poverty faced will vary from Order to Order; the chastity, once entered, will be non-negotiable; the obedience essential in any community adhering to even the slightest of discipline.

What happened in life prior to joining the Order is now irrelevant. But skills will be utilized in due course. A doctor will expect to look after the infirmary, an accountant to be bursar, a cook will find the way to the kitchen. Skills are a gift from God and, as such, not to be wasted. Not in any community and certainly not in this.

Above all, the religious life is just that – a life, an activity. It is not an escape from responsibility, nor inadequacy. It is life, different no doubt, but nevertheless existence with a purpose.

Religious life is a Catholic taking that path we talked of yesterday, the one that goes directly rather than crab-wise towards God. Fewer and fewer may take it nowadays but it is there; infinite in the variety of its character but always straight – to God.

18 May

ST JOHN I   ST ELGIVA

'*Veni creator Spiritus*,' roared the parish choir.

The bishop turned to the parish priest and smiled, 'They're playing my tune. Let's go.'

And on to the altar they went – the bishop to administer Confirmation, the parish priest to worry if all would go well.

The Council of Trent, meeting in 1547, did much to rationalize Confirmation as a Sacrament. In fact, due to Protestant denial of the Sacrament, the Council was particularly outspoken:

> If any one saith that the confirmation of those who have been bap-tised is an idle ceremony and not rather a true and proper sacrament; or that of old it was nothing more than a kind of catechism, whereby those who were near adolescence gave an account of their faith in the face of the Church; let him be anathema.

And then, to give even more credence to its determination to ensure the proper place of Confirmation amongst the Sacraments, the Council decided:

> If any one saith that the ordinary minister of holy confirmation is not the bishop alone, but any simple priest soever; let him be anathema.

Anathema translates as 'let him be cursed'. So the Council meant business. Originally, of course, the laying on of hands – as happens at Confirmation – derived from the apostles' actions at Pentecost. Then, their laying on of hands more often than not preceded a miracle. It still does in a very real sense, for when the bishop administers the Sacrament he passes on the power of the Holy Spirit.

To say that Confirmation reflects the Jewish Bar Mitzvah is tempting but not accurate, yet both ceremonies impress upon the young the reality of their religious obligations.

19 May

St Dunstan   St Peter Celestine

s the result of a deadlock over the choice of pope to succeed Nicholas IV the aged founder of the Celestine Order was elected Pope. His reign lasted from 5 July until 13 December 1294. Ring any bells? Try again then. He rode to take up the most important job in Christendom on a donkey. Almost immediately, the humble Peter Celestine was overwhelmed by the machinations of the powers surrounding him – both Church and secular. After five months of this, Pope Celestine became the first – and the last – Pope to abdicate.

He was widely quoted in 1978 when the bewildered Albino Luciani, former teacher and whimsical writer, died after just 32 days as John Paul I. The similarity owed much, not just to the shortness of his time in office, but to the vivid similarity of two simple men overwhelmed by the pressures of the papacy.

It may be near a lifetime, but I remember exactly when and where I heard of John Paul II's election. It was a clergy golf dinner outside Liverpool. The priest captain was called from the table to take a telephone call from Archbishop Derek Worlock. The meal halted, we looked at each other as the priests' grapevine – none faster – whispered who wanted the captain. When he returned he announced: 'We have a new Pope.'

Loud cheers.

'His name is . . . Wodge Tyler.'

Dismay. None knew the name.

Then the captain added: 'Derek knows him.'

Lots of laughter and very much louder cheers. Of course he knew him – Derek Worlock knew just about everybody.

Amongst those priests that night, one of few laymen, it was brought home to me how much leadership meant to the men in the field, how vital a part it was of their lives. Not just leadership at the very top, but leadership where they were – in Liverpool. And, that night, they were proud of both.

20 May

St Bernadine of Siena St Ethelbert

Bernadine was a Friar preacher. And his subject was the Holy Name of Jesus. In 'My God and my All', Faber gives us a hint of the importance of the Holy Name in Catholic life:

> O Jesus, Jesus, dearest Lord,
> Forgive me if I say
> For very love Thy sacred name
> A thousand times a day.

My generation was brought up with the habit that at every mention of Jesus the head would bow. It was one of those hidden marks of the Catholic and that little nod was the swiftest way to detect the Catholics in any prayerful group.

The respect, you'll find, has not survived into our new millennium – perhaps another of those petty pieties consigned to the dustbin of superstition? If so, it's a pity, for respect is the foundation of love.

A treasured document on stiff vellum is still preserved by me. It states that if Wilhelm Waldschmidt, at the moment of his death, should pronounce the word 'Jesu' he will go to Heaven and the presence of Jesus. My maternal grandfather did just that – he came out of a coma, uttered the Holy Name and died. My mother did the same. And such is my Faith – superstitious, sentimental, what you will – that I firmly believe both of them were uttering their first words to the One they had ever loved.

'Jesus' is, you have to suppose, the very shortest prayer you can utter. And it is enough. Like any prayer, it makes a direct address, it pleads, it invokes. Further words are redundant – your heart speaks what it is you need.

In support of this, on the Feast of the Holy Name, we pray:

> O God, Who didst appoint Thine only-begotten Son to be the Saviour of mankind and didst bid that He should be called Jesus; mercifully grant that we, who venerate His holy name on earth, may also enjoy the vision of Him in Heaven.

The Ascension of the Lord*

My goodness, this day, Ascension Day, was once so special in old England. A day of fiesta and joy, merriment and such laughter. All because, as the Roman Breviary puts it:

> God is gone up with a shout, Alleluia, Alleluia.
> God is gone up with a shout, Alleluia, Alleluia.
> And the Lord with the sound of a trumpet. Alleluia, Alleluia.

This is how the monks broke out in song in the seventh century and you can be sure they didn't spare the Alleluias. Nor, after, the celebration. Because they knew – *knew* – that where Christ had gone they would surely follow.

Remember the scene told both in Acts and in Luke? Jesus walked with the disciples from Jerusalem to Bethany, blessed them and then left surrounded by a cloud. Then, how human and likely, two men appeared to the disciples and urged them to stop sky-gazing and get on with the job Jesus had left them to do.

Then, in the Psalm, that exultant verse:

> God goes up with shouts of joy;
> the Lord goes up with trumpet blast;
> All peoples clap your hands,
> cry to God with shouts of joy!

Little wonder that if this was the tale the early Church told eagerly amongst themselves they were so fired up with the enthusiasm that carried them through insult and persecution.

Ask any leader, any teacher or any priest what it is they most desire in those before them. The answer's always the same: enthusiasm. If Faith should ever lose it, oh brother, it's a long way and a tough struggle to reclaim it.

God is gone up with a shout, Alleluia, Alleluia!

*If this movable feast does not fall today then see note an p. xiii.

St Rita of Cascia
St Helen of Carnavon

F̲ew cults are as active in Britain as the devotion to Rita, who ranks only second to St Jude in the matter of 'desperate causes'. Those devotions invoking Rita are mostly concerned with women – women who are sick, women whose married life is crumbling, women who are mothers.

She bore the stigmata of the Crown of Thorns after being widowed and joining the Augustinians where she cared for the sick and counselled those who sought her help. So widespread is her name in Britain that the Augustinians made their church at Honiton in Devon a centre for the cult.

In Catholicism, the phrase 'desperate causes' has a very special connotation. Quite simply, it means what it says. Saints like Rita, Jude or the Little Flower are not approached lightly but only after all other prayers have seemingly failed. These are the saints of the last-ditch stand before total despair numbs the mind to further progress in prayer. This implies no lack of faith in God's mercy. Rather, it is a huge humility acknowledging that what is desperate for the pray-er is but a speck in the universality of God's empire.

So the desperate prayer is addressed to an individual who, in the course of prayer, becomes an intimate, a friend, a shoulder to lean on that has ever proved sympathetic. 'St Rita, who art called the Advocate of the Hopeless, pray for me.'

The astonishing fact is that St Rita, called to intercede by those goaded beyond endurance by their anxieties, really does answer prayer. If you doubt this, then there is only one way to prove it if, indeed, you are in genuine despair:

O, glorious St Rita, who did miraculously participate in the sorrowful Passion of Our Lord Jesus Christ, obtain for me the grace to suffer with resignation the troubles of this life, and protect me in all my needs.

23 May

ST WILLIAM OF ROCHESTER

In the auction rooms I came to a halt, nonplussed. Among the stock of tawdry bric-a-brac there stood a tabernacle, doors ajar, dusty but unmarked. The silken curtain still lay limply about it. I had it photographed, and used it in a full front page with a few words about the sign of the times.

Archbishop Beck, horrified by the picture, asked me to investigate what had happened. It had come from a convent which had closed down. It had gone to a man who, intrigued by its design, placed it in the corner of his living room and used it as a bar. Perhaps he still does – unaware of the sense of desolation its sale had brought to an archbishop and a large number of his people.

The picture was on my wall and after a time I began to wonder what is holy and what is not. Can an object of metal attract holiness simply by association? Yes. But, after that association is over, is that object still holy?

I thought of the century or more hundreds of Sisters had knelt before that tabernacle – taking to Him their joy or their loneliness, their faith or their doubt. I thought how their eyes must have devoured the silken curtain in an attempt to see through to the loved One beyond. Then, it dawned on me, their attention was not the tabernacle but the Person it housed.

After that I found it increasingly hard to share the indignation stirred up by the tabernacle. Yes, it had housed Him. And, yes, it was holy. But when He left, it was then again a metal dome some two feet high and attractive enough in design to grace the corner of a room. It seemed to me a danger when metal, or bricks and mortar, became sacrosanct simply by virtue of past association. Even our bodies, we are taught, are temples of the Holy Spirit. Yet, when the Spirit departs, our bodies may be burned, buried or blown to smithereens without insult to the One who inhabited them. Had it been a storm in a tabernacle?

24 May

———————— ❧ ————————

There is another 'special' Sunday which we owe to the initiative of Derek Worlock, who to some seemed the architect of the Catholic Church in England for more than 20 years whilst Cardinal Basil Hume occupied the building.

Archbishop Worlock early foresaw the value of an informed media; even as secretary to three successive cardinals of Westminster he made the time to act as Chaplain to the Catholic journalists' society, 'The Keys'. Despite this association – or because of it – he instinctively mistrusted newspaper people. Not so much because he doubted their integrity, as mistrusted their ability to grasp the fine print of the Church's message.

So he deliberately set out not to censor the media but to see it had every facility to report the Church's point of view. In London, the Franciscan Agnellus Andrew had already started a television and radio studio which trained Catholic spokespeople. When he was promoted to Rome a rapid expansion of the Church's information services followed until today we have a professional team of journalists, headed by a priest, to field the obvious and the least probable queries the world's most sophisticated press can throw at them.

Time after time this expert base of the Church's venture into mass communication has proved invaluable in stemming the worst of media misconceptions. And, God knows, there were plenty of them. But it didn't stop at national level – by the end of the century every diocese had its own press officer, priest or retired lay journalist, and most had some form of written communication with the people.

All this was controlled by a tiny body known as the Catholic Media Trust. And all the work originally of Worlock, the priest whom, like St Paul he so admired, saw an urgent need to keep Christ in the news.

25 May

ST BEDE

Occasionally even our sophisticated world is thrown into confusion by the inexplicable. Such a challenge to rationality was born in Italy on this day in 1887. He died in 1968 having had the signs of the stigmata upon his body for 50 years. He was Padre Pio, a Capuchin monk whose hands, side and feet bled in imitation of the wounds of Christ.

As with Mother Teresa later on there was an immediate demand for his canonization, but it took Pope John Paul II, who had visited him in San Giovanni, to hasten his cause.

There were three peculiarities that drew thousands each year to San Giovanni, a town in southern Italy. Foremost, of course, like latter-day Thomasses they wanted to see the bleeding wounds. Then they wanted to share the strange perfume that so often filled the room where he was. All reported this as a sweet fragrance but for each who smelled it the perfume was different – violets, incense, jasmine? Opinions usually varied.

But these were the things curious people could experience. Their third purpose was to confess to the monk who was equally desirable of remaining anonymous. The Italians are emotional, especially in the south. And perhaps it was this uncontrolled adulation of Padre Pio that put his so obvious a Cause on hold for so long. Their devotion swamped the clear facts of this monk's holy life.

Padre Pio was by no means the first to bear the stigmata. Whilst many tried in the mediaeval Church to fake the signs, there is evidence that St Francis and St Catharine of Siena were visited with the marks of Christ's wounds.

In the case of Padre Pio, though, the wounds are not a tradition to be taken with some degree of faith; they existed for 50 years and were witnessed by thousands.

St Philip Neri St Augustine
of Canterbury

~

Two mighty names to conjure with. But conjuring isn't our purpose – although a little sleight of words might not go amiss with the founder of Canterbury and the Father of the Oratorians, who were to welcome John Henry Newman into the English Church.

You see, both were Europeans – Augustine was to adopt England and Philip Neri never saw it. Yet their influence was to dominate the path of the English Church both before the start of the second millennium and at its end. Augustine's conversion of the Saxon King Ethelbert and the Oratorians' appeal to Cardinal Newman topped and tailed a remarkable 1000 years of Catholic history.

One of the crosses Catholics in Britain have had to bear is their designation as RCs – Roman Catholics. In point of fact, there are no Roman Catholics, other than those in Rome, any more than there are ACs (American Catholics) or ICs (Irish Catholics).

But for 500 years in England, Norman, Plantagenet and Tudor rulers were rightly or wrongly highly suspicious of what crossed the sea from Rome. Henry VIII rectified it all by creating the English Church with himself as head and from then on our brand of Catholicism was designated Roman. For 300 years the description betrayed both suspicion and a need to alienate Catholics in their own country.

It's an irritating misnomer, probably at its worst in Northern Ireland where Roman so often carries an inbred slur. Even worse, Catholics themselves perpetuate the fallacy every time they sign a hospital admittance form or fill in a questionnaire.

Now, here's something I've longed to say, although it's politically incorrect: why should the Devil have all the best tunes anyway?

ST BEDE ST JULIUS THE VETERAN

The Venerable and the Veteran – strange that two such dissimilar men should share today's liturgy. A hint, perhaps, that we give to God only what it is in our power to give Him. Bede gave his learning and his gentleness; Julius, old soldier and brave with it, gave his life.

Time after time God makes clear that no two of His people have the same gifts to offer Him. We are, each of us, unique. And for this reason the Church fights hard to establish the right of every being to life.

Not even its parent has the right, once conceived, to deny a child access to life, however brief or uncomfortable its existence might prove. Disabled, mentally or physically, no man nor woman can usurp God's decision to create a human soul. Nor can anyone outguess God in that soul's influence upon those about it.

For the Catholic there is no half measure possible in this struggle for the rights of the unborn. The right to life is imbedded in granite. Not just in Christianity but in all Faiths that recognize the hand of God in every creation.

History is littered – and our own time too – with genius of all kind which some would have stifled at birth or before. And don't we all know of families where the birth of a disabled child has given all those about it a strength and unity that family would never otherwise have had? Even from what seems the direst blow endless virtue has flowed.

In so many ways we are all disabled. In some, the signs are apparent. In others, the disfigurement only rarely shows. No human being is ever perfect. Only unique. And it is not our task to make a choice between what disability survives and what soul is eliminated.

28 May

St Bernard of Aosta

~

Thanks to Bernard, a priest in the Alpine passes, we have the breed of dog with the same name. Whether we thank him too for the brandy isn't recorded. Like all fathers, Bernard was in the business of rescue and aid. Both can be sometimes heartbreaking. Take this letter from a Catholic father to his son at college:

My dear Boy,

It was so good to see you on that flying visit. And to meet Julia at long last. We both liked her instantly, a lovely girl. I'm just so very, very sorry you both felt you had to leave so abruptly. Peter, I know it's the modern way but there's just no way your Mum and I could think of you sharing the same room in our home.

When you both went, and so angrily, your Mum just sat down and wept. I have never felt so . . . so hollow, bereft. You must surely understand – this is your home, you grew up here, you learned to walk, to talk, to laugh here. And to pray. The very room you wanted to take Julia was the one we knelt about the bed every night you grew up, praying together. For big things and for little – but always in hope and always in love.

I know you love Julia. And we can so easily love her too. But, Peter, you ask the impossible of us when you take it for granted that we can't be anything but shattered when you anticipate that love here – or anywhere else.

Please, please, Peter son, bring Julia back soon. Tell her we love her, love you both. But we are what we are – and I think you are still. Our home has always been shared – the three of us and God. Peter – we can't slap Him in the face. Come soon, please, both of you – and try to understand.

All our love,
Dad

29 May

St Alexander, martyr

⟶

G ilbert Keith Chesterton, born today in 1874, died in 1936. Convert to Catholicism, master of paradox, apologist supreme, journalist, crime writer, poet with mastery of the art of sound, the Catholic writer who bestrode the world of letters in the early twentieth century.

Anti-Semitic? A touch – in the way most Catholics were about that time. Fascist? For a time he saw virtue in the way Mussolini built roads and kept his people employed. A learned innocent in so many ways, my guess is that, like Conan Doyle before him, he will be largely treasured in literature for his detective, Father Brown. Scamper with me through his observations:

On journalists (and he was ever a loiterer in Grub Street):

We do not need a censorship of the press. We have a censorship by the press.   *Orthodoxy*

On the Church:

The Church has been cruel; but the world has been much more cruel. The Church has plotted; but the world has plotted much more. The Church has been superstitious; but it has never been so superstitious as the world is when it is left on its own.

All Things Considered

On his conversion:

It is impossible to be just to the Catholic Church. The moment men cease to pull against it they feel a tug towards it. The moment they cease to shout it down they begin to listen to it with pleasure. The moment they try to be fair to it they begin to be fond of it. But when that affection has passed a certain point it begins to take on the tragic and menacing grandeur of a great love affair.

The Catholic Church and Conversion

30 May

St Joan of Arc · St Hubert

Joan of Arc must have shared the doggedness, the peasant obstinacy, of Mother Teresa, presently on her fast road to sainthood. Perhaps in future she'll share this day with the French warrior girl who acted in obedience to her visions.

Mother Teresa shone out at the moment an age was almost wholly without a sense of holiness. A beacon is always lightest in the dark and Mother Teresa was no exception.

The Church was lucky insofar as she was Catholic. In point of fact, there's no way she could have been anything else. The entire ethos of basic Catholicism radiated from her. Even her pigheadedness in the matter of healing was obstinately Catholic.

But tiny Mother Teresa was one shrewd lady too. And this showed in the way she chose those who would join her Order, the Missionaries of Charity. For ten years or so, whilst every other Order was desperate for aspirants, Mother Teresa was being deluged with would-be Sisters (and Brothers too).

One was a friend of mine – a highly skilled theatre nurse in a Hamburg hospital. Aged 30, she felt the time had come to burn her boats and give God what she felt she owed Him. She took a flight that landed her in Calcutta at midnight. Until dawn she paced the terminal floor, exhilarated that at last she was giving something back, apprehensive about the meeting to come.

In the Calcutta shelter Mother was bending over a woman; she glanced up and fixed my friend with a stare for all of five seconds. Then went back to her nursing. 'Mother,' cried my friend, 'I am yours.'

Mother arose slowly, looked her in the eyes again. 'No,' she murmured, 'go home.'

Tears flooding, my friend rushed out, back to the airport – just in time to board the same plane that had brought her there that morning. She is now happily married, mother of three.

31 May

PENTECOST SUNDAY*

I t's one of the most vivid pictures in all the Gospels – and the most incredible. You have to love Peter almost as much as you are overwhelmed by the Spirit that drove him. Imagine it, just put yourself there, in that square as crowded as all city squares are in the spring. Tourists from all parts of the world, jostling, inquisitive, almost unruly, just like the crowds you see in Trafalgar Square.

Slap-bang into that melee goes burly Peter – shoving, pushing with the best of them until he reaches a spot in the middle. Then this fisherman – solid, ignorant man that he was – with a voice that could be heard above the waves' roar, thunders out to this motley crew his love for Jesus. And, astonishingly, they all understand him, 'each in his own tongue'.

No wonder Pentecost is thrilling. And how I envy – deep, deep down – those still able to recapture the vibrance of enthusiasm that swept away Peter so long ago. And there are Catholics who can do this – obliterate self, give themselves utterly and become, in essence, spirit.

So many of us are embarrassed by the wholehearted freedom of those who can capture, or open themselves to be captured by, the Holy Spirit. We think like the crowds who said of Peter and his friends that they must be drunk and, in our fear, shelter in the shadows.

How I long to share that easy tactile freedom of the Pentecost Catholics, long to be part of their enthusiasm, their total faith in shared healing, their sure knowledge of God's presence in their midst.

But I cannot. I'm stolid, set in my ways, a lump of spiritual lard whilst they are cascading spring water. I know of God. Yet somehow, unlike them, I don't know God. Not the way I should, the way they do.

*If this movable feast does not fall today then see note on p. xiii.

1 June

St Justin

~

Profundity is not my scene. You'll know that by now. I'm an old hack whose life has been spent nibbling at the wisdom of others, selecting the bits I reckoned would be of interest to readers. Even as a factory welfare officer – which I was for three years – most of my time was spent in folks' homes establishing the extent of their poverty, their skiving or their terminal illness.

I had one Irishman amongst my clients. He had latched on to the rule that losing the top joint of a finger merited £25 under the Industrial Injury Benefit. Once a month – as his rent fell due – there would be an envelope on my desk. Inside was the third of a digit and the claim for £25. After two months I had him transferred from the metal shears to the foundry. To no avail – he simply moved from fingers to toes, dropping metal billets on his feet.

Then the reasonable supply of both dried up. The score was £250 in his favour. He came to me one day sheepishly. 'Sorr, I know I'm kinda clumsy. Me only daughter's First Communion is soon an' the auld lady – yer know how it is, yer one o' us – wants the best dress there is for her. We don't wanna be shamed afore the rest.' He paused. 'Could yer look up that wee book of youse and see what I get fer an arm?'

Relax – he still has his arm. Thanks to a lot of overtime and a little blackmail with the Foundry Manager who was of the Faith too.

It's June – the month of First Communions. Rightly or wrongly, Catholics will go deep into their pockets so that Anne-Marie or Timothy will approach the altar in finery they cannot afford. But it's not pride – it's instinct, Catholic instinct. Something timeless, bred in the genes, like so many things Catholic. Betraying weakness or strength? Who knows? Take your pick.

2 June

SS MARCELLINUS AND PETER

A priest I greatly love preaches a certain sermon about Pentecost time. It focuses on a man, a dedicated fellow, who all his life peered closely at the mountain paths he walked and the beaches he wandered. It had been profitable, he claimed in later life, for over the years he'd found some £22 and 20p and a French franc.

A man listening to him, about the same age, had never looked down – always up. There he had seen the visible universe – the planets, the stars, the moon and the sun. He knew well the surprise of a changing sky, the moods and magic of creation.

The first man asked him if he had ever found anything in life. The skygazer smiled. 'Only God,' he said.

Both kinds are living Catholic lives. The choice is our own. We can live dangerously as Catholics or we can live precisely, accurately to within the tenth Hail Mary in a decade, doing exactly what is expected of us. At life's end we will end up with either a pocketful of copper or a vision of what God really is.

Despite what critics say about it – constricting, authoritarian – the Catholic Church is a wide Church. It has to be when you consider the sheer variety of those it attracts. But it has to be much more than simply a mechanism whereby those who grease the works will open the gates to Paradise. Being a simple oiler and greaser may indeed be sufficient to enter – but at the loss of how much potential adventure?

Pentecost urges us to leave our tents' safety, to venture out in quest of the souls of the unchurched. There are so many ways to do this. Monks and nuns, even those enclosed, are very much part of the world as they present their prayers to God on its behalf. And the poor secular priest, faced so often with our apathy, is a visible apostle of the Pentecost challenge. Have you ever thought that what you have, by God's grace, is too big – like a Lottery win – for you alone? Faith has to be shared.

SS CHARLES LWANGA AND COMPANIONS

The Ugandan martyrs died in the best tradition. Offered the choice they chose Christ with the words, 'Until death'. Both Protestants and Catholics died together in the rage of their ruler Mwanga. Their Faith they owed to God; their knowledge of it to the missionaries.

Travel Africa – the real Africa of bush, mountains, scrub desert and tiny villages – and you'll meet these extraordinary men and women. Where once you found them in communities, now they are in pairs or even singly. Over the face of that continent they are scattered as stars in a distant firmament – together they make a huge array but viewed singly they are solitary.

One such dot on the massive face of Africa is Sololo. This is a forgotten township on Kenya's northern border with Ethiopia, centre for a small group of Verona nuns and priests. In this miniscule wilderness of rock and dust they maintain a hospital, a school-cum-orphanage and a church of mud and brushwood. Their parishioners are the Borani, a nomad people who know there is water at Sololo.

There is – one tap behind the priests' house. Before dawn the women come with their babes, balancing buckets, old petrol drums, on their heads. Then they sit patiently in the dust waiting for the tap to be turned on at dawn. Without it, they die. The spring supplying the water was dug by the priests during a seven-year drought.

To the north of Sololo there are only lions and bandits, the Shifta. These aimless remnants of Ethiopia's wars supply many of the hospital's patients. To the south – hundreds of miles away – is Nairobi, seat of a power that cares little for the worthless desert in the north and those who roam it. Yet at Sololo, when the tap has nourished them, the Borani women will seek the shade of the church and hear Mass, their children playing at their feet. It is then Christ reigns – where powers would not.

St Edfrith   St Ninnoc   St Petroc

Yesterday, Sololo and the desert. Today continue the journey apace and come to Addis Ababa – capital of Ethiopia, flower of the valley, a city of three extravagantly European avenues dominated by a massive palace and surrounded by the meanest poverty.

Three priests were my hosts in their house bordering the shanty area. Where they went by day I never clearly understood, just as I knew the learned Jesuits teaching at the University never willingly left the campus.

At night the priests returned. Supper was simple, pasta with . . . whatever came to hand that day. Lights went out throughout the city at 8.00 pm when the curfew started. We went to our rooms, mine was on the top. Throughout the night intermittent rifle shots, then the burst of semi-automatics. Some shouting, some screams. Next morning, walking up the grand avenue towards the palace there would be bodies hanging from the ornate Italian lampposts. They were never claimed by relatives.

My first night I heard scampering above my ceiling. I mentioned it to Fr — the next day. He shrugged. 'Rats,' he explained. The following night the noise was different, a rustling. 'Ah,' said Fr — when I described it. 'You are lucky – the snakes have come to eat the rats.'

At a convent I was impressed by the distinguished figure of the man doing the gardening. I pointed him out to the Irish Sister. Her finger went to her lips. 'Ssh, they are looking for him. He was the commander of the Air Force.'

In the end, I was arrested. It's a long story. But the upshot was that they did not really care who was in the cell. The Catholic Secretariate heard of my plight and suggested a young man should take my place there until the matter was cleared up. He did. I flew home. And he spent another month in that hole until my innocence was proven.

5 June

St Boniface

⁓

At a time when Europeans were pouring into England to save Saxon souls, Boniface, a Devonian, went to Germany to convert the pagans. Not only that, like many missioners since, he wrote home and begged prayers and material help for the new converts.

Having Christianized vast tracts of what we now call Germany he went on to reform the French Church. Note well the word – reform. And this was only the eighth century. What a wild, cantankerous lot we Christians are and have been!

Upon his death England proudly claimed him their special saint. But, poor man, he had been abroad too long and never quite made it into English hearts as Augustine had before him. But he left us considerable wisdom.

Generally speaking, English Catholics have steered clear of the continent. True, we did sneak in one English Pope – Nicholas Breakspear, later Hadrian IV, a clerk's son who entered the abbey at St Albans. That was in 1154 and his reign was short – less than five years. As the Irish might have expected from the only English Pontiff, Hadrian gave Henry II the authority to bring the Irish to heel and to make Ireland part of the English realm. Some things never change.

But in the latter part of the twentieth century Rome seemed to sense that the English Church was a safe pair of hands to deal with the sometimes unwieldy passions of the European bishops and Cardinal Basil Hume became leader for a while of the European Bishops. On the other hand, it could be that Basil Hume, with a French mother, was the first English bishop for a long time to speak French. Our hierarchy has never been blessed with the gift of foreign tongues.

But now – entering this magic millennium – perhaps all will change. Perhaps we are at the threshold of the rule of an English pope. St Boniface will be delighted.

St Norbert

A nother case: Norbert, a rich family's ne'r-do-well who saw the error of his ways and became a wandering preacher. More than that, he founded a group from existing canons called the Norbertine Canons – an association rather than an Order it still exists today in England at Arundel, Nottingham and Salford.

Preaching, of course, ranks high amongst the ways in which people can be led to God. Less so today than in the past but then today's most potent preacher is television.

But BT (before television), the century just gone had two preachers both outstanding in bringing Christ to the masses in their flesh – one was the Methodist Dr Donald Soper and the other a monk, Fr Vincent McNabb. 'The world is waiting for those who love it – if you don't love the world then don't preach to it. Preach to yourself,' declaimed the fiery McNabb at one side of Speakers' Corner in Hyde Park. Whilst, nearby, Dr Soper would rain Heaven's vengeance on the warmongers and the drunkards.

But outdoor preaching wasn't restricted to the clergy. The Church had the Catholic Evidence Guild – brave men, and a handful of women too – who would set up their all-too-flimsy platforms and preach a formidable form of apologetics to the rowdy, the lapsed and the professional atheists.

In Birmingham's old Bull Ring, at Hyde Park, on Liverpool's wind-slashed waterfront, they faithfully set up stall most days of the week and gave as good as they invariably got from the tipsy and the indignant. Perhaps they were encouraged by Arnold Lunn's comment in *Now I See*. 'Preaching,' he wrote, 'is heady wine. It is pleasant to tell people exactly where they get off.'

Alas, I've seen no evidence of the Guild for many years. Not too surprising for in the end Catholics are hugely embarrassed by the sound of layfolk preaching.

TRINITY SUNDAY★

I n my total, utter, crass ignorance, in my complete blindness
before theological exactitute, I have always understood the mystery of the Trinity. What is more, I reckon all those sitting around
me at Mass do too.

See how the mere suggestion of mystery produces a wodge of
words so crass you could stick salami in them and feast. A lot
of Church mysteries are the same. Bafflement for the theologians
but crystal clear for us plebs. The Virgin Birth? No problem – just
God thinking laterally. Transubstantiation – what simpler way could
God enter our souls? The Resurrection? How else would Jesus
finally convince us dunderheads that what He said was true?

Yes, there's a catch. The reason we very ordinary Catholics accept
such momentous miracles is that for 2000 years the brightest
amongst us have carved the minutiae of our religious creed into the
rock of belief. It is because of their inspiration, their endless chis-
elling of the word of God, that I say with surety today what Thomas
Aquinas taught: 'The Divine nature is really and entirely identical
with each of the three persons, all of whom can therefore be called
one: "I and the Father are one", St John.'

It isn't intellectual laziness that prompts Catholics to accept so
easily what their Church teaches. God's fools we may very well be –
but not knavish fools. The reason we grasp the gift of doctrine is
fundamental. It is because of a promise Jesus made to Peter that He
would be with His Church always – even to the end of time.

When we are satisfied God did make that promise everything else
follows. But that is not to say that the parish priest today will not be
hoping against hope that the bishop has sent a Pastoral Letter and
saved him preaching the sermon.

★If this movable feast does not fall today then see note on p. xiii.

8 June

St William of York   St Medard

W hy hermits seek their caves I cannot think. For the loneliest place on earth has to be the changing cubicle in the
X-ray section of an NHS hospital. With all haste –
because the sign on the door so instructs you – you strip away all
that is the exterior you. Then you struggle to do up the strings on
the back of the gown waiting for you. It's an impossible task, of
course, and finally you just wrap the thing around you, having
worked up a gentle sweat.

The urgency diminished, you sit on the stool and wait . . . and
wait. The walls are bare, a pallid green. No monk's cell was ever so
sparse. Sitting there, it's hard to credit that you are at the start of a
great adventure. And like the best of quests, this one has to be made
alone.

The trick is to realize that you are not on your own and never can
be. Yet it seems too small a space to accommodate both Mary and
Joseph who you keep talking to. Or Rita and Jude, saints of the lost
cause. But then space is a human concept, like time. Perhaps, after all,
a thousand angels can dance on the head of a pin. Perhaps they're
here now – if not dancing, then brushing you with their wings.

Dimly you hear the whirring machines, the muted voices from a
long way away ordering, 'Breathe in . . . breathe out.' But mostly you
are conscious of the solitude. It's not oppressive, you understand,
and perhaps the Freudian would see it as the return to the womb.
But it isn't security either. It's the opposite – you travel through
doubt, apprehension until finally you bump up against resignation,
acceptance.

On the wall is a little wire basket in which you've placed all your
valuables ready to take in with you. Your lighter, pipe, wallet, keys.
The sum total, in fact, of what you finally add up to. And when, in
your trepidation, you at last start talking to God then it feels as if you
are yourself in such a little basket, waiting for Him to pick you up.

ST COLUMBA ST EPHRAEM

C olumba was a Donegal man, and all that implies – stern, unbending, tough as old boots. Having done his best for Derry he was given, in reward, a tiny island off the west coast of Scotland. It was called Iona. He took with him twelve other monks and you can be sure their way of life was as spartan as sixth-century Irishmen could make it.

On the other hand, Columba was a man of talents, a bard. And as the gales buffeted their tiny rock you can be sure that he kept spirits high. Here is one of his compositions – they were all in Latin – 'Regis regum rectissimi', translated by H. Waddell:

> Day of the King most righteous,
> The day is nigh at hand,
> The day of wrath and vengeance,
> And darkness on the land.
> Day of thick clouds and voices,
> Of mighty thundering,
> A day of mighty anguish
> And bitter sorrowing.
> The love of women's over,
> And ended is desire,
> Men's strife with men is quiet,
> And the world lusts no more.

Just a touch of the chauvinist perhaps? That may be so because one of the strongest of the Catholic societies is named for the Irish monk – the Knights of St Columba, a very male bastion of good fellowship and an astounding record of generosity.

As for Iona – it has become, after Taizé, a magnet for compassionate ecumenism. The rugged Columba well deserves his heavenly crown.

10 June

St Ithamar

It's easy to get the feeling that if you blow hard enough it will all fall down – the creaking Welfare State, the world of pop and tinsel, the whole facade of glitzy nothingness. One puff, and, whew, all gone. There they go – floating in space. The Sunday papers obese with manufactured urgency, the phallic cars, the daily deluge of rubbish through the letter box. All gone.

Everything humanity once was – even the now forgotten once Bishop of Rochester, Ithamar – has been telescoped into us today. Yet, this change could be transient. A tide, a tempest, a quake, could change everything, and send us back to our beginnings. Send us back to the rock.

The rock plays a vital part in Catholicism, just as it did in the New Testament. Apart from Jesus' good-humoured pun on Peter's name the rock not only connates stability and strength, but timelessness. And for a Church that considers matters over centuries not years that's important.

In the end, said the maligned Jesuit Teilhard de Chardin, we must always return to the rock when we are disorientated. It was no analogy – just the plain truth.

Inside each one of us is the rock beyond which we cannot manoeuvre however much we try. In grief it is all too evident. It lurks there, at the periphery of despair. It is inflexible, immovable, hard – the granite core of the soul.

Born Catholics know it is in place from infancy – a protected, protective place, invisible yet tangible. Convert Catholics are more fortunate. By entering the Faith they imply they have found the rock and recognize it. They know consciously what the cradle Catholic only knows subconsciously.

From time to time we are forced to reach rock bottom. And it's only when our fingers clutch for the handholds on the rock that we're able to distinguish the trivia from the truth.

11 June

FEAST OF CORPUS CHRISTI*

——

The Latin every Catholic – even today – can translate: Corpus Christi, the Body of Christ. The most beautiful of the summer feasts and named that by the Bishop of Liège when he established the Feast in 1246. Renamed, oh so ponderously when the simple was best, the Solemnity of the Body and Blood of Christ.

The tableau of this day is always the same – the children go first, sprinkling petals ahead of the priest carrying the monstrance in which resides the Blessed Sacrament, the Body and Blood of Christ.

You kneel as He passes, you offer the only words possible, 'My Lord and my God'. And that is all that is required of you on this most wonderful of days – that you acknowledge, in full Faith, the presence of Christ.

Then you sing such a simple hymn, but one that expresses all that the mighty creeds ever demanded of you, a Catholic:

> O Salutaris Hostia!
> Quae coeli pandis ostium
> Bella premunt hostilia;
> Da robur, fer auxilium.
>
> Uni trinoque Domino,
> Sit sempiterna gloria;
> Qui vitam sine termino,
> Nobis donet in patria.

It is the most innocent of all processions ever walked, it is the gentle payment of homage we make the God we love for the summer that He brings. Come rain, come sunshine, as He passes you will most surely feel His blessing.

It's said that more converts have come to the Church through Benediction than through any other Service. On Corpus Christi you can well believe that.

*If this movable feast does not fall today then see note on p.xiii.

12 June

ST LEO II
~

If you came to Catholicism via Methodism (unlikely), or through Anglicanism (most probably), you will assuredly be disappointed if you had hoped to hear voices raised in song. Your average Catholic choir gives accurate meaning to caterwauling. It is well intentioned, probably meets during the week to try out a new tune and drink tea together. But the end result massacres the fresh tune and proves the tea was taken without sugar.

Apart from some cathedral choirs – the best in the field – and the Religious at Office, Catholic singing is at best a mediocre squawk, at worst a strangled bleat.

Today's saint, Leo II, was apparently something of a singer and encouraged Church music. It's lucky he didn't attempt it in England. How many priests have arrived at new parishes with the determination to create a singing congregation? And, after months of frustration, concentrated on forming an acceptable choir instead?

The plain fact is that singing aloud in church embarrasses all but the most gregarious Catholics. The night before, in the church club, they may well have roared the current ditty with gusto, crooned 'Take me home again, Kathleen' with sobbing vibrato. But put these same choristers in the church setting and they are dumb, none dumber.

Psychologists might argue – a bit desperately, I reckon – that it all goes back to ghetto days when Mass had to be celebrated as unobtrusively as possible, the only sound being the priest's quiet mutter. It may be that in the Old Mass, apart from formalized chanting, there was no space for community song.

Whatever the cause, dear new Catholic, be patient with us. It could be that if enough of you come – and are determined – Catholic singing will have a new future. Don't think we'll reckon you pushy – we won't. Because none enjoy singing more than us – if someone else is doing it.

13 June

St Anthony of Padua

O f all the superstitions beloved of Catholics the image of St
Anthony as recoverer of lost items is the strongest.
Naturally enough, we don't see it as a superstition – just as
unfailing, inexplicable fact. It's not enough, of course, to request the
Franciscan's help in locating the keys. You then have to bribe him
with an offering for his poor-box which is an essential furniture in
any church. However you explain it, St Anthony never fails.

It's strange that Anthony – a contemporary of St Francis – should
have such a seemingly trivial reputation. But there you are – and he
seems to enjoy it. Certainly his box is never empty.

In life he was a preacher of note. Churches were all too often too
small for the crowds he attracted and he earned himself a nickname
– 'The hammer of heretics'.

St Anthony was meticulous to the end. First, about his body
which was largely emaciated through his fasting:

> Let this word of mine be kept by you, so that no one shall know in
> what place my body reposes, for I shall receive it incorruptible from
> my Saviour in the resurrection of the dead.

Then he went on to dispose of his other properties:

> Distribute my garments thus: To Athanasius the bishop give one of
> my sheepskins, and the cloak under me which was new when he
> gave it to me; and to Serapion the bishop give the other sheepskin;
> and do you have the haircloth garment. And, for the rest, children,
> farewell, for Anthony is going, and is with you no more.

The least, then, we 'superstitious' Catholics can do is see that his
poor-box is never empty.

14 June

St Dogmael

Or, in the Welsh, Dogfael. A mystery man from Anglesey but evidently fond of children for if your child is slow to walk then get in touch with Dogfael. Yet children need protection in so many ways.

No one will convince me otherwise – the saddest passage ever penned in English comes at the end of A. A. Milne's *The House at Pooh Corner*. It concerns the passing of childhood when Christopher Robin explains to his lifetime companion that in future they will see little of each other. Like a fool, I read the passage at a primary school prizegiving. As I reached the end – where Pooh cannot understand what is happening – my chest started to pump. Tears were so close I couldn't finish. In my shame I hid behind the piano and sobbed.

The words had meant nothing to the children, of course. For, thank God, they were still children. They had yet to cross that magical divide between innocence and knowing. A divide we are urged to cross earlier and earlier. There was a time, in a good Catholic school, when childhood could make it all the way to eight. Now it seems our tots are lucky to make it to six.

There are times I wonder, as you must, if anyone really is in Hell. Then I think of those who manufacture pornography – on television, film, magazines, the Internet and even newspapers. Then I know for certain Hell is inhabited.

In just 40 years the pornographers have edged the bounds of decency so far forward that there is no longer a barrier to halt them. They have satiated generations until their evil is no longer recognized as the vile muck it is. They claim to portray life. And now they do – for the life that went before is no longer.

Over these years I grew angry that the Church did not fully combat the creeping filth for fear of being thought out of touch. Then my anger turned on myself and the rest of us who did nothing to stop the annihilation of childhood.

15 June

St Vitus and Companions St Trillo

T he two Faiths dominating Europe at the start of this millennium are Islam and Catholicism. Germany has its Turks, France its Algerians and England the homing residue of its empire. It is not beyond the bounds of imagination that by the end of this century Moslems and Catholics will be the only ones in this country to practise disciplined religions.

Already in England more mosques are built each decade than churches. And, between them, Catholics and Moslems occupy the only high ground left in the matter of public morality.

In common, the two Faiths share a concern for the inviolability of family life; campaign together for the unborn child; recognize the one God; reverence Jesus – the Moslems as a prophet, the Catholics as the Son of God. Importantly, both are proselytizing Faiths. Both are wholly convinced of their possession of the truth.

Inter-marriage has already commenced. But, unlike the mixed marriage between Catholic and Anglican, there is no common ground. Either both will lapse or one will accept the Faith of the other. Given the rigidity of the Moslem it is the Catholic who is more likely to give way.

Over 20 years ago Archbishop Derek Worlock wrote of the spread of Islam in Britain as the single most potent challenge to the English way of life and to Christianity. As in so many things, he was an accurate prophet. His solution then was the strengthening of ecumenical ties. The solution hasn't worked because the theology dividing the Christian mainstreams has tended to separate rather than unite.

If Britain, by 2100, is not to have a largely Moslem ethos it is only the Catholic Church here which can ensure the survival of Christianity and the tradition these days have been reflecting.

16 June

ST CYRICUS ST ISMAEL

If I'm going to be afraid then my preference is to be a fearful Catholic. Our obsession with supernatural support so often has its advantages. For a while I had use of a bungalow in the remote bush area of a central African country. The living, as the song goes, was easy. Until one night I woke to the staccato rattle of automatic gunfire. Peeping from the iron-barred window I saw it was a bunch of men on a drunken rampage. As I was the only European for miles it seemed that it was my rump for the rampage.

Naturally the phone didn't work, it was that sort of a place. In any case the nearest police post was 30 miles away. By the time they arrived my chums outside would be sleeping it off and remorseful. And I would be well fried for they were setting the lion bush fence alight.

The huge disadvantage of being an atheist is that at such delicate moments you have only yourself to rely upon. So can you wonder that mentally I gladly demanded and accepted all that Heaven could send by way of reinforcement. First, I saw the job as one for my guardian angel. Then, to be on the safe side, in case it was his night off, I enlisted Our Lady, St Joseph and, in the circumstances, St Jude.

After an hour or two the screaming died down, the fires burned themselves out and the lads crawled unsteadily off into the bush.

You could say – and some did – that it was just a prank that would have played itself out anyway. Yet I knew for certain that wasn't the case. I knew with every fibre of every jangling nerve that Our Lady herself had cast her mantle over that little house; that Joseph himself had soothed their anger and Jude had spat on their fires.

Being a Catholic is about never being alone. Never.

17 June

St Alban

A lban, a soldier, was beheaded for his Faith and the place where it happened became in course of time, St Albans. Truth to tell, you would scarcely know where you were in Britain were it not for the saints who bequeathed their names as well as their lives.

Wales is rich in such legacies. Llandrillo is named for Trillo, a fifth century abbot who left nothing but his name for us to recall him by. Llangollen reminds us that St Collen founded the church there, after killing a female ogre. And at Llanderfel there was once regular pilgrimage to the saint/soldier founder of the town, St Derfel.

English place names simply swap the Llan for Saint – hence St Mawes who first founded the fishing village or St Helens in Lancashire because the town grew up around a church dedicated to the royal saint who went in search of the True Cross. Interestingly, as you travel north you are less likely to find the saints remembered in place names although there are plenty of towns associated with saints. Pagan invaders and the Romans named the hardy northern townships centuries before the Church had taken root.

This kinship with the past is what makes for a Christian country, a country with its soul in the riches of the monks and saints. It is what has made England and Wales what they are and, therefore, us what we have become.

Roots like these we have in the old Faith are priceless – a constant reminder that the woods and pastures about us this wonderful June day are as much a legacy of the past as is our Catholic Faith. And neither the countryside itself nor its religious associations should ever be jeopardized. The saints, more often than not, were patriots too. For love of country and love of Church are so closely entwined in these islands.

18 June

ST JOHN RIGBY

When the vocations crisis began to bite hard the Archbishop of Liverpool, the ever pragmatic Derek Worlock, saw the situation not as a tragedy about to happen but as an opportunity sprung by the God of surprises.

If there are not enough candidates for the priesthood, he reasoned, then God clearly has something else in mind. It didn't take Derek long to come to the conclusion that God reckoned it was about time the laity did something more for Him than go to Mass on Sundays.

At first Derek Worlock came up with the Apostles Scheme. Simply enough, it asked for 12 men and women from each parish to take on many of the jobs done by the priest, including his task of evangelization. For some reason I never understood the Scheme died the death and was quietly put to one side.

Then the Archbishop went for something more specific and wholly male orientated – he went back to the New Testament and virtually resurrected the order of deacon as a clerical rank that could be undertaken by married men or single men who vowed never to marry.

He stressed that these men would not be 'lay' deacons – they would be reverend in both title and the place they occupied in the Church. Their training would be three years and, when ordained, they would do all that the priest could do apart from celebrating Mass and hearing confessions. Should they become widowers then they would not be able to re-marry and, no one doubted although it was never asserted, they could go the other two years and be ordained priests.

The experiment was largely based in Liverpool and its environs. There was no shortage of volunteers and today that diocese has well in excess of 120 deacons, many of them taking increasing responsibilities in parishes which are left without priests to man them.

It was sound thinking and put into practice with only a year or two to spare. But the notion was not universally popular.

19 June

THE SACRED HEART OF JESUS*

~

Slap-bang, here in the middle of June, the whole purpose of a month dedicated to the Sacred Heart. Here is the message by which we all hope – the lukewarm, the sinners and the damned. What is more, Jesus said it Himself: 'What man among you with a hundred sheep, losing one, would not leave the ninety-nine in the wilderness and go after the missing one till he found it?'

What expresses the Catholic's hope more succinctly? Inbred in us from birth is this notion that however low we fall there will be a hand to lift us up again. So common is the idea that we even gave this sense of hope a name – it's called presumption and it's a sin. But, God knows, we've all been guilty of it from time to time.

This devotion is peculiarly Catholic and, comparatively, recent. It was first celebrated by St John Eudes around 1648 and he termed the Feast a prayer to the Holy Heart of Mary and to the Adorable Heart of Jesus. The imagery for some reason appealed to the French and by 1674 had been given approval by Pope Clement X. Then a Visitation nun, St Margaret Mary Alacoque, saw visions in which the Sacred Heart figured prominently. It became a cult and a place for the new devotion was found as soon as possible after the Feast of Corpus Christi.

With the heart symbolizing the charity of humanity it was not long before any number of Orders sprung up named either for the Heart of Mary or the Sacred Heart of Jesus. And by the nineteenth century every home laying claim to being Catholic had the emblem of the Sacred Heart above the door.

For those within the home the Sacred Heart badge has many symbolisms – love, protection, guidance. But, at the back of our minds, what it is saying to us is that 'there will be more rejoicing in heaven over one repentant sinner than over ninety-nine virtuous men who have no need of repentance.'

*If this movable feast does not fall today then see note on p.xiii.

20 June

IMMACULATE HEART OF MARY*

~

The words which finally gave credence to the wild story told by the ignorant peasant girl, Bernadette Soubirous, were those she said were uttered by the Lady: 'I am the Immaculate Conception.' This put the vision in an entirely new light for the clerical sceptics.

Throughout the Church's history it has been vital that the mother of Jesus should be seen always as immaculate, spotless, without sin. It was a determination that later angered many Protestant sects who saw the elevation of the mother as some sort of slur upon the power of the Son. The inclusion of a Feast for the Immaculate Heart of Mary to follow immediately upon the Feast of the Sacred Heart of Jesus only added ire to their resentful ashes.

Because we are brought up with a love of Our Lady no different from that which we have for our earthly mothers, Catholics are simply baffled by those who would deny Our Blessed Lady the love and respect her Son would have wanted for her. For us, it is a simple matter of common sense that a son does all that he can for his mother.

Almost at a distance, we learn the end results of the heavy deliberations of the Fathers of the Church that Mary was both virgin and sinless. We appreciate the efforts they have put into this discovery but wink at ourselves and say, 'How could it have been any different?'

A Feast to acknowledge the loving heart of Mary is as natural as our haste to send our love to our mothers on Mother's Day. What matters is, that like all mothers, Our Lady is always there – ready to give balm to our wounds whatever shape they take and however horrific they may seem to those about us. She is the intermediary with the ear of her Son. Who else do we know – who else knows us? – to whom we can turn with more confidence?

*If this movable feast does not fall today then see note on p.xiii.

21 June

ALOYSIUS GONZAGA

This is the Feast of Aloysius Gonzaga, son of a marquis, patron of youth, who died aged only 23. Now listen to St Paul speaking: 'There are no more distinctions between Jew and Greek, slave and free, male and female, but all of you are one in Jesus Christ.'

Why is it, you have to wonder, that so few of our holy men and women came from what we term the middle classes? Discounting for a moment the martyrs – early and late – the people who gave the Church most emerged from the top and bottom of the social strata of their times.

It is as if sanctity attracted those at the extremes of society. The plight of the poor touched those most who had ample supply of wealth and the most to give and sacrifice. Those coming from the impoverished were beacons of hope for those about them. It's as if the challenge to be holy evaded the cosy, comfortable bourgeoisie. Sure, you can point to the exceptions. But they are rarer than you think.

In particular, in our own age, you are left baffled at the lack of vocations from the best of our suburban high schools and almost all of our Catholic public schools.

Up to the 1950s schools run by priests or nuns tended to take it as a matter of course that each senior year would produce a fine crop of postulants for either monastery or convent. Then, quite suddenly, the flow slowed and then virtually ceased.

What had gone wrong? Was it that the lifestyle evidenced by the monks and nuns was no longer an inspiration? Or was the fault deeper, something that had decayed at the core of the comfortable middle-class family?

Whatever it was, it was hardly surprising that more and more Catholic schools began to close. Almost as if God decided they had no function to offer. By their lights, He knew them.

SS JOHN FISHER AND THOMAS MORE

They were pre-eminent amongst their peers, both chancellors: John Fisher being Chancellor of Cambridge University and Thomas More the Lord High Chancellor of England.

Each emerged from the middle classes, relying upon intellect rather than patronage for advancement. They were contemporaries and friends of a kind although the bishop was an introvert whilst the lawyer was most certainly an extrovert. Fisher's execution preceded his friend's by just 15 days.

Their joint Feast is a reminder of the folly of kings and the everlasting integrity of two men. But it's something else too – a statement and a challenge. The statement is that, given the brevity of life, principle is vastly superior to glory. The challenge is to us – could we hack it given the same circumstances?

Many of our ancestors couldn't. Bishops, priests and laypeople alike tended to find good reasons to submit to the oaths refused by Fisher and More. The martyrs were few – remember this was a wholly Catholic country – in proportion to those who were pragmatic. They were not so much cowards as they were realists. And when the reality is impoverishment or even death then the tendency is to seek alternatives.

We're no different today. Mostly we find good excuses for accepting tainted profits, ignoring the filth on television, letting others make the sacrifice for integrity. In general, we are not the stuff of martyrs.

There are saints today too who, like Fisher and More, challenge our complacency. Some are breezes, some are tempests. But each and all of them throw down a gauntlet to our professed Catholicism. There's even the chance to die for the Faith – in China, parts of India, Indonesia. But what good's that to us if we can't even live for it?

23 June

ST CYNEBURG   ST ETHELDREDA
ST JOSEPH CAFASSO

~

A child cries out, instinctively its mother rushes to it. The world cries out, the self-same instinct ensures the Church responds. Few cries go unheard, for the Church has eyes from the slums of Mombasa to the jungles of Borneo; hands in the marginalized inner cities and forgotten shanties of Africa; ears in the councils of the great and the hideouts of the oppressed; over one billion hearts at least – and all of them dedicated to need.

The word 'power' is an ugly one, largely because it so often connotes a form of corruption. But power is what the Church has – and plenty of it. The Vatican has the largest number of employees in the world. Not directly, of course, but under control nevertheless. Every Catholic – directly or indirectly – works for the aims of the Church. And each and every Catholic – very directly – is under orders to serve the toughest Employer of all – God.

Most of us prefer to see the Church in microcosm – our parish, its priest, our local bishop. It's as if we are too timid to put our heads above the parapet and glimpse the awesome universal strength of our Church.

But it is there. And when it is needed it is mobilized, usually through the person of one man – the Pope. But for him to be effective we have to be willing to act as one, to react by instinct as the Church does to the needs of peoples everywhere.

It doesn't hurt, it won't give us swollen heads, if just once in a while we recognize what a mighty organization we are part of. And all, mark you, for the greater glory of God. That's the bit that counts – the ingredient that separates us from Esso and IBM. Our strength comes from weakness, not from increasing dividends. We seek income only so that we can spend it immediately for the ones crying out. It may be an odd way to run a business. But it's the only way to run a Church.

24 June

BIRTHDAY OF ST JOHN THE BAPTIST

Wishing John the Baptist a happy birthday is a huge breach of bad taste. There he stood in the desert – a wild man, clad in camel skins, feeding on locusts and wild honey. Not the sort you'd go up to and chant 'Happy Birthday, dear John, happy birthday to you'. My, he was tough, this cousin of Jesus. 'Brood of vipers,' he screamed at the Jewish elders when they came to see what he was up to. 'Repent,' he urged them as they went scurrying off to tell tales about the madman in the desert.

The best of us tend to distance ourselves somewhat from the fanatics every religion produces from time to time. Especially when they're telling us what we know is true but we don't want to hear it articulated.

Pope John Paul II, too, became a herald of Christ who could sometimes step aside from the cosy image of hugging children to the shrill denunciation of their parents. He enjoyed a lengthy honeymoon but in the end he was twigged for being a tough guy and there was no scarcity of those prepared to see him find a heavenly reward in the hope that his successor might soften the rough angles of Catholicism.

It's not easy to live with people who say what they mean and you know is contrary to what you want. Jesus was one of them, gentler than John and more understanding of our weaknesses. Nevertheless, like his cousin, He had to go.

Somewhere, at all times, the Catholic Church has a John the Baptist in full flight. He may not always – like John Pope II – be in the top ranks but he's there somewhere, urging, reminding, prodding. And most probably losing his head in the process. Remember Dom Helder Camara, the Jesuit slain in 1989? Always, then, the Catholic Church has voices that cannot be stilled. They may not, like poor John, lose their heads as the result of a royal tart's sense of grievance, but assuredly they'll live dangerously for Christ.

St William of Montevergine

I t was a June wedding like any other – until the bride abandoned the groom at the altar. One moment she was there, kissing her new husband in the traditional way. The next she had vanished, fleeing towards the door in the Lady Chapel. Priest and groom followed her flight, mouths agape. The congregation stirred in the many ways folk have of showing astonishment.

But then she returned, veil flowing and her face showing every sign of the triumphant bride. If she noticed the mutual expulsion of breath from the hundred or so there it didn't show. Instead, she whispered something in her husband's ear and, smiling, they left to sign the book.

Only the most observant had noticed that she no longer carried her bouquet. It lay there, in the Chapel, before Our Lady's statue. The first act of her married life had been to give thanks to the Mother who had thus far guided her. It was tough, no doubt, on the hopeful bridesmaids. But we were left with the feeling that Our Lady would have some way to compensate them.

A Catholic marriage should be different. It is, uniquely, for life, although the Catholic marriage is no more fortunate in its durability than any other. The national divorce average applies to Catholics in precisely the same proportion as for others.

Not every Catholic divorcing is lost to the Faith. Annulments too have increased, leaving the partners free to marry again in a Catholic ceremony. It is not that the rules have been relaxed, rather that the major ground for annulment – pregnancy before marriage – has become that more common, leading to the claim that marriage took place under undue duress.

Somehow, though, I know that the bride who gave the first minutes of her marriage to Our Lady will need no annulment. From the very start she had her priorities just right.

26 June

SS JOHN AND PAUL   ST SALVIUS

The manner of the way in which we celebrate Mass is now so familiar that it's hard to recall that just 35 years ago we bobbed and knelt in utter confusion. Besides which our ears were suddenly assailed with pedestrian English where once we enjoyed the magical cacophony of Latin, a language few understood but all loved to hear.

Over the years we have come to terms with it all. And, for at least two generations, there is no memory of the past. This is as true for most of our priests as it is for the laity.

Whilst it's impossible for something as unique as the celebration of the Mass to cause offence I suspect there are three moments in the Mass with which 'old' Catholics have difficulty. These are the Bidding Prayers, the Sign of Peace and the addition of the Anglican 'power and the glory' to the Our Father.

Mostly the Bidding Prayers are worthy, almost righteous, in a way that is not Catholic in ethos. There is unease, I sense, with the fulsomeness of the invocations. The best just don't reach the heart, the worst are sanctimonious to the point of embarrassment. Listen next time you're at Mass – see with what change of pace and enthusiasm the congregation will recite the Hail Mary, glad to be doing something they truly understand.

'Do we kiss?' we all asked 35 years ago, when the Sign of Peace became a part of the Mass. The uncertainty has not diminished for many of my generation. For us, the moment is still one of puzzlement as to which is the right alternative, it's a hiatus beyond us.

For so many years we could tell 'them' from 'us' because 'they' added 'the power and the glory' to the Lord's Prayer. It was a signpost we subconsciously searched for when we had doubt about the other's Faith. Now, after a little pause admittedly, we say the same. And in some peculiar way it is almost a betrayal.

Absurd, isn't it. But you have been asking what makes a Catholic!

27 June

St Cyril of Alexandria   St Zoilus

If you had been living in Egypt, at Alexandria, around the year 420, then the fiery Bishop Cyril would have presented you with plenty to talk about. He was a vigorous explorer of the truth, an aggressive guardian of the new Faith. His dissertations laid the foundation for many of our beliefs including the Real Presence and the Holy Trinity.

But today, because it is also the Feast of Our Lady of Perpetual Succour, it is best if you remember Cyril for what he wrote of Our Blessed Lady. It is racy, enthusiastic. It reflects what he was:

> Hail, from us, Mary, Mother of God, majestic common-treasure of the whole world, the lamp unquenchable, the crown of virginity, the staff of orthodoxy, the indissoluble temple, the dwelling of the Illimitable, mother and virgin, through whom He in the holy Gospels is called the Blessed who comes in the name of the Lord.

Fierce, fine oratory and none of the statements up for debate. And, you have to remember, only 400 years or so after Christ. Can you wonder that Christianity was to be the light that never failed?

For the devotion, comparatively recent, of Our Lady of Perpetual Succour we have to thank the Redemptorists. The original portrait of Madonna and Child came from the eastern Mediterranean and when it arrived in Rome was hailed as a masterpiece. It was placed and adored in the church of San Matteo and when the church burned down it was presumed the painting too had been destroyed. But after 40 years it reappeared – to the delight of Pope Pius IX who remembered it well. No doubt with his approval the Redemptorists instituted a confraternity based upon devotion to the picture copies of which then travelled the world. And today it is unusual for a Catholic home to be without the Byzantine treasure.

SS Peter and Paul (June 29)

You have to wonder why it is that opposites so often complement each other. Morecambe and Wise, Laurel and Hardy, Steptoe and Son. And today – Peter and Paul. Their partnership is as unlikely as the mating of an ox with a stallion. Yet, there they are, linked for perpetuity in holy alliance.

Burly Peter, the fisherman, the rock. Impetuous, courageous, learning on the hoof and from inspiration. Diminutive Paul, the tradesman, the scholar. Shrewd, informed, pragmatic, building a whole new religion from some undeniable facts.

Peter, happier at home amidst the familiar paths that reminded him of Jesus; Paul, traveller, linguist, missioner extraordinary, voyaging in some security as a Roman citizen.

Both were daring, both brave. Where Peter acted, Paul reacted. Between them a distance as behoved one with the character of iron and the other of quicksilver. Yet without their partnership the Church would have remained yet another sect of many in a remote Eastern province.

So the alliance was always intended by Jesus. Just as later the powerful Cardinal Ugolino would support the reforming Francis of Assisi or Mother Teresa would enlist the aid of the United Nations.

Both men were blessed with visions. For Peter it was the Transfiguration; for Paul the Damascus Road. The first astonishing, the second cerebral.

They clashed, but it said much for Peter's humility that he gave Paul full rein. But after the first Council at Jerusalem each great man went his way. Throwing together such differing characters was surely one of God's greatest jokes. And doesn't He do it still? Just as if the recipe for sound relationships depends more upon the sauce of variety than the stodge of sameness. As the French put it – vive la différence.

29 June

ST AUSTELL (TRNS. FROM SUNDAY)

Those of you planning your summer hols may give a thought to St Austell who founded the church in that Cornish village. Perhaps you'll pop in and see if his presence is still palpable there and if the memory of the Real Presence still lingers on in its old bricks.

It's always seemed astonishing to me how swiftly Our Lord makes Himself at home in even the brashest of our new churches, and how lacking He seems to be in some of the old ones. Astonishing, but reassuring too. For you come to realize that the presence of God owes nothing to the architectural toys we surround Him with and, indeed, attempt to imprison Him in.

In many Catholic churches today you have to look long and hard to discover Him in the Blessed Sacrament. He's been – as the saying goes – 'reserved' in some out-of-the-way spot. Put aside, as it were, as if He was not the real Host there, the One we expect to meet at once. From being the focus of His church he has been sidelined as an interesting afterthought.

In the frenzy of re-ordering Catholic churches throughout the 1970s, architects and liturgical experts finished off the job begun by Thomas Cromwell 400 years before. They ripped down the magnificent screens, hacked away the ancient altars. All was to be space and light as the Word took precedence over the Presence. In the end, of course, they were stuck. They had excluded God from His own home.

Some, shamefacedly, placed the tabernacle on the remains of the old altar. Others, hard-faced, determined that He detracted from the Word, hid Him away in a side chapel.

They forgot that whatever else God is, He is not 'reserved'. Wherever they tried to secrete Him He cried out, 'I am here!' And it was where He was that Catholics took as the centre of the church. In a Catholic place there's only one place to go – to Him.

FIRST MARTYRS OF THE SEE OF ROME

Midsummer is still fresh in our memories. A week or two back we enjoyed the longest day. Optimists saw summer stretching ahead; pessimists started counting the days to Christmas. But whichever we are we have that strange feeling that God has gone on holiday. It's an uneasy feeling – our church is emptier, familiar faces dispersed. Even the spider, nestling in St Joseph's arms, has taken his leave.

It's the start of summer ennui, of course, when our minds flit from Gloria to Creed scarce knowing how they got there. Only the shallow tinkle of the little bell at the Consecration reminds us that God isn't on holiday after all – He's here, and now.

So, senses numbed by unaccustomed sun, we have to admit that we are, after all, in the right place, at the right time, for the right purpose. Yet the time spent hosting Him in our hearts is that much shorter for the choir is gone, the organ silent.

Even as we respond, 'Thanks be to God', we are half-bound to the aisle and our escape to the sun outside. Perhaps this isn't so thoughtless. Perhaps in summer – a green, warm summer – God really is best found in the woods, in running water. Perhaps, beguiled by the soft drug of roses' scent, we can be forgiven if we dally a while with that old fraud naturalism.

At that point, I suggest, we should recall that midsummer madness is no fable. It's tucked away there, in our race memory – a wildness of spirit that was ancient long before Augustine reached us.

As a nation we are largely the creation of our environment. But what our forefathers knew through instinct we now know through knowledge. It is no magic, no druidical fantasy, that nudges nature from one mood to another – it is the hand of God.

1 July

ST OLIVER PLUNKET
SS JULIUS AND AARON

~

Perhaps Oliver Plunket, in combination with Patrick, provides the best, the only hope, for the island of Ireland. Because for sure no human agency will resolve that confusion of loyalties.

Appointed Archbishop of Armagh after studying with the Jesuits at the Irish College in Rome, he began, in 1669, to clean up the dispirited mess the Catholic Church in Ireland had become as a result of the monstrous penal laws imposed by England. The Church he inherited was similar to the state of the Church in England after the Black Death. The priests were leaderless, frightened, scattered the length of the country. They were ill-educated, persecuted and penniless. And the Catholic population was no different.

Unusually, Oliver could not turn to the Religious for help – the state of the clergy there was little better than the disorder of the secular priesthood. Add to this unpleasant potage another ingredient – the bitter rivalry between the Sees of Dublin and Armagh – and you can see the extent of the mess Oliver inherited.

When he was appointed to Armagh it was known that he was a brilliant scholar, but what was perhaps untried was his skill as a diplomat. And it was as a diplomat – rather than as the theologian he was – that he established for the first time in years a rapport with the Protestants of Ireland. But it was more than that – for the first time in centuries a Catholic bishop won the respect of both sides of the great divide and Armagh became the undoubted centre of the island's future hopes.

Seen from this distance, it is absurd that all he had accomplished should be destroyed in months in the pandemonium that followed the wretched lies of Titus Oates. Even more unbelievable that a man of Oliver's character should find himself arraigned as a traitor and hanged, drawn and quartered. Yet another foul wound in Ireland's history.

2 July

St Swithin

If it rains on St Swithin's Day, the legend has it, it will continue to do so for 40 days. It's an unusual way to mark the life of the innocuous Bishop of Winchester who died in 862. But if it even nudges folk to remember their saints then it is not in vain.

For PR has become part of God's armoury in the battle versus the secular world. It's not unknown for national Catholic Churches to employ highly paid agencies to produce predictions. It is then the churchgoers become As and Bs and Cs. They are classified by what they do and where they do it. They are North and South, East and West. Their giving is enumerated, their potential or lack of it is transcribed to a single line upon a graph.

As piety, sanctity and prayer are not measurable on a computer they have no place in the expert's scheme of things. At the end of the operation, with the wine chilled and the salmon smoked, they'll make a presentation telling the Church what every altar server could have told them – that what we need are holy priests and holy people, and a Church with its arms held out wide to welcome the needy outside who need its love.

The Church in Britain has largely escaped this PR scenario. Perhaps it is an English instinct for knowing when we are being manipulated or, worse, patronized. And worst of all, when we are being fooled. Our Lord got it about right when He said He knew His sheep and they knew Him.

You cannot advertise God – not the way the slick agencies would have the Churches do. Not with posters, not with ten-second slots on television. Not even with the permitted God-slots offered by the media which grow more and more evasive in their reluctance to 'over-sell' their Christian product.

Only Christians themselves can make others aware of the value of what they possess. And each and every time they scandalize the unchurched then, in the jargon we're using, they under-sell God.

St Thomas the Apostle

T hank God for Thomas and those five words of his: 'My Lord and my God'. We just cannot say that often enough – Thomas put the seal on the truth of the Resurrection.

So, you conclude, lucky Catholics. Smug, confident Catholics – so surefooted amongst the pebbles of doubt so many stumble on. If only that was true. Doubt is our constant companion until that moment we opens our eyes and see God. Doubt for the Catholic, as for the pagan, is the thread woven into every action we take. The reason for this is that we have free will – the gift of choice. And choice means that virtually every decision in life has an alternative. Glibly, we sometimes claim that there was no alternative. But there always is. And, as a result, the shadow of doubt falls over every single act we do.

Doubt is a human inheritance, a mark, if you like, of our humanity. So life is constantly signposted and the ultimate success we make of it depends upon the quality of our decisions - rich man, poor man, beggar man. But that decision is for the benefit of our secular lives.

What of doubt in Faith, doubt of God's existence, doubt about our own survival after death? Only individual Catholics can answer for themselves. We have the life and teaching of Jesus, we have the evidence of Thomas, we have the learning of thousands of wise and virtuous Christians. But finally we have to make a choice.

Put it this way: you want to marry. You love the girl, admire her family, your parents approve her, you are both of an age and with the means to marry. Do you then reject marriage because you cannot know for absolute certain what your partnership will become in 30 years time? No – all things being equal you decide to entrust your-selves to the future.

Belief is the opposite of doubt. It is belief Catholics should pos-sess. Not blindly, but after each brick in Faith's edifice has been examined. Even then, remember it's not a wall you're building but a bridge. To God.

St Elizabeth of Portugal

Ordinations are imminent. If you're lucky – very, very lucky – you may have one in your parish. But as it's unlikely more than 30 priests will be ordained in England and Wales this summer your chances are slight.

Which is a pity, because nothing galvanizes a parish like the ordination of one of its own. Dear Lord, the excitement! Much more than for the marriage of the year as here the Bride is invisible and the groom a rare species who would embrace the Church. Like a wedding, there will be gifts – from the parish fortunate to have nurtured a vocation; from the parishioners he served as deacon for the last months of his training; from relatives and friends, known and unknown. He will need the gifts – the job he's taking on doesn't pay very well.

The choir and the servers have to be rehearsed, the sanctuary filled with flowers. The parish priest has to research the rubrics for it's many a year since the last young man offered himself to God. All has to be perfect so that at the reception afterwards everyone can claim, 'Wasn't it just wonderful!' And it will have been that – full of wonder. At every stage, from the physical prostration of the man abandoning everything his peers hold so precious, from the austere definition of the priesthood outlined by the bishop, to the solemn oath taken promising the rest of his life to God.

At the conclusion of the ordination the new priest will hold out his hands to his parents and then bless them. It is a blessing which has been a long time coming. Giving it will dispel the clouds of uncertainty of the early years, the endless disputations between self and God of the recent years. A priest's first blessing for his parents may appear a slight thing. But look carefully. In that one gesture a man can represent God as He thanks the family for the gift of their son.

'Carry no purse,' Our Lord instructs the 72 as He sends them before Him. 'Carry no haversack, no sandals.' Things have changed. The Church needs a purse, a big one. Not to fill but to empty as soon as it is replenished. And we are the ones who do the filling.

Out of a Catholic population in England and Wales approaching some 4.5 million, some quarter of these attend Mass. Look closer – how many of these quarter represent frontdoors, families? At a guess, 312,500. Behind these doors is what wealth the Church requires to generate the resources managed by the bishops.

Given the generosity of practising Catholics the Church's cash-flow must be in the region of £650,000 a week. Not a lot. So each week the Church must go back to the same pockets, the same frontdoors, knocking for the extra £350,000 required for the upkeep of schools, seminaries and its vast network of social services. In addition, the missions and the charities are also at the same doors.

It's a fair guess that these Catholic homes give some £250 a year or about £80m. This sum, sadly, could be miles out either way. For besides income from legacies and investments there are gifts and grants. We can never know for sure because some 20 years ago the Church stopped publishing its balance sheet, the National Catholic Fund. And although required now by law to do so, few dioceses publish their individual balance sheets.

Three valid points can be made about Catholic finances in this country. The most glaring is what a difference contributions from those missing three million Catholics could make. It's particularly annoying because so many of them utilize the Church's resources whilst ignoring their obligations. Secondly, Catholics are mostly uninterested in how their Church manages, just so long as it does.

But finally, and most importantly, Church leaders know that if they need cash they have only to ask. It's the Catholic way.

6 July

ST MARIA GORETTI

Purity means a lot to Catholics. So Maria Goretti finds honour with us. Critics suggest we place undue emphasis on sins against chastity. They say our Faith is sex-orientated and, as a result, other sins are minimized. Sin for the Catholic, they say, is below the belt. For others it is cerebral.

Like all generalizations it's too simple a notion. Yet there is good reason why chastity – and, as they say, that covers a multitude of sins – looms large for us. It's a long story. In fact it starts right back in the first century when the Christian ethic was at war with the way the Roman morality was going. An early mark of the Christian was loyalty to one spouse and a life wholly dissimilar to the hedonism about him.

Purity of life – and of intention – was enthroned in Christian belief by the middle of the first century. It didn't come easily – remember poor Augustine's struggles with the flesh – but come it did.

Our Lady's place in the Catholic conception of chastity cannot be minimized. Her character pervaded all we were ever taught about the sanctity of marriage and the desirability of purity in life.

Skip 20 centuries and you see what happens when the moral ethic is relaxed. We are back in the decline of the Roman Empire but unhappily without its sense of fun – we are in dour pursuit of sex without the privilege and obligation of love.

And that is at the heart of the Catholic teaching, its emphasis on the difference between sex and love. Paradoxically, the Church view enhances the act of love, giving it a security and compassion it can never have as mere sex. It's not an easy lesson to teach hot-blooded youth but most Catholic couples will have discovered the truth of it for themselves. They will have learned what the Church gently professes – that sexual love is a duet sung best by just two.

7 July

St Thomas of Canterbury

L ast words must always be somewhat suspect. Accredited to St
Thomas à Becket in 1170 are: 'In the name of Jesus and the
defence of the Church I am willing to die.' Oddly enough,
Erasmus, three centuries on and no great supporter of the
Canterbury saint, had last words most of us would have no problem
assenting to: 'O Lord! O Lord! Make an end, make an end!'

On balance, given that he was surrounded by monks who agreed
the burden of his words, Thomas' last message was undoubtedly
accurate. And it was one which came to haunt his protagonist,
Henry II.

Last words are important because they carry the inference they
are true, a genuine summation of the dying person's views on the
life just passing. Perhaps Henry VIII's dying utterance proves this
point: 'Monks! Monks! Monks!'

St Teresa of Jesus' last words are not wholly verified but I like to
think they are true: 'Over my spirit flash and float in divine radiancy
the bright and glorious visions of the world to which I go.'

One pope, Eugenius IV (original name Gabriele Condolmero),
spoke to himself as he died – surely a message many other popes
would subscribe to: 'Oh Gabriele, how much better it would have
been for thee, and how much more would it have promoted thy
soul's welfare, if thou hadst never been raised to the pontificate, but
hadst been content to lead a quiet and religious life in the
monastery.'

Many last thoughts centre on confession, a frightened soul's
apologia for a life wasted. But with others you are led to believe that
what are last words here are, in fact, first words to the person of
Jesus. Certainly true of St Francis de Sales: 'God's will be done! Jesus,
my God and my all.'

---------- ⌒ ----------

He sat on a rock. Or perhaps a fallen tree – there were dense forests then in Judaea. The village folk had heard the rumour He was there. They wandered towards Him singly, as families, in groups. Those were the days before radio and you found your entertainment where you could. Rural workers, they were for the most part poor, humble. What delight, then, to hear the Man tell them they were blessed for their hunger, richer for being poor. It was simple, direct talk with Jesus.

Now, sometimes, it seems a mist has formed between Him and us. There have been too many voices telling contradictory tales. And it hasn't helped when some of them have been discredited, their injunctions no more than the gambits of the ambitious. Real communication, from Pope to bishop to priest to people, has too often failed. Our church walls have echoed with static as the message has bounced erratically in search of a clear frequency.

Ours is a Church of certainties. Take them away – under the guise of exploratory scholarship or intellectual pride – and you leave so many bemused. Blur the difference between the consecrated Host and a piece of bread and you have obliterated the most fundamental of all Catholic beliefs.

We have stood back and permitted certainty to be diminished. Some in the cause of free speech, some by stilling their voices when they should have been heard. The young – intellectuals or slap-happy teenagers – thirst for security. As a generation we have abused their needs, feeding them contention where there should have been surety. We have distanced ourselves from the Man on the rock and now many of us stand guilty before Him.

God help us. More urgently, though, God help our children.

9 July

ST EVERILD MARTYRS OF GORKUM

The Martyrs were 19 Religious, mostly Franciscans, who were hanged by Calvinists in 1572 despite an order from William of Orange that they should be spared. It was not a century renowned for mercy on either side of the religious divide.

As Christians we're always looking over our shoulders at history and wondering if we're any better now than we were then. The glance is seldom reassuring. Even looking forward three days to 12 July we know that politics hypocritically superimposed upon religion will cause anxiety in Northern Ireland.

If we're honest, there comes a point when we have to look objectively at Christianity and ask whether the world would not have been more peaceful, at rest with itself, without the Faith that so often divided society.

Then, having been that honest, we are forced to conclude that it was not Christianity that failed so often – it was us. It was our inability to accept Jesus' teaching in its entirety and without equivocation. The humanists attack the Messenger, in the person of Jesus. The Christians all too often defy the message.

In the heady days of ecumenism when it seemed that on this island at least Christians had found common ground, we talked of the 'scandal' of disunity amongst our Churches. It was an apt description. Yet the scandal goes on – a slap in the face for the Galilean who showed us all one way and one truth.

Perhaps it is, after all, arrogance we Catholics show when we insist that our Church still pursues – alone amongst the Churches – that selfsame path and that given truth. If that is so, then we must remain arrogant for Christ's sake. Yet, in truth, this arrogance is really desperation bred out of the knowledge that at the turn of a new millennium our Faith is the only one strong enough, convinced enough, to carry Christianity forward.

fter the Mass there is no more important an ingredient in the Catholic's life than the priest. In this month of ordinations, let's dally a day or two with the 'new' priest who, even in these days of shortage, will start his clerical life with a parish priest.

This first parish posting is vital to his future health as a priest. Knowing this, the bishop will look for a parish priest who still has the vigour of enthusiasm, who is not just a spirit figure glimpsed as he makes his way from supper to television. If a young priest lacks encouragement from his first parish priest he will surely lack it from the parishioners who are but a reflection of his personality.

The new priest's apartness must not become loneliness. If it does, then he's like a man starving in a bakery – he can stand amongst a thousand people and never hear a friendly word for his own sake. In such cases he too easily falls into a 'safe' house, the refuge of a good family in the parish. Whilst the relaxation is good for the man, it can mean death for his priesthood.

As priests tend more and more to be involved in social work there is one major difference between him and the professional. Unless his parish priest is responsive then he has no outlet for the tears and anxieties that have battered his ears all day. No wife to confide the sorrows he's shared; no colleague to turn to for encouragement.

As early as 25 the young priest is swamped in the peculiarities of human error and selfishness. He is always the recipient – he can never transmit his own feelings.

It's too glib to say that if properly chosen for their vocation priests should be healthy extroverts, able to fend for themselves. Few saints were ever this. And a priest first chooses his calling to sanctify himself rather than be the life and soul of the Union of Catholic Mothers branch meeting. If anything, the Catholic priest will tend to be an introvert. It is certainly true of him as he grows older.

11 July

St Benedict

S t Benedict created a loving environment for his monks. There's no such settled community for the secular priest. Unhappily, many Catholics seem unaware that if their priest had wanted poverty he would have joined a monastic Order. Poverty is thrust upon him as a result of circumstances, not because he has vowed to accept it.

Few priests can be termed well off. Most come from families already under financial strain and, unlike Anglican parishes, there will be no wealthy patrons to supplement the priest's income which nowadays averages about £50 a week apart from special offerings for his personal use at Easter and at Christmas. Evidence of this poverty is often put forward as the major reason for the lack of debate on celibacy. And, the Church being nothing if not practical, who is to say otherwise?

The young priest – apart from his Mondays with friends or family – will be guest at any number of social events following marriages and christenings. But there he is still the 'man apart'. The dancing is not for him, nor the bibulous jokes with the lads in the corner. Aunt Maud will corner him with the tale of her bunion, Uncle Tom with the rambling narrative of his 'doubts'.

Patron saint of the secular priest is the austere Curé d'Ars, not the companionable Benedict. And the Curé was a confessor first and foremost. Just as the young priest has to be – in or out of the confessional. At 26 he must be alert to the anguish of the woman on the change; the self-delusions of the elderly cynic. Ideally, he should detect too the onset of physical disease as readily as he recognizes paranoia.

If he has chosen his vocation correctly then as time goes by he will grow in compassion. If he has chosen unwisely then his sense of grievance will be a greater source of irritation to himself than to those who seek his guidance.

12 July

O n Sea Sunday, us landlubbers will blithely offer up prayers for those in peril on the seas we so seldom see or cross. It is a reminder to us that we were once great as a seafaring folk, just as the rare visit of a missioner to his parish is a reminder to the priest that his life could have been very different.

The missioner comes to beg, to take alms away. But he brings into the presbytery the heat of an African sun; the faintest whiff of a world far removed from the daily trudge down Ackerman Street in the drizzle.

As priest and missioner vest prior to Mass the difference between them becomes apparent. Muscular, bronzed arms scored with a dozen cuts and scratches, hands more accustomed to stripping down engines than to completing marriage forms. A face chiselled from sun and sand. Swift, impatient motions with the accoutrements designed to distinguish priest from people.

Later, as he listens to the missioner make his appeal, the priest wonders – not for the first time – whether he made the right choice. The missioner tells of a parish covering 100 miles, of people who walk two days to reach a Mass centre. He recounts the ravages of civil war upon his parishioners, their daily tussle to find food and water.

He begins to listen with only half his mind. Instead he looks down on his Sunday congregation. Comfortable, content folk – neither too bad nor too good. They'll pop a pound into the box when they leave; some will even be moved to make it a fiver. And then they'll forget.

But he'll be left with this buzzing in his head. Was his vocation with the physically starving or the spiritually undernourished? His doubt will diminish when the missioner leaves for another parish. He'll tell himself that we must grow where we're planted. And he'll be right.

St Henry the Emperor   St Silas

E ight hundred years before Bismarck, Henry's intention was to amalgamate the German states. To do this he needed the help of the Church and it was forthcoming. In return, he gave the Church properties. It must have come as little surprise when he was canonized after just a century. A simple quid pro quo unhappily too familiar over the early centuries.

Church dalliance with politicians has always been a tempting tightrope. It happened as soon as Christians had clout and continues up to this day. Just as it was then, so it is now – there are ample critics suspicious of such partnerships.

As recently as the days of Archbishop Derek Worlock there were those swift to condemn a real or an imagined link with both politicians and political parties. It was an accusation the late Archbishop vehemently opposed, saying that the Church had to be where the people were. And if that meant supping with people of power in both politics and industry then that was where he would dine. In simple terms, he would go wherever the power lay – not to share in it but to use it for the benefit of the powerless.

The problem for Derek Worlock – as it was for prelates down the ages – is that it is not power alone that corrupts but the very contagion of power. It can be argued that maintaining a constant proximity to the poor – which Derek assuredly did – will minimize the risk of infection.

Pope John Paul II, in the case of South America, felt compelled in 1979 to lay down clear rules upon what had come to be termed liberation theology. The rules were his definition of Christ's instruction that Caesar should have what is his and God what rightfully belonged to Him. It was a warning shot which echoed well beyond the continent for which it was intended. It was a reminder that any deals done in the eleventh century with emperors and would-be leaders had not created a precedent for the people of Christ. It was heeded – but at some cost to grassroots clergy.

St Boniface of Savoy St Camillus

Is it possible to be angry with God? Oh, yes. Is it possible to stay angry with God? No. God is the parent who denies you for your own good, edging you from one path to another without you knowing why.

St Camillus must have had a moment of anger for God. Short-tempered soldier, losing gambler, suffering from a diseased leg, there must have been a rebuke or two for God before he turned to helping others who were sick.

He was good at his new task, early to see the advantages of fresh air and diet, able to mobilize others in the service of the sick. It's little wonder that he is the patron saint both of nurses and the sick they tend.

There must be some good reason why Catholics tend to predominate in the caring professions. In England it can be traced to the opportunities nursing offered Irish girls with few prospects at home. The same was largely true for doctors. And both, of course, tended to be Catholic.

Yet there must be more to it than that. For the proportion of Catholics in every country serving medical needs is excessively high, too high to be mere coincidence. So you have to suppose that somewhere at the heart of our teaching is a stimulation of some kind to care for the needs of others. Women's Orders still maintaining a steady entry of postulants are largely those concerned with nursing. And the same goes for Orders of Brothers engaged in similar work.

I like to think all this a consequence of Christ's healing ministry which ran aside His teaching ministry, each gaining strength from the other. A ministry not ignored from the earliest times when Christians were foremost in taking skilled care as well as prayers to those in need of both.

St Bonaventure

Cardinal Bonaventure was a contemporary of Aquinas but very much his own man. A far-seeing man, for he prophesied the day when the creation of the world would be proved by human reason. Yet it is as poet that we best remember him today, through the beauty of his veneration of the Cross, 'Recordare Sanctus Crucis'. Here is the translation by D. Donahoe:

> Would'st thou dwell in joy abounding,
> All thy life with light surrounding,
> Make the Cross they constant care;
> On the rood of thy Redeemer
> Be thy soul an ardent dreamer,
> Bear it with thee everywhere.
>
> Be thou toiling, be thou sleeping,
> Be thou smiling, be thou weeping,
> Deep in grief or ecstasy;
> Be thou coming, be thou going,
> Pale with pain, with pleasure glowing,
> Let the Cross thy comrade be.
>
> Every sin and every sorrow,
> Every ill that life can borrow,
> In the Cross will gain surcease;
> In the Cross, though sore and grieving,
> He that humbly seeks relieving,
> Findeth refuge, findeth peace.

It was Bonaventure too who gave us the prayer once so prominent in the Roman Missal:

> O sweetest Lord Jesus Christ, I implore Thee, pierce the very marrow of my soul with the delightful health-giving dart of Thy love, with true, tranquil, holy, apostolic charity, so that my whole soul may ever languish and faint for love of Thee and for desire of Thee alone.

16 July

OUR LADY OF MOUNT CARMEL

O dd events happened to me under the shadow of Our Lady of Mount Carmel. A thief bowled me over into Haifa dock; children spat at my uniform as I walked their street; I helped carry a comrade's dead body down five flights of stairs when our station was blown up. And, all this time, above me and never visited by me, was the shrine to Our Lady of Mount Carmel.

Lots more too. But then you don't want to listen to an old policeman's tales. Except . . . except for one night when Our Lady proved to me she didn't take sides.

A Jewish immigrant ship, an illegal one, had been brought into the docks after the usual punch-up when she had been boarded a mile or two out to sea. The drama done, she had been tied up at the far end of a long causeway. An Arab constable and I were to remain on board until the morning in case someone still lurked in her depths.

It was a foul duty in every way: the detritus of 300 people packed tight like sardines for two weeks or more lay about the decks; the stink of urine and faeces mixed with the sweet odour of blood still laying after the brief fight. As ordered, I crept down to the bilges. A mass of indescribable filth floated there, the stink drove me up to the bridge, longing for the fresh sea breeze of night.

Then I saw him. Singlet, shorts, slime-coated. He was about my own age – 18. He grasped a baton taken, I expect, from one of the airborne soldiers earlier. The Arab constable cocked his Tommy gun, I took out the massive .45 revolver we'd probably inherited from one of Allenby's soldiers a generation before. He dropped the baton, but turned as if to run saying, 'I go'. Just that.

'La – no,' I told the Arab.

I dropped the heavy pistol to my side. He ran like a deer down the causeway until lost to sight. He ran – although neither of us realized it – towards Mount Carmel. Years on, I wondered – was Our Lady sparing us both? I think so.

17 July

St Kenelm

In the Irish village where I lived for a few years they called them the Usterbys – people who in another life used to be doctors, scientists, professionals of all kinds. Their conversations invariably started, 'I used to be . . . ' The simple gambit ensured they would always be newcomers.

But there was another breed of Usterbys – and they weren't necessarily incomers. More often than not they were villagers. Here the opening would be, 'I used to be a Catholic until . . . '

Then would follow the inevitable tale of the priest who knew nothing about the body he was burying . . . the nun who slapped the child with a ruler . . . the bishop who approved/disapproved of the IRA . . . the grocer churchwarden who gave short measure in his shop.

The most common target of the religious brand of Usterbys was the 'clawthumper' – the hypocrite who spent his weekly hour in prayer and then went home to beat his wife or cheat his neighbour. For these there was no quarter.

From time to time we discussed the futility of dismissing the huge virtue of the Church because of the actions of a few of those who practised its Faith. But the discussions – over Murphys or Jamieson – rarely moved further than the watery circles the glasses left on the table. Like them, we went around without conclusion.

Yet the indelible marks still remained. Stand in the village street as the Angelus rang out and you'd discern furtive fingers tracing the Cross like fleeting spiders. See the Usterbys pass the church and, unbidden, that same mark of the Cross reluctantly spanned some point in the chest.

The old truth still held – a Catholic can never be a Usterby however fast or far he or she flees. Catholicism – like Judaism – is a permanent signature on the soul.

18 July

St Arnulf

A rnulf did what so many bishops of the early Church did – he packed in the job and went off to the hills to become a hermit. But then, very little surprises me about bishops.

It was midnight. The Bishop and I sat next to one another in the gutter of the main street of Sao Tomé, capital of the tiny Portuguese island that lies off the coast of West Africa. The night air was no better than the dank, moist heat of the day.

We drank from our tins of tepid beer which instantly poured out of us as sweat. The fact was that I was very angry with this Holy Ghost priest who had the task of coordinating medical supplies for the Biafrans fighting only a few miles by air across that turgid sea.

For the umpteenth time I demanded that he arrange a flight for me to Uli. For the umpteenth time he shook his head, pointing out that they could no longer spare the space my 15 stone would occupy.

Furiously I pointed out that my erstwhile colleagues from both *Pravda* and *Paris Match* had been transported the previous day. Pragmatically he pointed out that they had larger circulations than my own newspaper, their support would be more valuable. He actually had the temerity, this Holy Ghost Father, to use the expression 'cost effective'. It was the last straw. I got up, stared down at him. I so wanted to shake his small shoulders.

Then he rose too, glanced at his watch. 'I must go – I'm meeting the Pope in eight hours.'

I looked at him astounded – it was the last straw. 'You're lying,' I hissed.

He smiled and walked away.

The afternoon of that same day I listened to the World Service, still angry that only 100 miles from Biafra I had to get my news that way. The lead story was about the meeting of three Nigerian bishops with the Pope. It was the meeting that finally brought the end of that evil war. I was ashamed. But I had learned something more about bishops.

19 July

MARY AND MARTHA

~

There'll be a chuckle or two, silent or expressed, at many a nuns' Community Mass at about this time. The Gospel tells of Martha and Mary – the plain story of women everywhere. For if you're fond of categorizing – and who isn't? – then all women fall into the guise of either Martha or Mary.

On the face of it, the incident has overtones of injustice. 'Martha, Martha,' chides Jesus. Note that double address, implying asperity.

'You worry and fret' – that double verb ramming home impatience – 'about so many things and yet few are needed, indeed, only one.'

At this point you have to sympathize with Martha. And, no sooner than you do so, than Jesus, a little mischievously I reckon, adds, 'It is Mary who has chosen the better part.'

Not half, every instinct urges you to cry out, not half she hasn't. There's poor Martha, hair askew, flour all over her face and blouse, hands red with pummelling dough. Then prim Mary, sitting so cosily at Jesus' feet, no doubt with a contented smirk, hair immaculate. Yes, you have to agree, Mary did all right for herself. Then, surprised, you must ask, didn't Jesus see this for Himself?

In every convent, in every home, there are the doers and the pray-ers. The woman who bakes an apple pie, the one who eats it. The giver, the taker; the grower, the consumer. If Sister Martha didn't 'worry and fret' how long would Sister Mary maintain her pious composure?

Within the incident – not a parable, mark you – there's a paradox, a contradiction superficially unfair. And because the apparent injustice is perpetrated by Jesus we're forced to dig deeper. When we do, we realize that Jesus is talking priorities here – not belittling Martha's labours but slyly pointing out that Mary's concern for her soul is preferable to Martha's worry about the cooking.

If housewives had a Charter – and why not? – this episode should form the preamble. Christ at His best – in the kitchen. Where the heat is.

$\dfrac{}{}$ ≈ $\dfrac{}{}$

A dultery is the soul's very own guillotine. It is that sharp, that final – a deep cut. And it is that cruel. In one stroke it severs the lifeblood of marriage. It's a betrayal so heinous that never again will the soul enjoy real peace. Its treachery affects at least four people, though usually it is many more. Adultery is the annihilation by one act – or many, it makes no difference – of trust, which is the bedrock of marriage.

Even so, Christ selected this particular sinner, an adulterer, for a spectacular reprieve – the most vivid example of charity He ever gave us. More than any other Gospel incident, it demonstrates the enormity of God's wisdom and the full depth of His mercy.

Which is as well for many Catholics. For adultery – by desire or by act – figures high in the list of sins we lay before God in the confessional for forgiveness. Should you wonder what happens in the confessional – and non-Catholics have some pretty odd notions on this – let me tell you.

The confession is made to God through His intermediary, a priest. Then God, again through His priest, repeats the words Jesus spoke so compassionately to the woman who had committed adultery – your sins are forgiven. But there is a rider to this, a vital one, for God adds, 'Go and sin no more.'

'Sin no more' may sound simple. But it means precisely what it says. There's no leeway here, no escape clause. Stop, demands God, here and now.

Confession is no easy path to a contented conscience. It doesn't work if you have a mental reservation to stop sinning in your own time, in your own way. Worse, if you have such a reservation then your sin is many times more grievous than when you asked forgiveness. The absolution is not only invalid, your act has been blasphemous.

All sin, Jesus Himself said, can be repented. The choice, as ever, is your own.

21 July

ST LAURENCE OF BRINDISI

⁓

S t Paul was being briefed before appearing on Channel 4 News. 'We're giving you four minutes,' revealed the producer proudly. Paul smiled. 'I only got three on ITN and BBC.'

The revelation didn't surprise the producer who smirked. 'Here on 4 we like to do things in depth,' he explained. Then, eyeing Paul, he added, 'But we do like to look for the story behind the story – if you see what I mean.'

A touch of suspicion crossed Paul's face. 'You're not dredging up all that stuff with the Galatians?' he asked.

For a moment the producer sensed a story the researchers had missed. But time wasn't on his side. He shook his head. 'No – what we wondered was . . . well . . . would any of this Christianity business have happened without you?'

Paul's face fell. 'Is that what people say?' he demanded.

A nod from the producer depressed Paul.

'But all I did was preach Jesus. Look how often I said I was His prisoner. You must know – I walked always in the chains He'd forged for me.'

The producer glanced at the supplementary question he had on his card. 'You're not saying, surely, that Peter and the others had the ability to do what you did?'

Paul hesitated. 'If I'm honest, no. It took us all – every one of the apostles and disciples, all of us. No one was dispensable – we all had a part to play. And we were all different.' Paul slapped his hand down hard on the studio desk. His eyes glinted. 'We only, each in his own way, preached what He had taught.'

The producer eyed the studio clock. 'There'll only be time for a third question. Looking back, what did you say that was of the greatest value?'

The little man didn't hesitate. 'If I lack charity, I count for nothing. When all's swept away all there is is charity.'

He looked apologetic. 'It's all I ever said really, you know.'

ST MARY MAGDALENE

~

Today, the Feast of Mary Magdalene, I'll be visiting my mother in her country cottage. It's her birthday – and she's a great one for birthdays. Her cottage is surrounded by yews. The grass is well tended. We'll have our annual chat. There's a lot to tell. She's a canny soul so I'll not get away with half-truths. She'll want to know the bad as well as the good. So there, in Bebington Cemetery, I'll lay before her the tangled bouquet of unrealized dreams, hopes that didn't quite make it.

With the breeze tickling the trees to provide her commentary it will be a pleasant half hour. We'd always talked of the Bebington grave as being the cottage country – a euphemism for what I always thought impossible. She had longed all her life for a cottage in the country yet somehow it was just always out of reach. Until, that is, she died all that time ago and the dream became a reality.

There is no headstone – she wouldn't want the weight of it. To be honest, I can no longer tell to within 20 feet just where she is buried. On the day she took up residence I knew I'd never be able to forget. But I have. Because time does that – blurs the sharp angles of despair. As the psalmist has it, time dries the tears and calms the agitated heart.

This annual visit is, my reason tells me, absurd. She's not at home, not in this cottage anyway. Yet it is the last place we went together. It was as far as a long journey had taken us. And for this reason alone the spot is unique for me.

And, let's face it, from time to time we have to share the tensions of living. And with whom better than someone for whom living no longer presents anxieties? But the visit isn't one-sided. I have to listen as well as chatter. Then there are pauses in our conversation. Short ones when I recall what she so often told me: 'Be still and know that I am here.' It's a hard lesson. Perhaps at times better learned there in the country cottage than in the church.

23 July

ST BRIDGET OF SWEDEN

Bridget was the daughter of a rich Swede who renounced it all to live in sympathy with the poor. She founded the Order named for her – the Brigettines – but was more importantly recognized as a seer, a visionary.

The Old Testament, of course, abounds with such seers and they are called prophets, not just because they see into the future but because they are aware of the influence of the present on that future. Since Christ there have been any number of Christian visionaries but seldom have we graced them with the title prophet. The reason is simple enough – most of the prophets were foretelling the coming of the Messiah. And He came.

Both visionary and prophet are terms with considerable cachet. The first is spectacular and the second is profound. Yet, oddly enough, aren't we all called on occasions to be both visionary and prophetic?

The parents must dream dreams for their children; the elders in the family must be prepared to reveal what must happen in certain circumstances. Then, as happened with all mystics bearing dreams, we must anticipate the dreams being shattered and the warnings ignored. Because we are not John of the Cross or John the Baptist the hurt is no less when our visions are ignored and our judgments dismissed.

In us all – as Jesus told us more than once – there is the capacity to be apostles if only we can grasp the reality that His way is usually the harder way. For this reason His seers and His prophets almost without exception had to suffer.

On this warm July day you watch your children running effortlessly across meadow or beach and your vision for them sparkles. Grandpa too sees them, nods contentedly and prophesies only the best for them. You have, perhaps without knowing it, acted religiously. Now you have to take it a stage further – and leave it in God's hands.

24 July

SS BORIS AND GLEB

*T*he *Oxford Dictionary of Saints* has an odd description for these two brother princelings killed by an ambitious half-brother. It seems they had only one of the usual requirements for sanctity – they were 'passion-bearers', innocent men.

Not at all like those of us Theodore Roosevelt described as 'those poor spirits who neither enjoy much nor suffer much, because they live in the gray twilight that knows not victory nor defeat.'

His words came to me as I watched a young mother come out of Tesco. There she was – all five feet of her, kiddy clinging to the trolley, not a care in the world. You can tell, can't you, in a glance if someone's at ease with themselves. It's more than the hovering smile, more than the walk declaring confidence. It's in the eyes, in the tot's unqualified confidence in Mum.

Dear Lord, it's so good to see. The more so because of the rarity. Give me an enthusiast, cries the Church, and I'll change the face of the world. It isn't clamouring for cults whose fanaticism burns out (remember the Jesus People?). It just seeks, in every parish community, one spark able to ignite the latent blaze. You see, goodness is everywhere in our small Christian groupings. It's evident in the care shown to the sick, the elderly, the disabled. Every parish has its simmering virtue. But from time to time the spark is needed to ignite ... passion?

The priest, the parish Sister, should be the professional animators. Hopefully they are. Yet simply because they are that, professionals, they are suspect. Their best role is in practical support of the enthusiast who displays that rare gift of sparkling awareness.

You cannot be sure, not positively, that you aren't that touchstone – the personality sufficiently unique to spark enthusiasm where there is apathy. Not until you try will you know.

25 July

ST JAMES, APOSTLE ST CHRISTOPHER

> Herod exerted his authority to persecute some of those who belonged to the Church. James, the brother of John, he beheaded, and then, finding that this was acceptable to the Jews, he went further, and laid hands on Peter too.

A brief enough note in the Acts of the martyrdom of the first apostle to die for following Jesus. For some reason never explained James became adopted by the Spanish and Compostela is still the site of a pilgrimage dating back to the twelfth century.

So engrossed have we been with celebrating our new millennium that we've forgotten what happened to celebrate the first. It was altogether more creditable than our own efforts. During the first decade of the year 1000 there was a frenzy of church building which reflected the sense of Christian renewal which the millennium had created. Not domes but spires. And following close on – and for the same reason, a new burst of Faith – came an increase in both the number of pilgrimages and the centres of pilgrimage such as Compostela.

We're permitted, I think, to compare our ancestors' sense of values with our own 1000 years on.

Helena, and her search for the True Cross, was probably the first pilgrim – a traveller who journeys to any place of faith out of love of God and atonement for sin. Her destination was the Holy Land and thousands followed in her footsteps. Later, Rome would almost supplant Palestine – it was nearer and had other attractions. And almost as old, and on our doorstep, was Lough Derg on the Donegal border and the island known as St Patrick's Purgatory. In England, since Saxon days, we had the Shrine to Our Lady at Walsingham. With the start of the second millennium pilgrimages took off just as package tours have today. At home, not just Walsingham but shrines at Evesham, Glastonbury, York and Canterbury attracted the pilgrim tourists. A wonderful way to travel – in hope.

26 July

SS JOACHIM AND ANNE

Have you ever wondered what it would be like being Jesus' grandparents? Would Joachim and Anne have fussed and bounced Him on their knees? Would He have heard His first stories from them? Would they have taken the toddler, so special a child, on walks about the busy streets of Nazareth? Or would He have been taken to stay with them, wherever it was they lived?

Questions, questions, questions – to which we never will have answers. There's legend, of course, in plenty, but fairy stories are not what Catholics want. Pop in a fantasy or two – as some say the Magi were – and you destroy the whole fabric of truth.

There was a move, as you'd expect, to link Joachim with prophecy but it came to nothing and the Church was reluctant to permit any form of cult to arise around them. And rightly so, surely.

Let's be content that the child Jesus had the love of Joachim and Anne. Let's presume, too, that they would be aware of the unusual circumstances of their daughter Mary's conception and espousal to Joseph. Let's be aware that, like us, they would have been just a little bewildered and in some awe.

One assumption we can make is that Jesus had grandparents. It was, remember, the Holy Family and the holiness of most families emanates from the influence of wise and loving grandparents. It is what has changed most today – the absence of that compassionate extended family of pre-1939.

For grandparents are the ones who collect miseries and heartaches. And, having gathered them, render them innocuous with a single kiss and a softly spoken whisper of encouragement. It's unbelievable that the child Jesus should not have had their shadows to shelter under.

———————— ⌒ ————————

The English may wear their Faith like an overcoat; the Irish like a skin. For the French it can be a casual drape, hanging loosely and so often in danger of slipping away. The Italians may don their Catholic Faith like a bikini – there only to hide the sensitive parts of their temperament. Spaniards can treat Catholicism as they would any dress accessory – there to glisten, to disguise the fabric beneath.

Only the African, let me suggest, grasps Faith for what it is – neither adornment, trinket nor disguise but the very essence of being.

Once you've discounted some superficial cynicisms about African enthusiasm for the Faith you are left with a belief that is soul deep, not skin deep. And this is as true for Africa's laity as well as it is for the clergy.

Cynicisms? Yes, some rushed to the priesthood for just the same reasons as some Irish did in the past. In the priesthood they saw status, dignity, security, a standard of living far in advance of what they had. For the women, the convent held the same attraction. Missioners – in their anxiety to count convert heads – looked the other way for a while and certainly there were abuses. No more and no less than had occurred elsewhere in poor societies.

But as the immensity of the obligation they had undertaken became apparent the false vocations were shed so that today the African Church and laity is as strong as any elsewhere.

It comes as no surprise that a few years into this millennium Western countries will be competing for priests and nuns from Africa. The process will be reversed – they will come to evangelize us. Their influence upon the regeneration of our faith will be impressive. They'll shrug us out of our protective clothing, rally and urge us to the fullness of Faith we have cosily forgotten. For the first time we'll realize the universality of the Church.

St Samson

I t's pretty revealing to examine a Catholic's neck. What's worn there indicates the direction Faith is taking. A simple cross is frequent – the wearer has Faith and is prepared to demonstrate it. The Brown Scapular of Franciscan origin denotes a more than passing devotion: a belief in the immortality of the soul. And then there is the Miraculous Medal – the wearer's expression of Faith in the desire and ability of Our Blessed Lady to protect.

It was in July 1830 that a novice with the Daughters of Charity of St Vincent de Paul went at midnight to the chapel of her House in the Rue du Bac in Paris. Her name was Catherine Labouré, and she was to live out her life in that convent without anyone knowing that in that chapel that night she saw Our Lady and spoke with her.

Her anonymity would have been preserved forever had not Our Lady visited her again four months later and instructed her to have a medal struck that would remind the wearers of the Virgin's concern for their protection.

Our Lady herself told Catherine what the design should be and what words should be upon it. On the front is a depiction of the Mother of God and the words 'O Mary conceived without sin, pray for us who have recourse to thee.' Our Lady is shown standing on a globe and around her feet there is the Devil, a serpent, writhing for mastery: the age-old conflict of good and evil.

On the reverse of the medal is the initial M and two hearts – those of Jesus and Mary. In no time at all it became known as the Miraculous Medal. And with good reason. Where it lay it brought comfort well beyond the means of human agency. Today it is the essential treasure in any Catholic's armoury.

Its power to comfort is inexplicable – it is, after all, a tiny piece of pressed metal. Yet I have clutched it so often in fear, left it beneath so many pillows in so many hospitals, and witnessed the ease it brings. For me, at least, it has been miraculous.

29 July

St Martha

Novena prayers are popular with Catholics because, unlike many prayers, they put a time limit on the response. The time is usually marked off in nine days, nine weeks, even nine months. Why it is nine I have no idea – like seven and three the number has gained a peculiar significance over the centuries.

A time limit on supernatural help? The idea is not as facetious as you may think. A time limit focuses the mind and the heart remarkably sharply. It improves the quality of prayer; it even prepares the supplicant for a denial rather than an automatic success. Unlike some other religions Catholicism encourages a pattern of prayer – most evident in the Rosary but also in the Novena. It's an intense supplication over a measured period.

Novenas need not be prayers, of course, they can be any form of devotion. Holy Communion over a specific period, attendance at Mass or Benediction, even acts of charity regularly performed – all these are forms of novena.

Novenas are prayers or acts of intercession, usually through the help of Our Blessed Lady or one of the saints. And as we've learned already there are saints with specialities, special interests.

For the housewife, as you might guess, there is St Martha. And in view of the drubbing she received from Jesus it is good to think that He relented and gives special attention to the good woman whose heart was in the right place. The novena to St Martha requires prayer on nine consecutive Tuesdays and a lighted candle.

St Martha, I resort to your protection and aid and as proof of my affection and faith I offer you this light which I shall burn every Tuesday. Comfort me in my difficulties and through the great favour you did enjoy when the Saviour rested in your house, intercede for my family that we may be provided with all our necessities. I beg you have pity in regard to this favour I now ask.

St Peter Chrysologus

There are times, sitting in Tesco's cafe, when I long for the articulacy and fire of today's saint. Times, cramped behind my bun and coffee, when I am tempted to leap up, snatch the talk I'm hearing and hurl it across the crammed Volvos, the pert Kias and those bumptious People Carriers.

The two talking were youngish wives enjoying the £1.75 genetically correct special lunch. I knew they were wives for they were talking about husbands. I knew they were youngish because they still had great expectations for their men. They were unaware that every plan they so carefully prospected showed no seam of contentment. They didn't know it, but thousands of years before a psalmist had prepared a prayer just for them:

> I waited, I waited for the Lord
> and he stooped down to me;
> He heard my cry.
> He drew me from the deadly pit,
> from the miry clay.
> He set my feet upon a rock
> and made my footsteps firm.
> He put a new song into my mouth,
> Praise of our God.
> Many shall see and fear
> and shall trust in the Lord.
> As for me, wretched and poor,
> the Lord thinks of me.
> You are my rescuer, my help,
> O God, do not delay.

As they went out they paused at the sign proclaiming 'Beans – two for the price of one.' It was the only new song they heard that day.

St Ignatius of Loyola

Man was created to praise, honour and serve God. We therefore no more prefer health to sickness, riches to poverty, honour to disdain, long life to short, but desire and choose only that which more surely conduces toward the end for which we were created.

And there, in his *Spiritual Exercises*, speaks Ignatius the solider – succinct, direct, peremptory. Thanks to a wound in battle which left him bed-bound, the soldier read a life of Jesus and the invalid who recovered had a new leader in life – Christ.

It was a huge gain for Christ's battalions, and for His Church then longing for something other than vacillating leadership. Ignatius formed an army and, so there would be no mistaking its leader, it was called the Society of Jesus. The first General was Ignatius himself. The army did not suffer through lack of direction. As a soldier, Ignatius knew the importance of clear orders. Here is one he sent to Jesuits in Portugal:

We may easily suffer ourselves to be surpassed by other religious orders in fasting, watching and other austerities of diet and clothing which they practise according to their rule, but in true and perfect obedience and the abnegation of our will and judgement, I greatly desire, most dear brethren, that those who serve God in this Society should be conspicuous.

It was done as Ignatius commanded although from time to time he had to send curt messages to his commanders in the field such as this: 'Prudence, my lord, is the virtue of those who command, not of those who obey.'

Christ, as we've discovered over these days, has a particular skill when it comes to selecting those He wants to serve. Seldom was his choice so conspicuously accurate as with Ignatius.

1 August

St Alphonsus Liguori

The Redemptorists, founded in the eighteenth century by Alphonsus, reached the summit of their influence in Britain at the very start of the twentieth century. Like their Founder, the Order's preachers strove for simplicity with a dash of fire and some little brimstone.

A quirk of one Redemptorist was to ask for written questions before the Mass at which he was to preach. On one occasion he unfolded the question and thundered it out before reading it. 'What's a handsome man like you doing as a priest?' it read.

In no way thrown he explained, 'What makes you think God likes only ugly priests?'

Redemptorists became renowned for the fire of their missions. There were few hiding places for the Devil in any parish the target of a Redemptorist blitz. Parishioners, dazed, would anticipate the Day of Judgment with an apprehension alien to them.

Nowadays the Order, like all others, is smaller. Its capability to shock diminished as the very Devil they preached becomes a reality. So Liguori's successors use the written word rather than the spoken. Mostly they supply the Mass sheets we use to rustle our way through the readings. But in many cases they also supply the homily for the day, reaching a congregation many times larger than any they attracted in the past.

There are still missions, of course – five days in which a team will take over the spiritual life of the parish, turning it inside out and upside down, revealing both its warts and its hidden ability to be holy and caring. They are rarer than they were, largely because they are expensive to host. But there's another, sadder, reason for their demise. The preacher – no matter how handsome, how articulate – no longer has much chance against the devils even Liguori didn't visualize: the Rovers Return and the Woolpack.

2 August

We were just talking about preaching and, behold, look at the reading: 'Vanity of vanities, the Preacher says. Vanity of vanities. All is vanity!'

Catholicism is no easy ride – this cannot be said often enough. And today we're told why that is. Today hammers home the lesson dinned into every Catholic heart from childhood, that the world is a fine affair, but a transient one. Just as a new pope is reminded, upon election, of his mortality, so we are nudged continuously with the almost nagging thought that here is brief and there is eternal. Today's Psalm is all about the brevity Catholics should understand:

> You turn men back into dust
> and say: 'Go back, sons of men.'
> To your eyes a thousand years
> are like yesterday, come and gone,
> no more than a watch in the night.
>
> You sweep men away like a dream,
> like grass which springs up in the morning.
> In the morning it springs up and flowers:
> by evening it withers and fades.
>
> Make us know the shortness of our life
> that we may gain wisdom of heart.
> Lord, relent! Is your anger for ever?
> Show pity to your servants.
>
> In the morning, fill us with your love;
> we shall exult and rejoice all our days.
> Let the favour of the Lord be upon us:
> give success to the work of our hands.

3 August

ST WALDEF

⁓

In search of a plumber I asked the lady next to me at Mass for a recommendation. She thought for a while. 'There's old Mr Ubend,' she said thoughtfully, 'or Sprockett and Winch.' Then she beamed. 'Ah, but you'll want Harpo, Tommy Harpo – he's a Catholic.'

I wasn't surprised. In the past I've employed joiners who couldn't join, brickies who asked me how to mix cement, builders whose creations crumbled overnight. All Catholics, every one of them. And taken on trust because of those magic words – 'He's a Catholic, of course.'

It's taken me the better part of a lifetime for the penny to drop that being Catholic does not make every carpenter a St Joseph, nor, sadly, does it endow him with honesty. Some of the more spectacular rip-offs I've suffered have been cleverly conducted by Catholics.

Yet, it shouldn't be so. At the back of my mind is the constant niggle that a Catholic won't sell me short. So when invariably I'm cheated once again by an incompetent Catholic I try to find excuses for him.

It's as if he had acted so out of character that there must surely be some good excuse for him. My sons are less accommodating. They embarrass me with the inevitable question when the slates fall off. 'What made you choose HIM?' Over the years they've learned to anticipate my answer – 'Because he's a Catholic.' It's a form of naivety they just cannot understand.

Nor can I. Because I still persist in clinging to the belief that a Catholic tradesman will make sure his Faith permeates both his work and his dealings. The reason is the ethic I hold dear – to work is to pray.

And what if the tap still drips, and the shed falls down? Why, the answer's simple enough – that Catholic just wasn't praying hard enough.

4 August

ST JOHN VIANNEY

agiology, the stories of saints, has been unkind to the common secular priest. It may indicate their humility, or more likely their lack of important friends in the right places. Whatever – John Vianney, simple curé, stands for all our unheralded saints who ever trudged a parish beat. No wonder he is, since his canonization in 1925, the Patron of parochial clergy – the secular priest.

Although no scholar, thousands made their way to his sermons each day in the modest village of Ars-en-Dombes. He had only a slight knowledge of the world, gained as a conscript soldier, yet so great was the desire to confess to him that it was not unusual for him to sit in the confessional from dawn to nightfall without a break.

So what was his secret? It could hardly have been his detestation of sin, because you'd have expected that in a simple priest. It wouldn't be his direct condemnation of all things obscene, since every priest is similarly condemnatory. What it was, was his insight into the human soul. It was his rare ability to pinpoint the area of stress in the human heart. In this he was as skilled as any surgeon, as healing as any physician. God had given him the gift of understanding. And, with it, the ability to cure the wounds people inflict upon themselves. He paid a high price for this gift. His style of life was austere, he rejected honours, and simple exhaustion took his life when he was 73.

Like all models, as young priests discover, he was unique. Priests may well address him in prayer and in their need but they know that to emulate him is well nigh impossible. In life – as in art and in literature – the hardest skill to develop is that of simplicity. It comes only with long, long experience and age; only rarely is it inbred. John Vianney possessed it in plenitude.

DEDICATION OF THE BASILICA OF
ST MARY MAJOR

T his somewhat clumsy title for a Catholic day conceals a deep concern with where and how the early Christians worshipped God and taught Christ. Mostly we have this vague idea of them slipping unseen about the catacombs. For the first 100 years or so this was partially true. But by the end of the first century worship was in the homes of the better off, and by the fourth century the large Roman halls which had once housed government offices or markets, called basilicas, had largely been taken over by the Christians as churches.

As Christianity flourished, the temporary basilicas were abandoned (or by then were falling down), and the name retained for the large churches now built for a common purpose: the worship of God. At that time, too, the Church developed the features that were to last until the present day.

The basilicas would be constructed in an east to west direction and usually cruciform in imitation of the Cross. Men would sit in the south aisle and women in the north. The main door into the church would, in memory presumably of another Gate, be called the Beautiful Gate. This would give entrance to what was called the nave.

But before you reached this point, you would pass an outer wall enclosing a quadrangle where there was a water basin for cleansing hands, feet and face and an area set aside for penitents who, because of their sins, would not be allowed further into the church.

It's August, so there will be flocks of tourists in Rome. If they wish to step 1600 years into Christian history they can still visit five original basilicas – St Peter's, of course, and then St John Lateran, St Mary Major, St Paul without the Walls and St Lawrence. If the sandal leather holds out, there are eight smaller basilicas. And, naturally, the most daunting 'basilica' of all – the Colosseum.

THE TRANSFIGURATION OF THE LORD

The Transfiguration does more to profile Peter – the living, breathing urgent Peter – than almost any other New Testament anecdote. He was such an ebullient man, so atypically human, so predictable in so many ways.

There he was, on a mountain top, 'where they could be alone', and what does Peter see – the Master chatting, yes, chatting, would you believe, with Moses and Elijah. The situation is mind-numbing, as if normality had ceased to exist and most certainly could never be the same again.

And what did Peter do? He babbled, just as we would have babbled in his place. He burst out with the first thing that came into his mind. He cried out how astonishing that moment was and then, betraying his own humanity, leapt at some way to celebrate the occasion. Just as we so often do, he insisted that something should be built to recognize the moment – build a temple, no, three temples – so that everyone in future would know what happened there on that mountain.

It's what we all jump to do when the fantastic happens, we long to make a permanence. A temple, a house, a plaque. God help us, even a dome.

Then, to cap it all for Peter, there is the very voice of God: 'This is My Son, the Beloved. Listen to Him.' Poor Peter, bewildered James and John, no wonder they fell down terrified. And finally, their ultimate frustration when Jesus tells them they are not to mention what happened.

Despite this – and so much else – it was that same babbling Peter who was to deny Jesus. If that doesn't reveal the crass humanity of the man, what else can? And for that we have to love Peter, to be ever grateful that, like us, he was able to betray the One he so loved. We all do it at some time or other. When we do, then Peter is there, the rock, to reassure us we are no different from him.

7 August

St Cajetan

W henever we feel inclined to write off the Church just prior to the Reformation bear in mind men like Cajetan. He was one of so many in those middle centuries who had so much to lose in order to gain integrity. Jesus' promise to Peter that His Church would endure was no empty one. For every ambitious, thoughtless, avaricious pope – and there were not so many as you might assume – there were always others amongst both clergy and laity to advance Christ's cause through His Church.

It would not be stretching the point to claim that Cajetan, in the 1530s, gave birth to the notion of Credit Union when he opened a chain of pawnshops whose purpose was to enable the poor to have a source of borrowing at rates which were not burdensome and would enable them to manage their own finances.

It's all too easy for us to forget that before the birth of what's termed the Welfare State immediately after the war, the major thrust of all altruism was in the hands of the Churches, notably the Catholic Church. Prior to the Reformation, convents and monasteries had provided what the State did ineffectively – they were the centres for charity, nursing and education. They were sanctuaries for the oppressed, havens for the dispossessed.

Today even Catholics have but faint recognition of what the Church in Britain does in their name for the needy and the powerless. And where the Welfare State so often assists anonymous recipients with only numbers to denote their existence, the Church agencies deal still with individuals, people unique in the sight of God.

Nursing is never so compassionate, teaching never so meaningful, assistance never so caring as when done by priests, nuns and lay-people in the conscious knowledge that what they do they do for Christ. Love of neighbour is forever the beacon mark of the Church.

8 August

St Dominic

B efore he died in 1221, Dominic was asked where he wished
to be buried. 'Under the feet of my friars,' he insisted. And
you have to wonder if he is not disconcerted by the magnifi-
cence of his tomb, decorated by Michelangelo, at Bologna.

Dominic was first and foremost a preacher who practised both
the humility and the austerity of life that he preached. Spotted by
the Bishop of Osma, who appointed him as his chaplain, Dominic
became accustomed to the subtleties of diplomacy and, more importantly, became deeply involved in combatting the heresies of several
small cults which banded together under the name of Albigenses.

When the Bishop died, Dominic enjoyed the freedom to live the
life of austerity which had first attracted him. In time he was joined
by other young men and, after considerable opposition from the
Pope, was eventually given permission to form an institute under the
name of the 'Preaching Brothers' with a monastic base at Toulouse.

The Rule, based on that of the Augustinian Canons, was rigorous. They wore wool not linen, there was perpetual silence, fasting
lasted from 14 September until the end of Lent, their poverty was
absolute. The Order, soon enough known as the Dominicans,
renounced all possessions and its members became mendicants,
wholly dependent upon the charity of others in imitation of St
Francis.

The charism of Dominic was intelligence supported by austerity.
It proved a heady mixture and the Dominicans grew rapidly, used, as
were the Jesuits, to be the instrument of the Church as far-flung as
the Americas and as near home as Britain where, at the dissolution
of the monasteries, there were no fewer than 57 Dominican friaries.

Whether the sensitive Dominic would have endorsed all that was
to be done in his name is open to argument. But then, so much
history is.

———— ∽ ————

T he discussion in the pub – when it isn't about soccer – still hovers about sex, politics and, thankfully, religion. When it's known you are Catholic then, as sure as monsignorii wear purple socks, someone will ask why the Pope doesn't sell the Vatican treasures and give it all to the poor. In effect, the one posing the question – the same one who is saving for a new Mercedes CLK – has this Gospel reading in mind:

> Sell your possessions and give alms. Get yourselves purses that do not wear out, treasure that will not fail you, in heaven where no thief can reach it and no moth destroy it. For where your treasure is, there will your heart be also.

In justice to the one asking the question, you can be sure that many a pope has thought just the same thing. Wealth, or rather the appearance of wealth, embarrasses the Church, as do the trappings of power. Yet, without resources, there can be no emergency aid through Caritas, no response when the masses cry out in anguish, no organization to support the massive machinery created to care for the powerless.

The Church's wealth always has to be available; it is a transient wealth – vast sums must enter the machine of Church but equally vast expenditures must come out at the other end. It is a cycle to which many millions contribute for the benefit of many millions who cannot. The Church is a heart through which blood must be continually pumped in order to reach every part of the body.

A Church rich in property? Yes, but what is the property used for? To educate in the love of God, to give shelter to the homeless, to house the disabled, to worship God. As for the old chestnut about selling the Vatican treasures, well, they are not the Vatican's – they are our treasure kept in trust. And where more safely?

10 August

ST LAURENCE THE DEACON

The Diaconate is as old as the day when the apostles, grown impatient with the business of administration, asked the disciples to choose seven men to do the donkey work whilst they got on with preaching Jesus Christ. But the men they chose were far from being donkeys. In many ways they were more intellectual than the apostles themselves, and certainly as prepared to die. Stephen, the first deacon chosen, was to be the first Christian martyr and Laurence would follow him.

In the course of time the Diaconate lapsed in the sense that it became simply one of the stages on the road to priesthood, until, in the 1970s, Derek Worlock urged the ordination of laymen as deacons in order to meet the challenge of a dwindling priesthood.

At any one time we have about 400 deacons assisting priests in their parishes. Most of them combine their work as deacons with their secular tasks. They come from all walks of life, represent a wide age range and are properly entitled to Reverend before their name. They are ordained ministers, not laymen.

They take their turn preaching, they can baptize, and perform marriage ceremonies. But mostly, as the apostles originally intended, they help take the administration off the priest's shoulders.

I often wonder why the revolutionary Derek Worlock stopped short at male deacons when women, in his time, were growing ever more strident in their demands for ordination to the priesthood. Just as he was largely responsible for restoring male deacons, did he ever play with the idea of bringing back the deaconess? We did have them, just as the Anglican Church has them today. Their tasks were, admittedly, limited – their main concern was with the poor, with teaching catechumens, being present at interviews between priests and women. It's a tantalizing thought – will women in time use this apparent loophole to attain their aims? Who knows?

11 August

ST CLARE

———⁓———

With my hobnailed boots, how could I talk of Clare? So I asked the Poor Clares at Hawarden, my Sisters, to write this day.

New woman, bright light, lofty candle stick of holiness: these were titles given by Pope Alexander IV when he canonized Clare two years after her death in 1253. Alexander, who had visited her on her deathbed, had wanted to canonize her during her funeral, but he let his cardinals dissuade him.

Clare stands, as it were, on the bridge between heaven and earth, before her the gospel by which she lived, at her side a bowl of water and a trowel symbolic of her Sisterly service, and in her hands the uplifted monstrance of the Blessed Sacrament, the attribute with which she is most often depicted, in tribute to her once repelling an invading army with it.

Born around 1193 to 1194, Clare came of a noble family in Assisi. Encouraged by St Francis, she ran away from home in 1212 and, after stormy scenes with her kinsfolk in which she clung to the altar cloths and bared her shorn head, she established herself at San Damiano's, one of the churches which Francis had rebuilt. Here she lived an enclosed community life in the highest poverty, which was imitated by more than 70 communities before her death. She fought a running battle with successive popes to avoid being coopted into Benedictine monasticism and became the first woman to write a Religious Rule, the confirmation of which she received only on her deathbed. Apart from her Rule, Clare left five letters and a testament. Short though these are, they reveal a unique approach to prayer:

> Gaze upon Christ,
> consider Him
> contemplate Him,
> if you would imitate Him.

J ohn Henry Cardinal Newman died yesterday in 1890. The impact of his conversion and then the richness of his mind's treasures just cannot be appreciated more than a century onwards. But we have to try:

> I recognise in the Anglican Church a time-honoured institution, of noble historical memories, a monument of ancient wisdom, a momentous arm of political strength, a great national organ, a source of vast popular advantage, and, to a certain point, a witness and teacher of religious truth . . . But that it is something sacred, that it is an oracle of revealed doctrine, that it can claim a share in St Ignatius or St Cyprian, that it can take the rank, contest the teaching, and stop the path of the Church of St Peter, that it can call itself 'the bride of the Lamb', this is the view of it which simply disappeared from my mind on my conversion, and which it would be almost a miracle to reproduce.
> *Apologia pro Vita Sua* (Note E)

Newman confessed, more than once, an unease with the devotion his new Faith gave to Our Blessed Lady. In the *Apologia* he admits that such devotion was his 'crux' as regards Catholicism. But in a letter to the Revd E.B. Pusey he made an important distinction:

> I fully grant that devotion towards the blessed Virgin has increased among Catholics with the progress of the centuries; I do not allow that the doctrine concerning her has undergone a growth, for I believe that it has been in substance one and the same from the beginning.

It may be trite to finish on a Newman truism but it is succinct:

> The one peculiar and characteristic sin of the world is this that whereas God would have us live for the world to come, the world would make us live for this life. *Sermons on Subjects of the Day*

St Hippolytus

W e know the big picture; we know, however vaguely, how the great creeds emerged, how doctrine was set like a cosmetic on the face of the Faith Christ left us. But what about the nitty-gritty, the little things that are so important in forming the charism of a Faith? One of those responsible for indicating the character of Christianity was today's St Hippolytus, a martyr priest of the third century.

He gave guidance – and it was largely followed – on a host of small matters that crafted the ethos of those early days. His advice could be sharp, for example, as it was for actors: 'If a man be an actor or one who makes shows in the theatre, either let him desist or let him be rejected.' Or it could be understanding: 'Let a catechumen be instructed for three years. But if a man be earnest and persevere well in the matter, let him be received, because it is not the time that is judged but the conduct.'

He throws an interesting sidelight on to the strict rules we once had for fasting before Holy Communion: 'Let everyone of the faithful be careful to partake of the Eucharist before he eats anything else. For if he partakes with faith, even though some deadly thing were given him, after this it cannot hurt him.' So fasting, at a time when poisoning was not rare, had a practical purpose.

Hippolytus laid down the early rubrics too – for the administration of Confirmation, for the election of a bishop (he was to be chosen by all the people), the questions to be asked of those seeking baptism and a whole list of 'little' things that are now part of the very fabric of Catholicism.

He even was the one who gave us morning and night prayers ordering: 'Let every faithful man and woman when they rise from sleep at dawn before they undertake any work wash their hands and pray to God . . . pray also before thy body rests upon thy bed.'

14 August

St Maximilian Kolbe

When you have given everything, just one thing remains. Your life. A Franciscan priest, Maximilian Kolbe, had reached that point in 1941 as a prisoner in the concentration camp at Auschwitz. It had been a long journey for the 47-year-old Pole, a life peppered with sickness – he had recurrent tuberculosis – and drama.

After a spell teaching in a Polish seminary he decided that journalism was the best way to serve both his Church and his country. With the help of other Franciscans he established a printing press, which first produced a Catholic magazine and then later weekly newspapers followed by dailies. He was a first-rate administrator, an outspoken journalist and a cheerful superior for his Franciscan brothers. So adept was he that he spent some time in the early 1930s founding a Franciscan monastery at Nagasaki in Japan. But his heart was that of a patriot as well as a priest, and he returned home in 1936 to be superior of a community of almost 800 priests and Brothers at Niepokalanow.

The German invasion of Poland in 1939 found him as independent as ever in the newspapers he still printed. Inevitably he was interned. But not for long. When the Germans released him he returned to his monastery which became a sanctuary for Christian and Jewish refugees. And still Fr Maximilian produced the newspapers that gave people hope.

As he knew it must, German tolerance was stretched too far and in May 1941, the Gestapo arrested Fr Maximilian and four of his helpers and imprisoned them in the camp at Auschwitz. Maximilian remained a worker - celebrating Mass, giving what Sacraments he could, always at the service of all. Until the day when men were selected for death by starvation. One was a former sergeant. When they came to take him Maximilian stepped forward: 'I am a Catholic priest. I wish to die for that man. I am old, he has a wife and children.' The request was granted. In the deathshed he comforted the dying until finally he died, injected with phenol.

15 August

St Tarsicius

T arsicius died in defence of the Blessed Sacrament which he was carrying and refused to give to his attackers. Perhaps this is a legend, but it has the ring of truth and has certainly been repeated since: the defence of what Catholics hold more precious than life itself – the sacred Host which is the Body and Blood of Christ.

At times of mealy-mouthed lip service to a pretend democracy it's comforting that the celebration of the Mass and the reception of the Blessed Sacrament stand out above all else as the only unquestionable democratic act left to us.

The Mass draws together all manner of people and the Host is there waiting for all who dare approach. The sheer availability of such munificence is startling when you stop to consider it.

It was not always so. At one time we were expected to receive Holy Communion three times a year. Then a rule was introduced requiring communicating – the proper name – just once a year at some period over the Easter season. That happened during the fourth Lateran Council in 1215. Over the next centuries there was good-tempered debate over the frequency, with some holding that daily communion was the ideal and others feeling that such familiarity would debase the uniqueness of the Sacrament.

St Catherine of Siena and then St Philip Neri were keen supporters for frequent communion but it wasn't until the start of the twentieth century that popes begin to urge us to receive Holy Communion as often as we were able. Pius X was prominent in this, instructing priests 'not to deter from frequent or daily Communion anyone who is in a state of grace and approaches with the right intention.'

Even in my youth it was unusual for more than a third of the congregation to receive Holy Communion. Now it is astonishing if there is anyone who does not. A wondrous step back to the early Church.

16 August

ASSUMPTION OF THE
BLESSED VIRGIN MARY

I n one sense Pius XII's solemn announcement in 1950 was
redundant. He defined as dogma: 'Mary, the immaculate perpet-
ually Virgin Mother of God, after the completion of her earthly
life, was assumed body and soul into the glory of heaven.' After all,
what son would have done less for a loving mother?

On the other hand, many of us could be bewildered by today's
strange reading from the Apocalypse:

> A great sign appeared in heaven; a woman clothed with the sun, the
> moon beneath her feet, and a crown of twelve stars on her head.

It's a description that appealed to Italian painters, the shame of it
being that in becoming entranced with the fantastic they tended to
overlook the ordinariness of the reality. Our Lady's strength for us
lies not in her remote grandeur but in her ever present availability at
the end of a prayer.

The oral tradition of Our Lady's assumption into heaven is almost
as old as the Church. In one way, Pius's decision to formalize the
belief pre-dated the ethos of the Second Vatican Council that came
15 years later – it was a decision not taken solely by the Pope but as
a result of the clamour from the world's bishops. They all felt, as we
the people did, that it was inconceivable that Jesus would have permitted His mother's body to decay. It was only common sense to
recognize what Christians down the ages had always taken to be
fact.

Our Lady's life – like our own lives – was a kaleidoscope of sunshine and sorrow. She endured much as the mother of Jesus. Who
could deny Jesus, the Son, the delight of this last favour for His
mother, the last gift He could give her in memory of His human
incarnation?

17 August

St Clare of Montefalco

~

The August days are hot, oppressively so. Our northern blood isn't attuned to it. So we question the reason for the heat. Is it the effect of El Nino, have bomb tests finally shifted the axis on which the Earth so slenderly tilts? We sweat on, our skins unprepared for the majesty of the sun. The newspapers run their scare stories – it's global warming, the icebergs are melting, the equator has moved, Africa will be wreathed in ice, Scotland will be a desert.

We are such a delicate planet, and can be such a fear-full one. An earthquake, a tornado, a flood, some sly trick of nature and we're dashing to the tomes of Nostradamus, hearkening again to the warnings in the Apocalypse.

We're prepared at any one moment to rush mindlessly into the pagan beliefs of our forebears, ignore the simple truths and warnings given us by Jesus amidst the restful hills of Judaea.

Be still, He urged us so often, be still. And so, sometimes, we can be, when the days are placid and nature shows us her kindly face. But let something untoward occur and then we're back in our skins and adorned with berry juices. Scratch us – with fear, surprise, realization – and we're sacrificing our offspring to the gods whose names we do not know.

The Church, in her wisdom, has always known how fragile is our concept of a knowing, loving God in Whom we can trust. The answers she has given us for these tremulous moments are usually sufficient and satisfying. But then, out of the blue, a child is killed, a city vanishes in a mountain of falling ash and we, and even the Church, are left without answers.

Because such tragedies happen so rarely doesn't mean that we must not be prepared for them. Even when the high priests stumble for words to excuse some appalling tragedy we have to be ready to alibi God rather than racing to the deep chasms of our racial memories.

18 August

St Helen

~

Catholics enjoy a special thrill when they see their football hero make the Sign of the Cross as he runs on to the arena. Consciously or not it makes him one of us, sparks off that other memory of that other stadium where Christians dedicated their lives to the Cross before dying.

The Cross has grown to be the strongest symbol in the world due, at least in part, to the efforts of Helena, the mother of the first Christian ruler, the Emperor Constantine. A late convert, she made it her life's intent to find the True Cross. She claimed to have done so in AD 326 and today part of the Cross she discovered is preserved in Rome at the Church of Sancta Croce.

Sceptics once said that if all the Catholic churches claiming to possess splinters of the True Cross put their treasures together you would end up with a forest. Perhaps. But, as ever, the cynics overlook what really matters to those who kiss the Cross: that their faith is not in the splinter but in the One who died on the Cross.

This faith of ours is ancient and pervades every act of the Catholic. Only about 200 years after Christ's death Tertullian wrote:

> At every step and movement, when we go in or out, when we dress or put on our shoes, at the bath, at the table, when lights are brought, when we go to bed, when we sit down, whatever it is which occupies us, we mark the forehead with the Sign of the Cross.

The Sign of the Cross quickly became the method of passing on a blessing and was an integral part of the celebration of the Mass, especially during the Consecration. On Good Friday the Cross becomes the focal point of every thought. The Cross is the burden which we help carry throughout life. And, at the end, it is the symbol we clutch.

19 August

ST JOHN EUDES

F ounder of the Congregation of Jesus and Mary, St John Eudes
was one of those in the seventeenth century who encouraged
devotion to the Sacred Heart of Jesus.

It seemed eerie when I was but a tot to be taught to say each
night: 'Most Sacred Heart of Jesus, have pity on the dying.' And that
prayer too had a rider: ' . . . have pity on my sinful soul, when it shall
depart from my miserable body, and shall enter into eternity. Obtain
for me, I beg You, the grace of a happy death.'

But the century between 1850 and 1950 was like that. At the
start, our Church having been underground, we inherited much
from the Germans who were beginning to flee to England to escape
military service in that expanding empire. They brought with them
a Faith dour and austere and sometimes downright macabre. The
emphasis was almost necrophobic – a stolid, unloving anticipation of
the agonies of death. In England where Catholicism had tended to
be merry before it was to be heroic this stolid foreign implant sadly
came during the Great Queen's widowhood and took root.

We had a long time to await renewal of Christian hope – and
Catholic belief – that death was a journey towards and not a journey
finished.

Today a Catholic funeral of someone of mature years is very
nearly a celebration in the true sense. We celebrate the life but we
also celebrate the life living on. True, where once we were despairing we now tend to be presumptuous. But if that is so, then it is in
fact a very little sin indeed and one we commit almost gaily on
behalf of those left to mourn.

It is as if nowadays we have learned to be on friendly terms with
the Son when only yesterday we could get no further than our fear
of His Father. Of course there are dangers inherent in this new
familiarity. But none, surely, that the Son cannot control.

20 August

St Bernard

———— ❦ ————

I t's not what you'd expect from the Abbot of Clairvaux – a monastery so austere that even the twelfth century Cistercians were uneasy. Yet St Bernard, well born, was as much at home with the wealthy as he was with the poor. Listen to this advice:

> Silk and purple and rouge and paint have beauty, but impart it not. Every such thing as you apply to the body exhibits its own loveliness, but leaves it not behind. It takes the beauty with it, when the thing itself is taken away. For the beauty that is put on with a garment and is put off with the garment, belongs without doubt to the garment, and not to the wearer of it.
>
> *Letters*

Much of the Cistercian ethos was based upon humility – not just physical humility but humility of the intellect too. It must have come hard to Bernard, son of a knight, a charming man-about-society in his youth, to preach this virtue, but it showed his own humility when he did:

> Humility is that thorough self-examination which makes a man contemptible in his own sight. It is acquired by those who set up a ladder in their hearts whereby to ascend from virtue to virtue, that is, from step to step, until they attain the summit of humility, from where, as from the Sion of speculation, they can see the truth.
>
> *The Steps of Humility*

Despite the seclusion demanded of his monks, St Bernard was himself no recluse. His interference in politics almost led to his total loss of influence when he fervently urged the Second Crusade which not only failed but splintered Christian alliances.

His legacy, however, was the strength of the Cistercian Order whose vast network of monasteries was to be the source of civilization for centuries to come.

21 August

St Pius X

P ius X died a hugely disappointed man just a week or two after the start of the First World War, which he had tried so desperately to prevent. But the Church he left behind was far from dissatisfied with his work 'to restore all things in Christ' – the motto he chose for his pontificate from 1903 until 1914.

To this end he enlisted the services of the remarkable Spanish Cardinal Rafael Merry del Val as his Secretary of State. They made a formidable duo taking on France, Ireland, Portugal and Poland in general assertation of Catholic rights over state supremacy. In Italy he put an end to the cold war between State and Vatican.

But in the end modernism was his target and to this end he enlisted the aid of the laity, turned the Curia upside down, swept away the obsolescences gathering dust in the Vatican and rewrote the Church's rule book, the Code of Canon Law. He was in so many ways a complete paradox. He was the scourge of the intelligentsia, of scholars intent on broadening Church attitudes on moral theology. At the same time he gave new zest to religious practice, commending frequent Communion and making the Sacrament available to children as soon as they reached the age of reason. He revised the missal Catholics use at Mass and urged the return of music, particularly the Gregorian Chant.

He became a rallying point for a clergy that had begun to become demoralized and opened the seminary windows to a breath of fresh air. Pius was in a true sense an early template for John Paul II in that he proved a radical could be at the same time a conservative. More importantly, for us in this age, he evidenced that in the Catholic Church there can be no 'wings', right or left, just the Church and her teaching. In him many virtues met.

22 August

QUEENSHIP OF THE BLESSED VIRGIN MARY

The Bishop frowned at the nun. The nun grimaced at the chaplain. And the chaplain looked upward in the general direction of Heaven. A telephone call was the immediate cause of their dismay. Cupping his hand over the mouthpiece the Bishop hissed, 'What made you say I was in, Sister?'

Sr Mary Joseph of the Apparition swiftly cast her eyes down, pretending to the long defunct rule about custody of the eyes. 'It seemed urgent, Father,' she excused herself.

'Isn't it always?' grumbled the Bishop as the flow of vitriol poured without interruption into his ear. A deluge, reckoned the Bishop, that should have been re-directed to his vicar-general.

As the torrent seemed unlikely to abate of its own accord, the Bishop spoke firmly, silencing his caller. 'I share your sadness over the closure of Our Lady, Queen of Peace,' he enunciated slowly, 'but it's a matter of resources, using them to the best advantage of the diocese and the inner city.' He spoke over the protest he knew would come. 'No one loves Our Lady's more than me – not even the 30 people who still attend Mass there.'

The caller agitatedly shrieked, 'Forty!'

'All right, forty,' agreed the Bishop. 'But it's just not practical, nor possible, nor even just, to spend £150,000 on the basic repairs needed to keep Our Lady's open.'

His caller – a widow pensioner living on £75.55 a week – screamed back so that the chaplain, at the door by now, winced. 'We could find the money – me and the others, we'll find it.'

That night the Bishop – neither a hard man nor a sentimental one – laid his problem before the Cross by his bed. 'Those people will probably never set foot in a church again – even though St Pat's is only ten minutes away,' he protested. But, even as he spoke, he knew he would be forever the 'vandal' who tore down Our Lady's. It would become folklore, his cruelty, for thousands as yet unborn. It is the dilemma that haunts every bishop at the turn of the millennium. And it is insoluble.

23 August

My elder son, a pilot, tells me that in the air he is always mentally targetting alternative landing places should the worst happen. As a writer – we are all anxiety-ridden – the knowledge comforts me when I'm aloft. But, grounded, I'm stymied. What happens if tomorrow I cannot recognize God? Where do I land then? What are my alternatives?

The possibility of this forced landing is not so remote as we might think. Faith in God is a gift, we're instructed. But it's not a one-off gift we treasure for life. It's a perpetual gift we receive hour by hour, day by day – like water from the tap, power from the electricity. But just as we have to turn on the tap and switch on the light, we have to prompt our Faith in God.

He doesn't make it easy. There are times when pain can be so exquisite that we scream, 'How can God do this?' There are moments when grief all but tears your chest apart and you cry out, 'How can God do this?' There are anxieties so numerous you no longer have the capacity to absorb them. Then your mind simply turns off, gives in. And in the ensuing blankness there's just no room for God.

Little wonder the Church so swiftly listed despair as a serious sin. Real despair is totally corrosive: it decays any image of God, leaves no room for hope, no alternative landing place for the soul.

So, we have to plan ahead of the moment when we need one. And here the Catholic is lucky. There are saints whose dark nights of the soul have been even darker than our own. They will understand because they have been there and landed safely. There is Our Lady herself – who had darker days? But always there is Him – there in the tabernacle. Always ready to aid the flier flying blind.

ST BARTHOLOMEW THE APOSTLE

The Churches represent the finger in the dam of the welfare state. Without them, the dam would surely split and the leak the Churches prevent would all too soon become a torrent. In my own diocese – and in yours – the Catholic organizations beavering away for the weaker ones is multifarious. Just think of a need – the Church has its finger in the leak.

Even so, I know Catholics – and so do you – who say the Church has no place supplementing the State's inadequacies. The Church, they will insist, is there to give spiritual succour; its priests are there to celebrate the Mass and not to supplant the DHSS. These, they allege, are the priorities. What is left over when they have accomplished these tasks can be distributed as the do-gooders think fit.

It's a point of view, I suppose. The state is a greedy beast – do its job for it and it will be delighted to transfer the funds to a new squadron of tanks.

But it's a viewpoint that disregards Jesus' own priorities. He was the Man who gave the blind sight, the dead life, the leper a cure. He wasn't just doing that to establish His credentials as the Son of God. Like everything He did it had a purpose, it was meant as an example. Just as His most memorable sermon, the one delivered on a mount, indicated so clearly the way He was nudging us.

So I'm proud – in the better sort of way, of course – that my diocese offers homes for the homeless, groups for the disabled and their parents, schools for the disadvantaged, help for the blind and the deaf. And just about every other need you can imagine.

It is God's work it does. And if some doing it aren't always seen at Mass then I venture to suggest Jesus regards them as Catholic in their actions as the rest of us are in our formal devotion.

ST LOUIS ST JOSEPH CALASANZ

I t's a fair guess that there were some contemporaries who did not perceive the sanctity in King Louis IX of France, apart from several thousand Moslems against whom he led two crusades. He was a just administrator but even that virtue in the thirteenth century would be sure to create critics. You might say the same about today's other saint. Calasanz did nothing but good for children and for the sick and yet found himself, in his old age, at odds with the Holy Office.

People say much the same about Rome where, it's generally recognized, it's hard to keep your Catholic Faith. If, they say, you can keep your Faith after three years in Rome it must be good. The sad truth is that the nearer you get to the skirts of power the more likely you are to be offended.

Rome is such a powerhouse. But then, to a lesser degree, so is every bishop's house, presbytery and convent. You should not get too involved with any of these unless you are prepared to realize that from pope to assistant priest those who serve the Church unless indeed they are saints, are just as human as we are ourselves.

Popes can be irritable and bishops too. Priests have periods of disillusion and even Poor Clares surprisingly can have off-days. But in Rome, what you can perceive is the taint of ambition tinged with a degree of opportunism. Look closer and you will encounter lobbies, factions, groups intent on following specific agendas. The Church's bureaucracy, in fact, is no different from the barriers you'll come up against in every civil service. At worst you will be scandalized; hopefully you will be understanding.

The Vatican is not, thank God, the Church. We are. The Vatican is no more and no less than the administrative set-up any organization as large as the Church requires. It is necessary but not necessarily evil. Just men and women at work, and all that involves. Be neither scandalized nor surprised that they're just like us.

DOMINIC BARBERI

B ack you come this week, back from secluded bays, mountain lairs, country cottages. Back to commuting, getting the children to school, working all hours to enhance the pension that will permit you to return to the blissful spot you've just left. And stay there.

You won't, of course. Common sense tells you that a cottage one mile from a village full of strangers puts you at a huge disadvantage both physically and socially. The betting is that you'll stay just where you are, in contact with the acquaintances made over the years, familiar with the church which has seen so many of your joys and sadnesses. Yet something will change. You – you will change.

Retired, you come face to face with a stranger: yourself. Life's masquerade is over. The wheeling, the dealing, is done. None of the old excuses apply any more. There is no boss to satisfy; you have all the time in the world. The mask you've worn for life's ball is taken away and the face you see in the mirror is the one you have tucked away in the attic for so long.

The Bible tells us that 'your old men will dream dreams, your young men shall see visions.' But old age is viewed differently today. It's no longer the cul-de-sac it once was. It's a new direction, a new perspective without old limitations. In many ways it can be the emancipation of the soul which is now wholly your own, not to be bargained for any other's gain.

Most of all, retirement is the moment when ambition is flavoured with humility making it the easier for the wisdom you've gained on the way to be more apparent. That's how St Augustine saw it – a man impatient with those who simply saw old age as a time to anticipate infirmity. Just sitting in your church so that the doors will stay open is preferable to dozing away hours as precious to you as they are to God.

27 August

St Monica

⁓

Monica's Feast today precedes her son's tomorrow. It's a sensitive thought by the Church. But then the Church has always had a soft spot for mothers, and Monica was a very good one.

In fact, the whole ethos of the Catholic family tends towards a matriarchy. The dominance of the Jewish mother may be the butt of many a joke but in the Catholic family it's reality.

Perhaps at this moment I should admit a bias – I had the best mother in the world. And, oddly enough, I suspect you had too. My father was there, of course, largely in the background, a silent presence which took the form of oracle in major decisions. But the home centred about my mother, and her love which pervaded everything.

The Catholic home is very much the reflection – or should be – of that home in Nazareth. Our image is that of Joseph the patient carpenter and Mary, the busy mother at the core of things. The model, even if idealistic, is at the very core of family security.

A great many factors contribute towards the well-being of the family. But central to the cocoon protecting it is the stability of the mother. She is both protector and animator and invariably her guise is that of arbiter. She is the reason a Catholic accepts without question the honour heaped on Our Lady for, unconsciously, heavenly Mother and earthly mother are inextricably bound, one within the other.

This association in the past produced a chivalry designed to protect all women. Oddly enough, feminists found the last vestiges of this gallantry denigrating, patronizing. They fought for equality seemingly not realizing they already had superiority. For a Catholic man – and son – this was truly an enigma.

28 August

St Augustine of Hippo

~

P erhaps the greatest of the Church Doctors, Augustine's road to conversion was wild and erratic, and well chronicled in his *Confessions*. As he admitted there: 'I thought that continence was a matter of our own strength, and I knew that I had not the strength: for in my utter foolishness I did not know the word of Your Scripture that none can be continent unless You give it.'

Just as a reformed drunk is the most puritan of teetotallers so Augustine turned violently against the joys that had pleasured him:

> Nothing so much casts down the mind of man from its citadel as do the blandishments of women, and that physical contact without which a wife cannot be possessed. *Soliloquies*

Augustine – in *The Good of Marriage* – lay down the basic tenet which today rules Catholic marriage:

> The marriage of male and female is something good. This union divine Scripture so commands that it is not permitted a woman who has been dismissed by her husband to marry again, as long as her husband lives, nor is it permitted a man who has been dismissed by his wife to marry again, unless she who left has died.

It was to Augustine also that the encyclical Humanae Vitae leaned so heavily:

> Marriage itself among all races is for the one purpose of procreating children, whatever will be their station and character afterwards; marriage was instituted for this purpose, so that children might be born properly and decently.

THE BEHEADING OF JOHN THE BAPTIST

T he 'voice of one crying in the wilderness' was stilled when John, cousin of Jesus and only a few months older than Him, criticized Herod Antipas for his unlawful marriage to Herodias. It's unlikely that Herod would have had the gall to kill a man his people saw as a latter-day Elizah, had he not been tricked into it by a promise made to Herodias's daughter, Salome.

If the story is familiar then it's not entirely due to Hollywood. It's because men like the Baptist – and Jesus too – invariably end up dead.

Archbishop Oscar Romero, Gandhi, Martin Luther King, Sadat – the list is as long as their memory surely will be. And, oddly, it was not their actions so much as their words and their convictions that ensured their deaths.

We admire them, we respect them. We will even follow them overtly if the risk is minimal, covertly if we stand to lose something. We are, for the most part, the mute bystanders. When a union bullies a member, we are silent. When an employer wrongfully dismisses a colleague, we stand by. When hooligans attack someone, we cross the street.

Yet the Faith we follow demands of us the occasional heroism; it insists that our lives are secondary to our principles. What if God judges us, after all, not for our peccadilloes but for our cowardice, for our omissions and not our commissions? Most of us could be in for a shock.

It's for this reason that we're urged not to judge for then we shall be so judged. There's something wrong when a society – or a religion – produces more snipers than it does hussars. We are more likely to be judged severely for our silence than for our protestation.

———— ❧ ————

Humility is a virtue not apparent in Catholics nor, for that matter, in Christians generally. Neither is it the mark of the Jew or the Moslem. You have to travel very easterly for even a sniff of it and even then it is suspect. Let's face it – human kind is not innately humble.

Even the Gospel story – taking the lower place at the table – has a sop for the proud contained within it. For at the end, doesn't the host come along and say, 'My friend, move up higher'? So Jesus, too, knew we had our limitations and needed a carrot to induce us to be self-effacing.

Even the missal has to make a distinction – 'true humility is not false modesty', it introduces the Mass, 'it means acknowledgment that the talents we have come from God.'

Like most Catholics I look for the imitation of Christ in the pastors who presumably are closer to Him than I am. And whilst I've discerned much of His wisdom and some of His enthusiasm in the bishops I've met I've seldom come across His humility. To find that I've had to look to the lower ranks – some parish priests, some Sisters and a few monks. Even then it has been hard to distinguish pragmatism from humility.

We have to talk about humility because the act of being humble has been forever muddied by the character of Uriah Heep who, we all know, was humble only to disguise taints in his character.

If this Gospel reading is to have meaning we have to assume that it is unlikely that anyone other than God will ever say to us: 'Friend, move up higher.' If we can do that then at last we will have discovered humility. But I have to confess the virtue is rare – perhaps only found in the houses of the contemplatives where, indeed, all things done are done for the greater glory of God.

St Aidan

A idan was yet another Abbot of Lindisfarne who was canonized for his work in the north-east of England. It's hard for us now to envisage just how vital that uninviting, windswept island was to the spread of Christianity in the early centuries. Reached only by boat or, at low tide, by a causeway, it sent out monk after monk to brave Vikings or the impetuous cruelties of pagan kings. Yet the time of its greatness passed and so did the need for its holy men.

The same might be said for a movement known as Catholic Action, first conceived by Pius X but only as a thought. Pius XI gave it form and support and for a while it flourished here in England, most actively during the 1930s, the Second World War and only slightly into the 1950s.

Pius XI said that Catholic Action was to be outside and above every political party. He did more: he claimed that Christ Himself had 'laid the first foundations of Catholic Action.' At the same time he was anxious that it should act under the guidance of the hierarchy of whatever country it operated in. That inspired and battling editor Count Michael de la Bedoyere jumped in with a distinction: 'The object of the new Catholic Action movements is not to widen the ecclesiastical function of the priest, but to Catholicize the secular function of the layman.'

Catholic Action went on to borrow – or was it otherwise? – the cell notion from the communists. Catholic Action members were known only to a small number within their group. They acted secretly within industry, where they would combat communist elections to trade union posts, and in the armed services. Their intention was simple – to Christianize human society at every level they could.

Like Lindisfarne, the Catholic Action movement served its purpose at a time of social upheaval and then quietly passed into history. If it has an equivalent today, it is the Catholic Union.

1 September

St Giles

―――⟡―――

The travelling's done for another year. And can there be any sensation more delightful than getting back to your own bed? The lumps, the cavities are the ones you've made yourself. The knick-knacks, that old statue of St Joseph, the Cross above the bed – all familiar landmarks you have missed. Once something of a traveller I'm content now to sit and listen to other folk's tales. But the truth is that jaunting isn't what it was. The sense of surprise is lacking when every foreign city has its McDonald's and even the desert, they tell me, is littered with empty Coca-Cola cans.

Surprise is a vital ingredient of any religion. And you get plenty of surprise within Catholicism. In the lifetime of many of us the Second Vatican Council was the biggest surprise of all. Right from the start, who would ever imagine a 77-year-old Pope, John XXIII, to be anything but a caretaker Pope? And then, within two months, calling only the second Vatican Council?

Here was an old man calling for a new Pentecost, prepared to see the Church he had aged in opened up to the vastly dissimilar visions of some 2865 bishops and prelates of all kinds and from all races.

The Council rumbled on from October, 1962 until December 1965. 'Good' Pope John had died during it but his successor, Paul VI, ensured the impetus didn't wane. The paper generated must have consumed many a forest and the hot air probably caused global warming. But at the end there was stark achievement – three new constitutions – vital ones – on divine revelation, the liturgy and the Church.

The Church as generations of Catholics had known her was wholly changed, as the result of an old man with one foot in the grave but a soul possessed by the Holy Spirit. Surprised? We all were.

2 September

ST WILLIAM OF ROSKILDE

The Church has dedications for the months. In September the Holy Cross once predominated. Less so today, but Shelley caught the ambience of September and autumn when he wrote:

> The day becomes more solemn and serene
> When noon is past – there is a harmony
> In autumn, and a lustre in its sky,
> Which through the summer is not heard or seen,
> As if it could not be, as if it had not been.
>> 'Hymn to Intellectual Beauty'

The Church seasons, perhaps to console the new converts, mirrored nature's seasons. But not quite. Autumn, apart from the Harvest Festival, had it beat. There is something innately pagan about this little segment of the year. Trees cast mellow shadows we cannot quite penetrate; the greenery is of a texture too secretive for us to name. There is a hiatus in nature that seems to exclude us, just as if shrubs, trees and grasses withdraw into themselves and ask, just briefly, to be alone.

The Church, ever sensitive, takes the hint and seems to pause. There are no great solemnities other than a reminder later on of the power of the Cross. And even that Feast, dedicated to plain wood, reflects an exquisite understanding of the strength of nature in September.

People are less impressionable. Almost gauche, surrounded by so much natural mystery. Out of tune with the delicacy of the month they begin to busy themselves with raucous matters that have no place in the hush of September. They troop back to bingo and fayres, disturb the autumnal gentility with clod-hopping practicalities. It's as if they throw down a gauntlet to their pagan past, refusing to dig deep holes in the leaves where they can be warm and escape the coming winter. Placid, mysterious September is not for the Christian, but it reminds us of the stark creatures we once were.

ST GREGORY THE GREAT

S t Gregory shares his Feast with the start of the Second World War. In his day Pope Gregory I was every bit as important to the people of Britain as the start of the war was momentous. Shortly after his death in 604, he was dubbed 'The Apostle of the English', for it was through him that Augustine was despatched with a small band to Christianize these islands. In the event, Gregory's part in our conversion took second place to Augustine's efforts.

It was Gregory, too, who gave us the Gregorian chant which a year or two back was number one in the pop charts. How he must have chuckled in Heaven when the news reached him.

It's the fiendish mark of old age that I recall this day in 1939 vividly. I had turned 11 only yesterday. My treasured gift had been a clockwork tin bomber and the joy of possession hadn't diminished over 24 hours. It was a fine, warm day and I wanted to be off in the garden. Instead my mother asked me to listen to the radio. By the time Chamberlain uttered those words 'and a state of war now exists' I was already on my feet heading for the lawn.

Then I realized my mother was in tears. Astonished, I went to her. But she took my tin bomber and flung it into the fireplace. For the longest time I was numbed with the shock of it – the action was so out of character.

It was over a year later, sitting by that very fire one November night that I began to understand her treatment of my tin toy. But by then I had grow up quite a lot and the bomber no longer had the attraction it once had.

I would like to write that on this day, so many years ago, we knelt and prayed. But to the best of my memory we did not. Not then. The prayers were to follow.

So, in the perspective of history, which event today is the more important – Gregory's love for the Angles or Hitler's fury for them?

4 September

St Ultan

~

Whatever the consolations offered, the end of a life, a venture, can only be sad. And when a community faces
extinction it is heartbreaking. The Sisters I visited epito-
mized what is happening in so many convents. There were 22 of
them in all, with an average age well in excess of 70. Their House
had been founded almost a century and it had been their home
since their late teens.

From that House over the years they had sent off Sisters to found
two other convents and a medical centre in Africa. These were still
thriving – particularly the convent in Africa which had more vocations than it could cope with.

The service these 22 nuns had rendered their community since
1902 was inestimable. Their nursing skills had made their hospital a
centre of excellence. Their maternity wing had seen the birth of a
large proportion of the local Catholic population. But when surgical
equipment became so expensive they could no longer afford to
maintain excellence they pulled back and turned their House into a
home for the aged.

Alas, there were no more vocations. Then the time came when
they could no longer afford the large secular staff needed, nor the
improvements the law required. So there they were when I visited –
indomitable ladies who had spent a lifetime together and who now
faced the disintegration of their 'family' and the fact that they no
longer had the resources to keep their convent and maintain their
prayers together.

Having given all for upwards of 60 years each nun faced loneliness and possible penury. Yet none was sorry for herself, only for her
companions in Christ over the years.

The time is surely come when the remnants of the Orders can
be gathered up into the Church's generous arms and given some
powerhouse of prayer where each group can keep its own charism
in security.

5 September

---~---

In 1997 Mother Teresa of Calcutta died on this day. Not just the Christian world mourned her but those of all Faiths. And that was as it should be, for Mother Teresa made no distinction in those she and her Sisters served as Missionaries of Charity, the Order she had created. Perhaps by now she is canonized – certainly her cause commenced the day she died.

A little lady, she possessed what is called charisma. A simple lady, she saw all things in black and white and had no pretensions to either scholarship or diplomacy. She created shelters for the destitute worldwide and despite the stench of poverty in which she lived she left behind the sweetest perfume of sanctity. In many of her convents this credo was displayed:

> Life is an opportunity, avail it;
> Life is a beauty, admire it;
> Life is a bliss, taste it;
> Life is a dream, realize it;
> Life is a challenge, meet it;
> Life is a duty, complete it;
> Life is a game, play it;
> Life is costly, care for it;
> Life is a wealth, keep it;
> Life is love, enjoy it;
> Life is mystery, know it;
> Life is a promise, fulfil it;
> Life is sorrow, overcome it;
> Life is a song, sing it;
> Life is a struggle, accept it;
> Life is a tragedy, brace it;
> Life is an adventure, dare it;
> Life is luck, make it;
> Life is life, defend it.

6 September

You turn men back into dust
and say: 'Go back, sons of men.'
To your eyes a thousand years
are like yesterday, come and gone,
no more than a watch in the night.

Physics has a comparatively new theory – that chaos is only order in another form. When the Master Weaver wove His tapestry it seemed that it was a chaotic pattern. It wasn't. Throughout the canvas was a design. And no part of this design was more important than the thin thread that was the Family . . .

Five thousand years ago, in a cave in the Quantock Hills, mother, father and three children prepared for the onset of autumn. They would move to the caves farther south where they would be warmer.

The youngest son was whingeing – he loved the hills and despised the custom that enforced their trek to make sacrifices at the Stones. His sister too was angry – she had met the man she wanted as mate and knew they might lose each other on the journey. There was no joy either for the middle child – a boy who had lost his arm to a boar and would surely be sacrificed. But tradition was tradition. The parents knew it. And, if they too felt reluctance to travel, they knew they would, knew they must. The sun that daily grew colder required it of them, demanded their obedience and their worship.

Between them, they had few words. Mostly signs and grunts guided their actions together. Yet they had strengths as a group. The hunting was easier, they tended to protect each other, each had a given task which made their rough life that much easier.

As they assembled for the trek the father surveyed them. He felt a special feeling for his mate, and a similar though different emotion for his children. He longed to put his arms about them all and hold them close. He wanted to call them . . . he could not find a noise for it. But the word he sought was Family.

7 September

ST TILBERT

———— ✎ ————

Those returning from their annual trek to the auld country shake their heads sadly. 'It's not the way it was.' No, Ireland is different from the memories we have of her. Different too are heaps of other things. We've priests who can't speak Latin; cars that will do 100 mph at the touch of a toe; astronauts who reach the moon; a Church that speaks of love rather than fear; cabbage that no longer tastes cabbagy; drugs to enable us to live to a 100 years old; babies that no longer need a womb; sins we never thought of as sins; children who know more of sex than we do; tea that comes in perforated pyramids.

Why, then, the surprise that Ireland has entered the twentieth century just in time for the twenty-first? Perhaps it's because we always thought Ireland the last surviving Catholic country. Perhaps, our visits were so short, we were beguiled that the Angelus Bell still rang and that the old churches we saw were Catholic not Anglican. Perhaps too we thought the Irish immune to the lure of contraception, the ease of abortion, the enticement of drugs, the temptation of easy divorce.

The English Catholic with Irish roots visits Ireland with huge preconceptions only to discover they are misconceptions. We find it shamefully disappointing that they have our own greed, our own lusts, our own inclination to put comfort before sacrifice. We expect them to be different. And they are not.

Just like us the Irish cannot find enough priests and Sisters, their churches are beginning to empty, their laws – based on a Catholic morality – are changing. Like us they already have only a memory of what it was like to be a Catholic country. They have even thrown out the leprechauns with their Catholic ethos and we find this as hard to bear as their determined stride towards unchurched Europe.

We long to point out to them the error of their ways. But we have no such right.

8 September

OUR LADY'S BIRTHDAY

The age-old quandary: what present do you give someone who already has everything? And the answer – for a mother – is always the same. All a mother ever wants is our love and the assurance that all is well with us.

So, dearest Lady, here is our love for your birthday. We would love to add the assurance but it would be a lie. For we are just the same as ever. A quarrelsome, meddlesome, agitated family forever striving for we know not what. Right at the very start of time we wanted just three things – food, warmth and shelter. Today, some of us, at least, have more food in more variety than we know what to do with. A press of a button, for some of us that is, gives us enough warmth to curdle our toes. Shelter, for some of us you understand, varies from the more than adequate to the downright luxurious.

Ah, dear Lady, you spotted the evasion. Thousands of years on and there are still those who have neither food, warmth nor shelter. I was going to be patronizing and say how astute of you to spot the qualification. But then I realized you are not one to be fooled by our semantics. Neither are we – the well fed, the cosily warm, the secure – your whole family wishing you Happy Birthday today. We are, if statistics are correct, only the minority of your family.

Yes, yes, I get your point, dearest Lady. You're pointing out that there is therefore a gift we comfortable ones can give you besides our love and our assurances. You want us to realize that the Family of Man has a heck of a lot of relatives. So many, in fact, we don't even know their names.

But you do. And so too does your Son. And all our Sunday clawthumping doesn't mean a dicky bird if we forget the rest of the Family. Point taken, dearest Mother, and as usual, instead of giving you a birthday gift, we're here yet again asking one of you. Pray for us, dear Lady, that the Family of Humankind will one day gather beneath your blue mantle.

9 September

ST PETER CLAVER

⁓

I n the last analysis what matters most to men and women is their sense of dignity. The shrewdest of the tyrants have always known this. That's why Nero was such a simpleton in the matter of cruelty – he allowed the martyrs to die with their dignity unimpaired and thus helped, rather than hindered, the birth of Christianity.

Other tyrants were much more oblique. They robbed the persecuted of rank, status, wealth, reducing them to paupers amongst their peers. The process was too slow for the SS – in the concentration camps they stripped their victims, used fear to eliminate their innate sense of honour, created conditions which made dignity impossible.

The Jesuit, Peter Claver, spent a lifetime sparking the dormant dignity still lingering in black slaves who had been torn from their villages in West Africa, ferried like beasts across the Atlantic, then put up for sale at Cartagena in Colombia.

For more than 40 years, in early seventeenth-century South America, his mission was amongst the oppressed and abandoned who flooded through the slave centre in vast numbers before being sent to work silver mines and the jungle plantations.

It was not slavery he preached about – the condition at that time was morally accepted in both Christian and non-Christian countries – but the equality of the worth of souls before God. And, despite the slave masters, he struggled to tend the conditions of his black parishioners. He would have preached Benedict's Rule to them: 'Whether slaves or freemen, we are all one in Christ, and have to serve alike in the army of the same Lord.'

It was to be another two centuries before a pope, Leo XIII, appealed to the Brazilian bishops to 'put an end to that kind of traffic, than which nothing is more base and wicked.'

Nowadays it is only the State which can truly impose slavery, perhaps in unconscious memory of St Ambrose who said: 'The peculiar characteristic of slavery is to be always in fear.'

10 September

ST AMBROSE BARLOW

The Benedictine Ambrose Barlow, born in comfortable affluence, finished life on this day in 1641 after being hanged, drawn and quartered at Lancaster. In Lancashire he has never died but still rides the flat lands there, celebrating the forbidden Mass, carrying the Holy Host, preaching. He, like so many martyrs of his age, was given the opportunity to retire gracefully into oblivion having done more than his fair share for the Faith. If he had, then his county would never have honoured him as they do still today.

It is likely that the oft-imprisoned Ambrose would have read the book that had become second only to the Bible for Catholics, *The Imitation of Christ*, Thomas à Kempis's dialogue with Christ. Writing of the judgments of men Thomas says:

> Who are you, to be afraid of mortal man? Today he is here; tomorrow, his place is empty. Fear God, and then the threats of men will have no terrors for you. What harm can a man do you by his words or his wrongdoing?
>
> It is himself he is harming, rather than you; and, whoever he may be, he cannot escape the judgement of God. Keep God before your eyes, and do not get indignant and argue. You may seem for the moment to be losing the battle and suffering undeserved disgrace; but don't let that make you complain, don't, for want of a little patience, dim the lustre of your heavenly crown.
>
> Instead, look up to heaven, to me; I have the power to rescue from all shame and wrong, and to give everyone the reward his deeds have deserved.

Ambrose, then, chose to ignore the terrors of man and so found his heavenly crown. So why do so many of us get a crick in the neck looking Heavenward?

11 September

SS PROTUS AND HYACINTH

⁓

I f anyone told me that Cain borrowed the cash to buy the cudgel
to batter Abel I'd not be one whit surprised. Usury has been
with us a long time.

About now our children, young adults, set off for their first taste
of life away from home. For most the journey to college involved
their first encounter with usury by way of a student loan or suc-
cumbing to the campus banks' encouragements to help themselves
to plastic cards and the promise of fixed overdrafts.

Consumerism marred the second half of the century just gone.
And, worse, it has made captive most of the youth who will grow
mature in this new millennium. Debt is a ruthless warder, a corrosive
companion. It enslaves young minds that should be running free
amongst the ideals only youth can, for so little a while, conceive and
nurture.

John Paul II warned often enough of the dangers of the con-
sumerist society. He urged that 2000 should be a Jubilee marked by
the cancellation of the Third World debt. But the weight was not
lifted fully and captive nations entered the third millennium as
impoverished and burdened as any student leaving college.

Perhaps the priest in his pulpit, the bishop with his influence,
should have hammered harder at the poisonous growth of the credit
card and the notion of whole generations forever indebted. Yet the
priest was too busy paying for his church roof and the bishop too
hassled with the needs of his diocese to warn of the ethical morass
their people were sinking ever deeper into.

Religion isn't a separate activity we practice on Sundays. It is part
and parcel of our lives. It is something to take into account whenever we make a decision. Owing God a death should be debt
enough for all of us.

12 September

ST AILBE

───⌒───

My admiration for the Catholic convert is immense. Me? I was lumbered from birth. The prohibitions that would chase me down the years were apparent by the time I reached the age of reason.

The practising Catholic's life is lived by the rules. Call them the gentle bonds of God but they are, in the last analysis, rules. So today I received a shock when I learned that the other dominant Faith in England is prepared to modify its rules in the face of changing social conditions. The headline in my newspaper read: 'Church eases its stance on remarriage of divorcees.'

There are two words there that told me immediately the Church was not Catholic. 'Eases' and 'stance' are really near euphemisms designed to mollify Anglicans who have to accept this situation and Catholics who can only regret it.

For starters, it's not a 'stance' that is affected by permitting the remarriage of divorcees – it is an age-old doctrine. Then again, you cannot 'ease' a doctrine – it is 'any truth taught by the Church as necessary for acceptance by the faithful.'

From what I read the Anglican bishops seem prepared to shoulder responsibility for declaring when a second marriage is 'appropriate'. As a legal interpretation it sounds like shoddy legislation; as a religious statement it is impossibly naive. Try putting it up against St Augustine's peremptory ruling, 'If a man leaves his wife and she marries another, she commits adultery', and you see how mealy-mouthed it is to talk, as they do, about 'a responsibility to discern'.

Of course Catholics – and many priests too – would welcome any relaxation permitting the divorced to remarry and receive the Sacrament. But the Church, however compassionate, cannot 'ease' what Christ so evidently taught. The result – as Anglicans may have found – is utter moral confusion for a world already ethically bewildered.

13 September

———————— ∽ ————————

A round this time is another of those specially designated
Sundays – this time it's Racial Justice Day. In truth, I'm baffled that Catholics need to be reminded. Our Church now
numbers in excess of one billion members. And, you have to believe
it, most of those are not Anglo-Saxon whites, nor handsome, swarthy
Europeans. They are of every shade and from every corner of the
globe. They are Hispanic, African, Asian, Oriental. But, and this is
what really matters, they are Catholics.

They are our brethren – a wonderfully descriptive archaic word
that translates as brother.

Each one of them are witnesses – just as we are – to the very
same miracle that is the Mass. They profess precisely the same Creed
as we do, Sunday after Sunday. They worship the same God, receive
the identical Sacrament, share in the same hope for salvation as we
do.

Their devotion to Our Lady is no less than our own; their respect
for the saints, their concern for their families, the sacrifices made for
their children's education – all these are identical with our own
yearnings.

For a Catholic to harbour a sense of racism is not just incredible,
it is impossible. Nothing convinces you of the absurdity of racism
more than the recollection that Jesus was a coloured, Middle Eastern
Jew – a racial origin even the liberally minded Romans found hard
to swallow.

Hopefully the Bidding Prayers will give more weight to the dangers of nationalism and tribalism than to the cultural origins of
Catholics – a difference that should not be given the oxygen of
recognition. Jesus would surely agree.

THE HOLY CROSS ST CORNELIUS

It's odd that having just spoken of the firmness of the Church's teaching authority we should come face to face with the twenty-first Pope, Cornelius. His major conflict in mid-third-century Rome arose from his desire to be compassionate towards those who had baulked at the thought of martyrdom and then desired to return to the Church. In this he was opposed by Novatian, a hard-line bishop who was an anti-pope during Cornelius's reign.

Cornelius insisted that all sin was forgiveable – including second marriages – whilst Novatian had no time for those who had denied the Faith to save their own lives. It was a messy dispute and a major crisis so early in the life of new Church.

Today there are no such doubts. The Church's arms are wide in welcome even if there is just a touch of Novatian still in the way in which they are received. There was talk – it came up at the National Conference of Priests in 1999 – that perhaps the promised Jubilee for the new millennium might include an amnesty for the million or more Catholics in England refused the Sacrament following re-marriage. There is no doubt whatever that the Church would have witnessed a huge return of its children.

But the cost would have been loss of integrity and a mounting doubt over the new century of the Church's teaching authority. Whilst our hearts longed for the compassionate view, our minds told us that the Church could not barter its validity as custodian of morals even for the three generations of Catholics who would so happily have returned.

Perhaps Cornelius would have permitted the amnesty – he did so for those early Christians in second marriages. But 2000 years on he may have come to realize that the rock he represented had to be firmer than the waves buffeting it.

15 September

OUR LADY OF SORROWS

W edged in my pocket between tobacco pouch and penknife there is usually a rosary. It is something Catholics carry as naturally as the medal around their necks. Yet some, like myself, are not happy with the Rosary as a form of prayer. My mind just cannot attune to the repitition involved. And I'm prepared to admit it is my loss.

The rosary itself, a bracelet of beads each representing a prayer, is not, in Catholic terms, ancient. It first was used in the thirteenth century and the name was in all probability Mary's rose garden which was abbreviated to rosary.

The full Rosary is 15 times 10 decades of Hail Marys, each preceded by an Our Father and concluded with the Gloria. The intention of the repetitive prayer is not so much the prayer itself but the meditation that accompanies it.

Today the Rosary said will be the Sorrowful Mysteries, which are the Agony in the Garden, the Scourging, the Crowning with Thorns, the Carrying of the Cross and the Crucifixion. There are also the Joyful Mysteries and the Glorious Mysteries.

Given the date of its origin it is conceivable that the rosary itself reflected Moorish influence and the beads carried to this day by Moslems.

So potent a powerhouse of prayer is sure to have a tradition and the one always current about the Rosary is that St Dominic had the system of prayer revealed to him by Our Lady in a vision. Whether it is used for its proper purpose or not, the Rosary is the constant companion, the prayer tool, of every Catholic – throughout life and on that final journey to meet Our Lady and her Son.

16 September

ST GILES

———❧———

The first of the Christmas brochures will come any day now. Masses of gift suggestions for those of us that have everything already. Not to be outdone, the Church has had special gifts on offer all the year round. Like the brochure from Harrods this morning they are carefully catalogued.

There is the gift of wisdom: the ideal present for the contemplative. Most of us are content with simple truths. This gift urges us to dig deeper – to explore why truths are truths and then to judge them on their merits.

To go with this gift you will have to receive another – the gift of understanding. Whilst faith enables us to accept teaching without dissent, understanding gives us the ability to get to the bottom of matters more profoundly.

You will probably find the gift of fortitude especially useful – it proffers you strength of character when you are put to the test. It comes in little packets: faithfulness to your vocation whatever it may be; courage in sickness or adversity of any kind; a readiness to suffer for what you know is right. Expect a big parcel when this comes.

Oddly enough there is a gift of fear. No, not the snivelling apprehension of pain but the proper respect we must have for God. With this gift comes awareness of God's true majesty and our own humility in the face of such awesome reality.

Piety, too, is a gift. It is the distinction between kneeling, standing, sitting at all the right moments and actually feeling an overwhelming sense of love for God. Don't expect to open the package and use this gift straight off – you'll need to study the instruction book first!

There are other gifts the Church offers – counsel, integrity, tongues, knowledge. But the Church is only the middleman, just like Harrods. The gifts all come with the love and encouragement of the Holy Spirit. Shop early for Christmas!

17 September

St Robert Bellarmine

Bellarmine was an atypical Jesuit – learned, shrewd, disputaceous, austere. When Pope Sixtus V reconstructed the Vatican Library he called on Bellarmine, then Archbishop of Capua, to be its Prefect. Despite this recognition there was not much love lost between the Franciscan Pope and the Jesuit scholar who wrote extensively upon the distinction between the pope's spiritual and temporal powers. At the time, the end of the sixteenth century, Sixtus was aggressively cleaning up the mess the Papal State had become. When that was accomplished he turned his attention to the Church's administration.

Bellarmine was at hand – the most distinguished scholar of this day – to offer definitions of papal authority that would last well into the future.

> The pope has not the same kind of right to depose temporal princes, even though they might deserve to be deposed, as he has to depose bishops, that is as their legitimate, ordinary judge. Nevertheless he may, as the supreme spiritual authority, dispose of kingdoms, taking away the power from one monarch and conferring it on another, if such a change be necessary for the salvation of souls.
>
> *De Romano Pontifice*

Whilst supportive of the rights of monarchy, Bellarmine frequently laid their duty before them:

> This is the first duty that must be found in the heart of princes, to love their subjects as sons, to procure peace and plenty for them, to protect them from unjust treatment at the hands of officials.
>
> *The Duty of a Christian Prince*

Today we would pass off such strictures as of passing interest. In the sixteenth century they had the force of moral law – coming from the pen of such as Robert Bellarmine. The Church influenced society's actions. Today, no less than then, it must continue to do so.

ST JOSEPH OF CUPERTINO

B y any standards, the Franciscan Joseph was a huge embarrassment to all he came into contact with. Not only was he
given to astonishing feats of levitation – he once, it is
claimed, flew 30 feet to help hang a cross – he would frequently dis-
solve into trances as he did when brought before the Pope. In the
end, as folk usually do when baffled, the Church hid him away.

But for students the world over he is the saint of final appeal. The
little prayer to him is rather shrewd. It doesn't ask for miracles but
for understanding. 'Dear St Joseph', it goes, 'let me only be asked the
questions to which I know the answers.' How's that for casuistry?
But it works – I know.

On the whole, the Church is more exacting when it comes to
miracles than the people. Bernadette very nearly slipped into oblivion. Many of the miracles at Lourdes are unacceptable to the
Church's scrutineers; weeping statues of Our Lady are instant targets
for Church scepticism just as they are rallying points for those in
need of conviction.

Happily the modern view tends to consider people's actions
rather than their miracles when canonization is under consideration.
Or perhaps we just have a more realistic view of what a miracle is.

In the past we looked for an emulation of Christ's miracles – the
truly supernatural acts of healing. Nowadays perhaps we look for
natural acts which require spiritual heroism in some form or
another: and act of self-sacrifice like Kolbe's at Auschwitz; the acts of
love of Mother Teresa; the dedication of missioners who stay put and
face death. These are all miracles in the sense that they are performed beyond the natural obligation we all have, one to the other.

Not that any of that would stop me, if I were still a student, from
invoking the aid of the little Franciscan so many misjudged.

19 September

St Januarius St Theodore of Canterbury

Talking of miracles, which we just were, today you can take your pick between the fantastical and the practical. Januarius may have died around 305 but on certain occasions during the year his blood, kept in Naples as a relic, liquifies. There are few exceptions to this thrice-annual occurrence but one was when Naples elected a communist mayor. That's the fantastical. What about the practical?

For that, let's go to Theodore, a Greek, who was appointed Archbishop of Canterbury in 666 when he was over 65 and a stranger to Britain. This active elderly man did the nigh impossible by uniting the three core strands of Christianity on these islands – Saxon, Irish and Roman Catholicism, as unlike each other as a nearly common Creed would allow.

Theodore, perhaps because of his age, was a patient, diplomatic priest who avoided the quarrels of the time by granting each of the warlord kings a respect they probably neither deserved nor understood. With hindsight, it was a great pity Theodore was not used to settle the Irish Question back in 675 – he appears to have been the only diplomat in history capable of doing so.

As Canterbury was important then, Westminster and who occupies it is vital today. The Catholic Archbishops of Westminster, since the Restoration in 1850, have with few exceptions been pretty cack-handed when it came to relations between state and established Church. It was why Cardinal Basil Hume, the Benedictine from out of the blue, made such a momentous impression upon Faiths of all kinds and people without any faith at all. He was in total contrast to his immediate predecessor, John Carmel Heenan. Hume had no pugilist ancestor, no touch of the Irish, no impregnable stubbornness. Apart from a French mother, he was English through and through. And it showed. As this century proceeds whoever holds the Hat at Westminster will be every bit as important to Britain as was Theodore.

———————— ⌒ ————————

Around this time is Home Mission Sunday and, like it or not, we are all part of this mission – increasingly so, as the Orders and secular priesthood fail to attract vocations.

The lay mission is to take Christ to the unchurched. Not, note, to the pagan and the heathen, but to people who have had brushes with Christianity, may even have a quiet sympathy for it, but have long lost touch with the caring hand of God.

In many ways it would be easier to start from scratch with a riproaring pagan. Like building a house – if someone else has started the construction, and done so badly, then it takes twice the effort to finish it.

For most of us, embarrassed by the thought of actively preaching Christ, the simplest option is example. We have to be the open arms to which people bring their troubles; we have to be the ones to whom race is the 2.30 at Kempton; we have to be the solitary voice urging life when others clamour for death; we have to be the first to end a quarrel and the last to start one; we have to be Christians.

Succeed in that, then we can think about being Catholics and do what our Faith demands of us – spread the knowledge we have.

In the meantime, and in confidence that God does not intend us to be wholly without priests, we have to look within our own families. God knows, we cannot enforce vocations. But we can provide the climate of care and Catholicity that might, just might, breed them in sons and daughters.

With so much emphasis on priests, we need to remember that the need for nuns is just as desperate. Almost unseen over the past three decades we've lost the merry, virtuous presence of so many good women in schools, hospitals and parishes. This is when we nudge God and assure Him we'll play our part too.

21 September

ST MATTHEW

———⁓———

'What's your name? What do you do?' It's the invariable way people meet. The name's essential, of course, to make the new acquaintance in some way unique in your mind. But equally vital is the second question. People's occupations tell you so much about them.

'What's your name?'

'Matthew.'

'What do you do?'

'I'm a tax collector.'

Urgh! It's not your fault, that reaction. It's instinct. Here is one of the breed that keeps you poor. Worse – one of those whose job it is to delve into your most private affairs. And, in this particular Matthew's case, he was working on behalf of an authority you both resented and despised – the Roman government.

An odd choice, then, for a young Rabbi to select as an intimate. But He did. And Matthew himself told us how it happened:

> Jesus saw a man called Matthew sitting at work in the custom house and said to him, 'Follow me'. And Matthew rose from his place and followed him.

That's it. Just as simple, just as complex. It is the only time in the Gospel he wrote that Matthew referred to himself and to his call; he was withdrawn, confidential, reserved. But he was also analytical, and well-read too, for he was the one who mostly used the Old Testament as proof that Jesus was the expected Messiah.

It must have hurt him when, after his selection, he invited Jesus to his home only to find his neighbours tittle-tattling about his new leader. What sort of fellow, they whispered, would go into the house of a publican?

His Gospel, as you might expect from a civil servant employed by the Romans, is concise, almost nit-picking.

22 September

St Thomas of Villanova   St Maurice

Thomas, Archbishop of Valencia, was nicknamed 'The Almsgiver', so we have to assume he knew how to raise the alms he gave. There are any number of parishes with this passion for raising money. Sometimes you feel that what happens at the altar is less significant than what is happening in the porch.

You see, very often the parishes best at raising money don't have any special need for it. They have a watertight roof, an organ with sweet notes, all the hymnals and kneeling pads they'll ever need, and no expensive school to maintain.

Yet, at the drop of a whisper, there's a committee formed, then a sub-committee and the rolling moneybox is on the road. Imagination knows no bounds for the Catholic-on-the-make. First, there are the hardy annuals – the Christmas Fair, the Autumn Fair, the Harvest Festival, the Grotto, the Summer Fete. Then there are Bring-and-Buys, jumble sales, car boot sales. There is Bingo. There are sweepstakes. There are raffles.

Anyway, you get the idea. And, let's be fair about this, these fundraising schemes are practical euphemisms for Catholics saying, one to the other, let's get to know each other.

Over the ramshackle tables laden with bric-a-brac we do just that. We reveal the smiles you'll not find in church; we slip the veil on our secret selves. The church is for Him. The parish hall is for us. It's not the way it was in the early Church, of course, and it's not the way it is in the liberating masses of the African Church. But it's the way we self-conscious, reticent Anglo-Saxons dole out our personalities – this for God, this bit for our neighbours. So why worry – it's the way we are. If it takes a dog-eared copy of 'Forever Amber' to induce us to see the Samaritan in our midst, so be it. Amen.

23 September

St Adomnan St Thecla

Like all freelancers – mercenaries, journalists, locums, entrepreneurs of all kinds – farmers are uneasy people. If you believe – as St Paul did – that God can be proved from nature then farmers must be people of exceeding faith. Their well-being depends entirely upon the transient seasons doing as they ought to at the right time and in the correct quantities. A sun too long or too soon, a shower misplaced, a sudden storm, and they are ruined. Get it right and they are rich.

My own little parish is farmer-based and it's hard not to comment on the satisfaction I see on the faces about me as we celebrate the Harvest Festival. Should I make the serious social error of telling them the summer has been kind to them, their eyes will cloud over. 'Ah, but . . .', they'll say. What was good for the rape was bad for the barley; what inspired the pigs depressed the cows.

But it won't stop them decorating the church with corn-dollies, the robust apples, giant cabbages and all the rest that perpetuates our happy links with the pagan past. And in church there will be that pervading smell – scent of rich earth, perfume of the fields, all mingling so naturally with the faint odour of sweet incense left over from Benediction.

We are what we are. And what we mostly are is a generation four times removed from our peasant forebears. Most of us – we are not for the most part landed gentry nor noble – are at heart serfs or possibly yeomen by stock. If we could trace our ancestors back 150 years they'd be there, in their little stone homes, hedging and ditching, furrowing and farrowing. Peasants all.

They would have enjoyed the summer just passed. Although they would not have recently returned from Tuscany or Madeira they would have shared our pleasure in the Catholicity of the harvest season when folk would share the merriment with more than just a casual glance in the direction of the altar and the Man who made it all.

24 September

OUR LADY OF RANSOM

A remarkable priest, Monsignor Anthony Stark, is the animating influence behind a society that, in a sense, defies political correctness. The Guild of Our Lady of Ransom exists to pour prayers into Heaven for the conversion of England and our awareness of our Catholic heritage in this country. Besides which the Guild has ever been a generous donor to poor parishes.

The title, Our Lady of Ransom, dates back to 1218 when St Peter Nolasco founded an Order of priests and knights to ransom Christians held by the Moors. When the reason for its existence petered out the title for Our Lady still remained and in late nineteenth century two men, Fr Philip Fletcher and Mr Lister Drummond, revived it to name a society dedicated to the conversion of England.

An early success for them was the inclusion after each Mass of a special prayer for this intention but with the coming of ecumenism it fell into disuse.

Yet the notion of England as Mary's Dowry is still strong amongst us, as strong as when it was first spoken of by Thomas Arundel, Archbishop of Canterbury in 1399:

> The contemplation of the great mystery of the Incarnation has drawn all Christian nations to venerate her from whom come all the first beginnings of our redemption. But we English, being the servants of her special inheritance and her own Dowry, as we are commonly called, ought to surpass others in the fervour of our praises and devotions.

Suddenly, at this turn of the century, the conversion of England is no longer the pipe dream it was for our grandparents. England may not at first be converted to Catholicism but certain it is that Catholicism will have to speak for Christianity. In a decade or two the choice of Faiths will rest between Islam and ourselves. And we will have greater need than ever to be Mary's Dowry.

25 September

St Finbar St Cadoc

F inbar is a name to be reckoned with in Cork. Like the county
itself he must have been a hermit crafted out of rock – the
hard, hungry rock you find about Gougane Barra where he
established his little home which is now a place of pilgrimage.

I lived for a while near there on a Cork mountain just a little less
daunting than the one that overshadows the lake at Gougane Barra.
On one of those Irish days of heavy, overcast, sleeting rain, when you
could well believe all you knew were dead, I'd go across to Gougane
there to shelter in the little chapel aside Finbar's grave.

Considerable waves would lap the island that is his resting place,
rattling the shale and stones of the beach around the chapel. There
you could be alone and savour what it meant to be an Irish hermit
in the seventh century.

There would have been nothing. Just the massive mountain sub-
siding into the depths of the lake and that feckless sky which can
change mood and colour in the twinkling of an eye. Of course,
there would be fish to eat, and water in plenty. Perhaps berries. And
pilgrims in good weather would wade across the little causeway to
sit outside Finbar's stone hut.

On the gentle side of the lake his followers built a school but,
presumably, far enough away not to disturb the good man's
thoughts. Finbar did leave that lonely spot for a while to walk to
Cork where he had built the monastery around which the later city
was created. But after that he returned to his hut in the fastnesses of
solitude.

Go to Gougane Barra when you're next in Cork. Sit on the
tombs of the few men strong enough to join Finbar there in that
desolation. And ponder, as I did so often, the massive stolidity of
those early Irish monks, their astonishing strength of character to
carve Christ out of sharp rock. And stay with Him there.

SS COSMAS AND DAMIAN

Whether Cosmas and Damian were canonized as a result of their martyrdom or because they treated their patients free of charge is something we will never know. I like to think that, between them, they initiated the first free health service. It's satisfying to think of them slinking about the catacombs providing their medical skills to the underground Church. Whatever the truth of the matter today they have honourable status as patrons to the medical profession.

We've drifted so far from that early Church in which – we have Paul's word for it – everything was held in common, each person contributing personal skills for the general good of all.

Somehow we've drifted into the 'them' and 'us' syndrome with 'poor' parishes and 'rich' ones, some priests in considerable comfort and others on the breadline, often enough and, shamefully, within the same diocese only a mile or two from each other. And the paradox is that so very often the 'poor' parish is the richer one in terms of what matters – the spirituality of its people and clergy.

If society is not to be scandalized – or ourselves – then we have to try to adjust the balance. In the diocese I know best this is done by pooling resources – not just cash but the skills of one set of parishioners being used to benefit the others.

If this appears a long way removed from the twin healers, it's not. It's as hard to heal the broken heart, splint the fractured spirit, as it is to cure the body. We still need the patronage of Cosmos and Damian.

Remember, though, that doctors are fortunate, since they have another patron, one of their very own: Luke, the Greek physician turned evangelist. And of the four Gospels Luke's is the one that expresses best the huge compassion of Jesus for the sick.

ST VINCENT DE PAUL

T he harvest is in, which will please the saint whose Feast day it is, St Vincent de Paul. If the first half of the seventeenth century boasted a Robin Hood then it was Depaul, his original name. Although he did not rob the rich, he charmed them into a realization of their needs. He was 24, already ordained a priest, when he was captured by Barbary pirates and kept as a slave in Tunis for two years before being freed.

St Vincent had three vital gifts he was to give the Church. And they would be lasting gifts, right up to our own times. His first gift was a congregation, the Vincentians, who would live close to the people for whom they worked. His second was an Order for women, the Daughters of Charity, who would do the same. The third gift was late in coming, some 170 years after his death. But it was well worth the wait – it was the lay organization of the Society of St Vincent de Paul founded by Frederick Ozanam strictly along the principles outlined by the saint. It was to become the flagship of lay Catholic charitable action for 200 years up to the present.

Vincent's stratagem was to form confraternities of charities in ever-increasing centres. If you think the plan was welcomed, you'd be wrong. A royal lieutenant complained bitterly of 'a priest called Vincent who, disregarding the king's authority, and without informing the court officials . . . is holding meetings for a great number of women whom he has persuaded to join a confraternity which goes by the particular name of a Charity . . . a matter which cannot be tolerated.'

Today there is no such objection to the work done by the Society of St Vincent de Paul. It's estimated that worldwide some million priests, Sisters and lay people practise what Vincent preached. He has given them the opportunity to serve God through good works in the anonymous way in which God so often works Himself.

28 September

St Wenceslaus St Laurence Ruiz

The cremation of a friend today. And how I wish the Church had continued to refuse it for Catholics. However delicately the operation is done, however subtle the stagecraft accompanying it, however lulling the taped music, I am disconcerted by the euphemistic horror of the whole thing.

Christians shared with Jews a horror of burning the body. It was originally a pagan practice. It denied the dignity of the body as the repository of the Holy Spirit, and could be construed as an atheist's way of denying the future life of the soul.

The Church's excuses for finally permitting cremation were pragmatic and very recent. Apart from bowing to political correctness – burial was unhealthy and wasted land space – the Church had to acknowledge that modern warfare all too frequently cremated its victims, even annihilated all trace of the body. It seemed reasonable, therefore, to make clear to the faithful that the soul made its entrances and its exits independently of the body.

So, in the fateful 1960s, Catholics were given the choice of burial or cremation – another little mark of Faith that slipped into abeyance It's not a choice I welcome. As with so many other decisions I was happy always to say Rome has spoken and leave it at that. Apart from anything else it meant I didn't have to take so momentous a decision myself. After today, though, I've decided that I want this aching old lump that is me buried not burned. I want those few present to smell the fresh soil, have their hair ruffled in the wind, feel sun or rain on their faces and know the finality of earth thudding onto coffin.

I don't want them solaced with computerized hymns, dulled by the brisk efficiency of a softly drawn curtain meant to veil reality. Not when they can witness the easy simplicity of a person returning to God.

SS MICHAEL, GABRIEL AND RAPHAEL

Michael the Archangel holds a daunting title. He is the Prince of the Seraphim, those angels who compose the highest choir in Heaven. He is more: not only is he the messenger of God – like Gabriel and Raphael – but also he is the mighty leader who led the heavenly host in battle against Lucifer and his rebels. And you can only wonder at the magnitude of that encounter.

The three archangels have had specifically momentous tasks on earth. Michael has been summoned at times of bloody crisis – 'defend us in the hour of battle' – not just against foes but against the Devil himself. Raphael cured Tobias's wife from her possession by the Devil. Gabriel had the most important task of all – he was the one, at the Annunciation, who told Mary she was with child.

You could be excused for finding it easier to comprehend God than to envisage His angels. Yet, if our Faith means anything, it indicates that God is not a solitary; rather, He is surrounded by the faithful of whom we pray we may one day be one.

Despite the conception of an archangel being beyond my understanding it is a notion with which, as a Catholic, I have grown up. It is not something I can examine or reason with – as I can the reality of God – but at the same time it is not a notion that gives me a problem. It is too comforting to query and, when we come to the feast of the Guardian Angels, I'll tell you why, like Faber, I am only too happy with the thought that unknown to me there is a presence that cares for me despite my unawareness.

> Dear angel! ever at my side,
> How loving must thou be
> To leave thy home in heaven to guard
> A guilty wretch like me.
> F. Faber, 'Hymn to my Guardian Angel'

St Jerome

Freud thought differently, but I like to think that God, or perhaps my Guardian Angel, takes sleep and dreams as an opportunity to speak to me. St Jerome had a dream in which he felt a sense of betrayal of Christ so deeply that he became a desert hermit for five years whilst he sorted out his feelings. The respite was highly productive and when he returned it was to become one of the most erudite scholars of the fifth century. His study was specifically of the Bible and he produced the first real Latin text translation. As he said himself: 'A man who is well grounded in the testimonies of the Scripture is the bulwark of the Church.'

So we have to listen to Jerome, Doctor of the Church and scholar, and perhaps you'll be surprised just how much of his learning is familiar:

So true is it that, where there is most law, there is most injustice.

I praise wedlock, I praise marriage; but it is because they produce virgins.

The character of the mistress is judged by that of the maid.

You make a virtue of necessity.

A pearl will shine in the midst of squalor and a gem of the first water will sparkle in the mire.

It is no small gain to know your own ignorance.

God is the only one who has no beginning.

It is the intention which makes a gift rich or poor, and gives things a value.

True friendship ought never to conceal what it thinks.

He who is educated and eloquent must not measure his saintliness merely by his fluency. Of two imperfect things holy rusticity is better than sinful eloquence.

1 October

St Thérèse of Lisieux

~

There are few closer to the Catholic heart than this Little Flower of Jesus, Thérèse of Lisieux, whose life was victim to tuberculosis at 24 but who filled each of those short years with the fragrance of her presence.

A Carmelite nun, her brief life would have passed unnoticed had it not been for her autobiography, *The Story of a Soul*, which her sister edited and published. 'If you will the end,' wrote the young nun, 'you must will the means.' And the means for the Little Flower were reflected best in her poetry.

> O Jesus! give me wings of white, then I
> Can come to You, by soaring in the air:
> To those Eternal Shores I want to fly –
> I want to see You, God my Treasure there.
> I want to fly to Mary's arms – for, near
> Her on her throne I'll find such rest in store;
> And there she'll give to me, my Mother dear,
> The gentle Kiss I've never had before! . . .
>
> Loved Jesus! soon, so tenderly (above
> As never yet to me) Your smile impart,
> And I, in a delirium of love,
> Will (let me!) hide myself within Your Heart . . .
> Oh, happy moment! What a joy to me
> To hear You speaking – gently. I'll adore
> When first I glimpse Your Face, and in it see
> That Glory which I've never seen before . . ..
>
> St Thérèse of Lisieux, *Poems*, translated by
> Alan Bancroft

St Thérèse – who better to usher in the month dedicated to Our Lady of the Rosary?

THE GUARDIAN ANGELS

A day to listen for the flurry of angel wings. Not the mighty ones of the archangels but the gentle ones of the Guardian Angels, drawn in their million perhaps from the Heavenly Choir of Angels and given the task to be there when needed.

In all likelihood the notion of an intellectual spirit without form (the theologian's description) cuts little ice with our new caste of crypto-scientists. And this despite the fact they admit of a wind they cannot see, a universe they cannot measure, a force they cannot name other than the clumsy title 'Big Bang'.

Can we help feeling just a little smug that mysteries that elude scientists are to us just everyday events? I, for one, am wholly convinced that at conception my life was entrusted to an angel with the task to watch over me without in any way interfering with my free will. It's been no easy task for him – as, in due course, he'll be the first to tell me – but I know that at moments of fear, evil and plain stupidity he has been there to advise, encourage and sadly sometimes to turn away rather than see my shame.

If you want to be pedantic, you call my angel 'conscience' and write him off as the result of conditioning or genetic inheritance. But I won't. For when I am still I can hear him as clearly as I can the breeze; I can sense him just as I can sense the turn of the tide.

A Guardian Angel is no more a diaphanous, elusive mystery than all the others we Catholics have to accept on Faith and on Faith alone. The living Church – from Pope to humblest layperson – can be but a poor yardstick by which to measure mysteries. At best the Church can guide; at worst it can sometimes scandalize. But between exhilaration and despair there is always the unseen sanity of the Guardian Angel, a sentinel to guard errant souls until he can lead them into Paradise.

3 October

It was a little item tucked away amidst pages of so-called 'big' stories, in the briefs of my morning newspaper. It reported that an Italian priest had been shot in his bungalow at Archer's Post in Northern Kenya. He died before reaching medical aid at Wamba, 50 miles away.

The one-man mission at Archer's Post is a natural stop before starting the hairy journey across the desert either to Wamba or to Marsabit and finally Ethiopia. I had stopped there three times on journeys north and on each occasion had to camp in the compound because 'Father is off on safari'.

This remote spot is set in prickly, untidy bush, featureless in all directions. And it was, in nothingness, that Fr Luigi Andeni, a Consolata Father, was shot in the stomach by a marauder after a dollar or two. It was a long way from Genoa or Rome or Naples or whatever Italian town reared him, to this scruffy wilderness of stone and thorn. You would think that with scorpions, snakes, lions, he had enough to contend with. But, no, man was the greatest hazard.

I imagined the bumping, lurching journey he would have endured on the track to Wamba – itself no more than a cluster of tin roofed huts amidst scrubland. Little wonder he died on the journey, his stomach burning as blood and entrails oozed out. Even as he lay dying a horde of flies would have gorged on the rich banquet of his blood.

The little news item taught me something new about God. He was unlikely to apportion ten pages to a Clinton story and one paragraph to Luigi, Consolata missionary. Suddenly my mind focused with huge clarity and I knew, with utter certainty, that God would have a fine sense of priorities. Why does it take us so many oblique turns to realize finally what is of consequence and what isn't in this life of ours?

4 October

ST FRANCIS OF ASSISI

The brothers shall appropriate nothing to themselves, neither a house nor place nor anything. And as pilgrims and strangers in this world . . . let them go confidently in search of alms . . . This, my dearest brothers, is the height of the most sublime poverty, which has made you heirs and kings of the kingdom of heaven; poor in goods but exalted in virtue. *Rule of St Francis*

The story has lost nothing in the telling – the young man about town who sold some of his wealthy father's goods to pay for the repair to a broken-down church near Assisi, San Damiano. When his father was angry with him the young Francis tore off his own clothes and started not just a new life but a new Order of considerable austerity.

San Damiano was indeed built despite Francis's espousal of the Lady Poverty. In course of time former friends and others joined him in his frugal lifestyle which, eventually, Pope Innocent III approved by accepting the simple Rules of Francis which centred on the basic injunction:

The rule and life of the Minor Brothers is this, namely, to observe the holy gospel of Our Lord Jesus Christ by living in obedience, without property, and in chastity.

But San Damiano was too small for Francis. He took off to convert the Saracens, fell sick, and was taken to Acre. There he was one of the few churchmen who saw the crusaders for what they had become – cruel adventurers in search of wealth and not Christ.

When finally he returned home it was to find that his simple Rules had sparked the imagination of a whole generation and his Order had flourished with more than 5000 joining.

Dying young, Francis left the instruction: 'Let the brothers ever avoid appearing gloomy, sad and clouded, like the hypocrites; but let everyone be found joyous in the Lord, gay, amiable, gracious.'

5 October

SS MAURUS AND PLACID

A t Mass yesterday the theme throughout was faithfulness and we responded to the Psalm with a refrain curious aside our general indifference – 'Harden not your hearts,' we intoned. But looking about church I saw the very opposite of hardness and plenty of evidence of faithfulness.

There were the two sisters, both in their 70s, who sat as near to the lectern as possible for the one was nearly blind and the other deaf. Over the past 20 years or so I've watched their conditions worsen and their reactions to that. I've seen how one will supply sight and the other hearing for the other. I've caught their brief moments of impatience, one with the other, and seen how swiftly, with a touch of the hand or a smile, they've excused each other.

There is the man who brings his wife to Mass, guiding her every move, his hand about her. She has Alzheimer's disease and hasn't recognized him or the church she knew so well for almost ten years. When she stands to wander during the homily he takes her gently to a side chapel where they sit silently, side by side.

Nearby, the youngish couple and their daughter born ten years ago with Down's syndrome. From time to time she'll scream, her fists will fly. Seconds later, her smile and giggly laugh will recompense her mother for the bruise on her cheek. The father takes her and cradles her in his arms where, momentarily, she dozes.

Near the statue of The Little Flower the parish's newest war widow – her husband killed in Croatia – sits as she so often does and talks with the one who knew so much pain yet still loved in the ecstasy of love.

Every parish is but a microcosm of the world outside. But because we are there, closely closeted, we see everything with clearer eyes and greater understanding. It's as if, for a short time, God's captives, we can see things with His eyes and comprehend with His compassion. 'Lord, harden not our hearts.'

6 October

ST BRUNO ST FAITH

Carthusian customs, virtually unchanged since 1133, ensure that the contemplative Order founded by Bruno remains the hardest path a man or woman can take to discover God. It calls for total renunciation of the world and a life of complete mortification. It's no surprise then that these essential hermits, vowed to silence, are now thin on the ground although their famous liqueur is still in abundant supply. In England the only remaining monastery – or charterhouse as we corrupted the word Chartreuse – is at Parkminster in Sussex. John Skinner was one of those who, briefly, sought a vocation there and he described what a monk there seeks:

> The Carthusian monk seeks silence. He has entered the solitude of his desert, that man-made seclusion that signals to himself and to the outside world what he is about. He has gone there to find God; or rather he comes to the desert of his innermost self to permit God to find him. And his main path is the way of silence.   *Hear our Silence*

It is just possible, John Skinner concludes, that the Order may adapt its customs. But there is a big doubt there, although it has slightly modified since this description of Carthusian life by a visitor, the Abbot of Cluny:

> Their dress is meaner and poorer than that of other monks; so short and scanty, and so rough, that the very sight affrights one. They wear coarse hair-shirts next to their skin; fast almost perpetually; eat only bran bread; never touch flesh, either sick or well; never buy fish but eat it if given to them as alms ... their constant occupation is praying, reading and manual labour, which consists chiefly in transcribing books.

It is all far distant from our consumer society, the one we cannot avoid outside of the cloister. Yet isn't there a hermit of kinds inside us all? Tomorrow, Feast of Our Lady of the Rosary, is a good time to find out.

7 October

OUR LADY OF THE ROSARY

W̶e're scarcely aware of our total enslavement to time and space although we are conscious of our dependence upon our bodies. Perhaps it was to escape this bondage that so many of the saints we've visited together were, for a time certainly, hermits. Christ Himself needed those 40 days alone, free of time, space and bodily demand. As ever, He would not have exiled Himself in that way unless the action had some sort of message for us.

Sadly, life isn't geared to hermitage. Far from being a frugal act of Faith, it's an indulgence few of us can share. From womb to grave we live life by time. Our lives, apart from a few exceptions, are spent within a 20-mile space within which we work, eat, and take pleasure. It's such a narrow confine when you consider the enormity of our earth, the magnitude of our universe.

Time, like space, we docket, pigeonholing what we regard as essential. Sunday Mass may be one of these – just as is car cleaning and mowing the lawn. Time too is docketed for prayer – a brief memo to God to register thanks and add a shopping list of requests.

We kid ourselves by saying that when we are old we will have the opportunity to ignore both time and space. But then that other tyrant steps into it – our body. Its needs now predominate.

Perhaps, regardless of aches and creaks, we should attempt to live those last years as the saints did. But could it be that what was for a saint the mark of sanctity, becomes for us yet another indulgence?

It's unlikely we will ever know for certain. One day a knock will come, a call that recognizes neither time nor space and we'll be off to where there is eternal time and limitless space. And, best of all, these wretched bodies of ours will no longer call the tune.

8 October

———— ✒ ————

Call it snooping if you must, but it's what old hacks do best. And anyway I hadn't meant to eavesdrop. It was just that I was sitting on one side of the wall in that Nazareth square, on the verge of a quiet snooze, when I heard this snippet of conversation from the other side.

Man (I'd guess him thirtyish): 'You're worried – that frown has no place on a pretty face like yours. What's the matter?'

Woman (younger, early 20s): 'It's Mamma. She's brought up six of us. I'm the youngest. She's not all that old, only 50. And, Rabbi, she's so tired. I long to take her up in my arms, hug her close, sit her down and tell her to rest.'

Man: 'What's stopping you?'

Woman: 'Why ... I don't know ... She's Mamma. She does that to us. She'd think I'd gone crazy.'

Man: 'You're going to marry soon.' (Surprised start from the woman.) 'Yes, I know, you're not sure. But his name is David – a good man who'll make you a good husband. You'll have children and, like Mamma, you'll be tired. Then, wouldn't you like your daughter to take you in her arms?'

Woman: 'She'll be too ... too shy, just like me now. She'll think, like me, that mothers are indestructible.'

Man: 'And you'll know – as your Mamma knows now – that they're not. Mothers give of all their love, not just little bits at a time. And giving of yourself, all of yourself, is exhausting. In time it leaves a void, an emptiness you think you'll never fill. It's then, Rachel, that someone like yourself comes along to fill that hole with love, and kisses, and hugs. And appreciation. Go home, Rachel, do it now.'

From my side of the wall I heard her rise. I looked for the Rabbi but he'd gone. Then I wondered – how many personal encounters had He had, apart from His public ministry, that we knew nothing about?

SS DENIS AND COMPANIONS

et another scientific breakthrough today in the race to discover how God put us together. Already they have announced they have mastered His blueprint for human beings. Now they will challenge the Church with ethical questions which will need answering.

They will ask: If we go to a gene bank and pay a deposit, can we then take out the bits of people that most offend their neighbours? Is there a moral reason why someone, due to inheritance, should be a sinner when they can so easily be a saint? A pervert when he could be a wholesome teacher? A poet when he could be a stockbroker?

Human beings are like a computer, they'll allege. Change the chips and you change the output. In a generation or two you'll have near perfection. We will, say the scientists, make up for the deficiencies of this original plan of God's which was so prone to error.

The Church, of course, has its own scientists, some of them as high in the art as the best there are. Many of them are Jesuits, skilled not just in science but in the Church's apologetics on science. And they will know well Thomas Aquinas's assertion:

> Every Christian is bound to hold that acts which issue from a man's own will, namely all his human acts properly so called, are not subject to determinism. *Letter to Reginald of Piperno*

And they will see the quandary the philosopher St Justin asserts:

> If man does not have the free faculty to shun evil and to choose good, then whatever his actions may be, he is not responsible for them. *First Apology*

We are on the verge of the first creature being born without what we term free will in its full meaning. When it happens, it will turn the Church upside down. But God will chuckle at what the scientists have missed.

St Francis Borgia St Paulinus of York

Y ou have to wonder about genes. Francis Borgia was a Jesuit, the great-grandson of a Pope, Alexander VI, who the Catholic Church would much sooner forget. A voluptary who bribed his way to the papal crown, Alexander, originally Rodrigo Borgia, fell victim with his son Cesare of a poison they had intended for a guest at their table.

Perhaps it was God's intention that the sins of Alexander should be expiated by the grandson. Who can out-guess God? But the fact is that Francis was everything Alexander was not, although Ignatius of Loyola spotted the same ability for organization and was his patron.

Most Catholics feel hard-put to it when critics point to the bad popes – not as many as they infer, but just one is bad enough. We have an apologia for it, of course, because 2000 years of history tends to throw up matters best forgotten. It is no different with a family's history over a century – there is much to forget and forgive.

Usually we end up saying that Christ's promise was to ensure the Church would survive whatever the Devil threw at it. And this promise He surely kept.

There is much in the Church's past that is indefensible. Our mistake has been in attempting to defend it. That in itself has shown a lack of faith in God's promise. But in a very real sense the warts on the Church's face have just been that – external blemishes that, whilst repulsive, have not altered the message of the Church.

The physicians called in by God during these leprous moments were the saints – men and women who knew well the message and intended, whatever the opposition, to carry it forward. Because of them, down the ages, the essential purity of Christ's Church remained untarnished. For every Alexander there was, in the wings, a Francis to even up the score. Today, too, it is the enthusiast who blows away the corrosion of the apathetic.

Like a lot of people who failed miserably at maths I enjoy getting my own back by using a calculator to do sums I would never be able to do otherwise. Anyway, I've just worked out that I've attended Mass some 4000 times. Note that word there, 'attended'. Many of the occasions were not, as they should be, celebrations. Any number were services to which I lent my physical presence but not my heart and soul as you should.

A number of the 'attendances' were during schooldays when we were marched in and marched out. In the intervening time I tried to recall history dates or measured my chances of scoring a try that afternoon. Other times I was at Mass because not to be there would condemn my soul to Hell fire. Truth to tell, even today there's just a touch of that at the back of my mind. Mostly though I went because not to do so would be an affront to Him and leave a great hole in the place where my heart should be.

As I grew older, though, the purpose of Mass became the opportunity it gave me to have Him to myself for however a little while it was. Almost to my surprise, I found myself looking forward to my date with Him and even arranging to meet Him out of hours as it were. Daily Mass for a while was a huge enjoyment – the more so as it seemed He and I were meeting on the sly, not at all like our formal Sunday engagement.

On a rare occasion, I couldn't get to Mass. So I read today's reading and there He was – slipping a note into my soul as He often does:

> If we have died with him, then we shall live with him.
> If we hold firm, then we shall reign with him.
> If we disown him, then he will disown us.
> We may be unfaithful, but he is always faithful
> for he cannot disown his own self.

Fair enough. See You next Sunday then – God willing.

12 October

St Wilfrid

~

Few of us ever stop to consider how sophisticated life was for some in eighth century Britain. Wilfrid's long life – he was 76 when he died at his monastery near Oundle – was astonishingly well travelled and quite often luxurious. He journeyed to Europe and Rome, he confronted kings and founded monasteries throughout the length of the land. He enjoyed and patronized the arts, he shone forth for his brilliance in a way few do today.

Now, if remembered at all, it will be for his connection with Pip and Squeak – if your memory is that good. Yet our English Church is built on men like him and women too who, from the confines of their convents, exerted influence which would be denied them today.

Catholics in Britain tend, on the whole, to be too modest about their Church's achievements, and know little about the extraordinary virtues that have been bred in these islands. Today, even, the Church in Britain is probably the most vital bulwark of Catholicism in Europe. But seemingly we are unaware of this. It would be satisfying to think our unconcern is humility. But it isn't – it's mostly ignorance. Ignorance of our past and more especially our unawareness of the vital part our Church plays and must play in the defence of Christian morality.

We have current difficulties, it is true. But in the end it is inconceivable that the legacy and the groundwork of such as Wilfrid and Thomas More should be squandered because either we don't care enough or have forgotten too much.

Whatever our feelings may be upon the political European Union there is no doubt whatsoever that the spiritual union of Europe depends heavily upon the example and leadership of Catholic Britain and Ireland.

Wilfrid, no stranger to Europe, would, and probably does, agree.

13 October

ST EDWARD THE CONFESSOR

'**V**apulet v. severely' was a note I carried with great frequency to my housemaster. It translates simply enough –
'Let him be whipped very severely'. It may have been for
an error in Latin prosody, or an inability, which was never rectified,
to understand why x should equal y, or, as on three occasions, my
failure to eat my breakfast of fried bread silently enough.

The Catholic schools of my youth all had a reputation for favour-
ing corporal punishment. My prep school, where such punishment
was meted out in dour cruelty, and my monastery school, where
the strap was given with mutual chuckles on either side, were no
exception to the rule.

Some schools fared worst when the reminiscences were doled
out – notably the Christian Brothers and the Jesuits – but none,
including the convents, escaped the bottled-up rage of past pupils.

It is a rage I find hard to share. Not because I am a natural
masochist, assuredly not, but because, at the time, it all seemed so
natural, albeit unpleasant. It did not breed in me a sense of sadism – I
never lifted a hand to my own sons but had no marked objection to
someone else doing so. It did not later cause me to fester over a
sense of injustice (except for the fried bread incident). I hope it
never encouraged me to be a bully. In short, corporal punishment –
and I was no stranger to it – was just another academic event
amongst so many.

If the thought of it actually caused damaging fear then it was
being improperly used and must be condemned. If the one adminis-
tering it took pleasure in the task then clearly he/she should *never*
have been permitted near children.

If it was – as is sometimes alleged – a Catholic tradition then I see
little fault in it when it was used justly. As an introduction to life,
which so swiftly punishes the sinner, it even had virtue.

14 October

St Callistus St Selevan

W e'd be here all night if we try to sort out Pope Callistus, the anti-pope Hippolytus and confusing tales of schism around the year 220. It's an unpleasant jumble of charge and anti-charge that only Rome could inspire.

Instead, a tale of a simple Cornishman I first heard when I lived for a while in Polperro and would while away the nights in the Three Pilchards where, besides the gossip, I heard tales of the Cornish saints. One of these was St Selevan.

He gave his name to a tiny hamlet you can still visit – St Levan, just three or four miles as the pilchard swims from Land's End.

Go there, off season I suggest, and you'll find his well and the stone heaps that were once his hermitage. Neither will you miss the block of wood on which two fish have been carved. Put all these together and you have the beginnings of a gentle legend.

It seems he went fishing from the rocks and, perhaps because he was a holy man, he caught not one but two fish on his hook. For reasons the legend doesn't tell he threw them both back into the sea. The probable guess is that he was not a greedy man and fished just for his immediate needs.

So he cast again and – would he believe it – the same little fellows came back on his hook. As any hermit would, he saw this as a challenge and back they went again into the ocean, perhaps a bit bemused by then. Another cast and, yes, you've guessed, there were the two determined fishes again. Like Abraham before him, Selevan knew when he was beaten. He took the two fishes home ready to make a glutton of himself and who should be there on a surprise visit but his sister and her two children – and extremely hungry.

I believe the tale. Not because of the strength of the brew at the Three Pilchards but because I know, yes, *know*, Jesus works in little ways.

15 October

St Teresa of Avila

In a Church so often chauvinistic, Teresa of Avila is an astonishing figure. In her autobiography she makes clear why she was regarded as someone somewhat extraordinary even for a Carmelite:

> I wish I could explain with the help of God, wherein union differs from rapture, or from transport, or from flight of the spirit, as they say, or from a trance, which are all one. I mean that all these are only different names for one and the same thing, which is also called ecstasy.

If ecstasy is a rarity few of us have ever enjoyed then hear Teresa on another experience sadly unknown to almost all of us:

> Rapture, for the most part, is irresistible. It comes, in general, as a shock, quick and sharp, before you can collect your thoughts, or help yourself in any way, and you see and feel it as a cloud, or a strong eagle rising upwards, and carrying you away on its wings.

After 25 years at the Carmelite convent, Teresa longed for a more exacting life and finally was permitted to open a house of her own for reformed (Discalced) Carmelites. And here she wrote:

> When that sweet Huntsman from above
> First wounded me and left me prone,
> Into the very arms of love
> My stricken soul forthwith was thrown.
> Since then my life's no more my own
> And all my lot so changèd is
> That my Beloved One is mine
> And I at last am surely His.

A romantic? No – a determined woman of singular common sense who led her new communities from the front, serving as they did with every common task, driven by the one Love of her life.

16 October

St Margaret Mary Alacoque
St Gerard Majella

P ope John Paul II was elected Pope on this day in 1978. Less than a year later he paid Ireland the tribute of being one of the first of many countries he would visit – Britain had to wait until 1982. Anyone in Dublin when he arrived – and that included a quarter of Ireland's population – would never forget the day. A new Pope, a man brimming with charisma, a friendly, humorous man, a man who had suffered, who was approachable. He captivated the hearts of not just the Irish but of the world.

And what did he do? As you would expect, he went down on his knees and begged the secret armies to forsake their terror. His plea could not have been made more publicly, more trenchantly. The inspired crowds cheered, applauded, followed him over the island in their droves. And, when he left, the terror began again. It was as if he had never begged for peace.

It was a phenomenon which was to become ever more apparent. The person of the Pope drew adulation whilst what he said was largely ignored. The scenario repeated itself in the Americas, on the great continents of the world. Even in the halls of the United Nations. Love the messenger, so many seemed to say, but to heck with the message.

Sometimes the message was peace – ignored. Often it was for a return to moral certainty – ignored. Always it was for the right to life – ignored. It began to dawn on people that Pope John Paul, personally charismatic, was urging them to practise what so many had long since abandoned – their Faith. What is more, their Faith as it had always been taught, without one concession to the demands of a world now largely without the old moralities. Behind the undeniable love emanating from the Polish Pope they discerned the iron which is the true stuff of saints, the stubborn rock on which the Church has to stand or be overwhelmed. As years went on, love for John Paul did not diminish. But it was for the man, not what the man stood for.

ST IGNATIUS OF ANTIOCH

Ignatius was a man of letters – quite literally. He wrote hundreds of them, just as Paul had only 50 years before. It's understandable. For before the days of media the letter was the only way of keeping contact and reinforcing whatever personal teaching had taken place.

You gather some impression of what the letters had been from the saint's last words: 'I am the wheat of Christ; I am going to be ground with the teeth of wild beasts, that I may be found pure bread.'

Ignatius set forth some of the ground rules that would influence the dignity of the bishop and his rights in the new Church. The bishop, he insisted, should be received within the community he visited as if he were the Master himself. In the same way, and for the same reason, the bishop required total obedience and should be kept fully aware of what was happening. He even encouraged Christian groups to start their own choirs, so that they could sing in unison with their bishop.

Ignatius made it clear that the Church in the making was to be one Church, not a medley of discordant opinions, a Church founded by Peter and Paul inspired by the truth that Jesus was the Son of God.

> For faith is the beginning and the end is love and God is the two of them brought into unity. After these comes whatever else makes up a Christian gentleman.   *Letter to the Ephesians*

His warning for those ready to tamper with the truths expressed by Jesus was earthy and pulled no punches:

> Heretics mingle poison with Jesus Christ, as men might administer a deadly drug in sweet wine . . . so that without thought or fear of the fatal sweetness a man drinks his own death.   *Letter to the Trallians*

Ignatius died in an arena, devoured by lions. Only the body, not his spirit.

18 October

St Luke

he truth is that you probably know more about Luke than you think. After all, you share his writing week after week and however a writer tries to stand back from his work there is a part of him in it that cannot be disguised. And Luke was a prolific writer – not only his Gospel but the Acts of the Apostles came from his pen.

We know that he was Greek and a physician, probably not Jewish, and well ahead of his time in regard to political correctness. We know, too, that he was a companion of Paul on several of his journeys and that he started his Gospel whilst on these travels.

Clues to his Gentile origins lie in his sympathetic treatment of the Roman centurion and of the Samaritans, a people despised by the Jews. Throughout his Gospel the references to the women involved in Jesus' life are both gentle and compassionate without any hint of the patronizing which would have been as common then as it is now.

Because of the way Luke 'draws' his story there is also tradition that insists he was an artist as well as a doctor. There was sound source material for him as he would have read Mark's Gospel and perhaps too he could have sourced information from the mysterious 'Q' document so many think existed, although no evidence of it has ever been discovered.

Whilst Luke was compassionate – Paul called him 'my dear friend, Luke, the physician' – he was never sentimental. We can be sure that his Gospel was painstakingly documented and it is again likely that the bulk of it was written whilst Paul spent two years in jail in Caesarea and Luke found himself with time on his hands.

It's virtually impossible to believe that Luke was a man to take any hearsay evidence, that he was not a man for whom truth and accuracy were paramount. This being so, we have to concede that the clearest picture of Jesus comes from the pen of the 'beloved physician'.

St Paul of the Cross

T he Passionists, founded by St Paul of the Cross in 1737, added to the customary three vows of poverty, chastity and obedience a fourth – the promotion of devotion to the Passion of Christ.

The Passionist's vocation is largely concerned with preaching vivid missions and giving retreats. Alternatively, Sisters of the Passionist Order are strict contemplatives.

Although born in Genoa, an early ambition of Paul was to achieve the conversion of England and in 1842 the Passionists obtained their first foothold. Today they have seven houses here, the most well known being at St Helens in Lancashire, which is the centre for the canonization of Bl Dominic Barberi who received John Henry, Cardinal Newman into the Church. He was a typical Passionist – articulate, scholarly, well mannered and courteous. Their contribution to missions may be less than it was but I shall never forget the Passionist who read these words from Isaiah:

> We had all gone astray like sheep,
> each taking his own way,
> and the Lord burdened him
> with the sins of us all.
> Harshly dealt with, he bore it humbly,
> he never opened his mouth,
> like a lamb that is led to the slaughter-house,
> like a sheep that is dumb before its shearers
> never opening its mouth.
> By force and by law he was taken;
> would anyone plead his cause?
> Yes, he was torn away from the land of the living;
> for our faults struck down in death.

My Passionist preacher did not only read the Passion – he had lived it.

St Maria Boscardin

S ome saints are so ordinary they give us all hope that one day we might touch the hem of His garment. Maria was one such saint. A girl none too bright, from a poor family, who was probably lucky to secure a place in a convent and find the security of the veil. Even there, life was not unlike home in that she worked as a scullery maid until her Profession in 1907 when she was 19. Then she was allowed to work in the children's diphtheria ward where she caught the virus that would finally kill her.

She had a 'good' war insofar as she found a real talent nursing the Italian soldiers wounded at the great defeat of Caporetto. In the noise and confusion of modern warfare there was a place for someone like Maria, someone like us. As sometimes happens within Orders, her superior must have felt she was getting too big for her boots and once again Maria found herself a skivvy, this time in the convent laundry.

The war over, she returned to the children's ward but, at 35, the earlier virus caught up with her and she died in 1922.

Not much to offer God, you might think – a few dishes washed, some babies comforted, some soldiers encouraged to smile again. Yet seemingly it was enough for Him because people began to visit her grave, first to pray there and then to go in hope of a miracle. Their faith in Maria was justified when she was canonized in 1961.

So, we're learning something about saints as we slip through this year of ours. We're beginning to see that they are not necessarily outstanding intellects nor are they steeped so thickly in sanctity's odour as to be unapproachable. They are men and women chosen from our midst to be that little bit more compassionate, that extra bit generous that most of us cannot achieve. Many of us hover on the outskirts of sanctity all our lives only to die having rejected the grace, always there for the taking, of doing that little bit more.

21 October

St Fintan Munnu

In my haste to celebrate Luke the other day I missed out World Mission Sunday, which, given Luke's travels with Paul, would be unforgiveable. It was a Sunday for both pride and bewilderment: pride because we could recall the thousands of priests and Sisters we sent to what's now called the Third World; bewilderment because our Faith is now stronger where they went than it is here at home.

It's no longer a pious jest that we must look to Africa for our priests. It is reality. Early in this millennium the source of Britain's evangelization will be Nigeria and Goa. And there will be other consequences. Not least of them the probability – not possibility – of a pope from the Third World. If not next time, then certainly the time after.

We must accept that those coming here as missionaries will face the same problems ours did in their countries. Problems of language, culture and certainly finance. It will give us Westerners a chance to practise a virtue we've lost touch with – humility. And yet there are those who say God has not got a plan.

A pope from a continent more preoccupied with survival than greed will have novel priorities. Heading the list will surely be a desire for a better distribution of resources, greater emphasis upon the spiritual strengths of Catholicism, certainly a deep sympathy with the universality of the Church.

Will such a pope feel uneasy amongst the detritus of European society that Rome, the city, has become? Will such a pope, conscious of the swing of the pendulum of Faith from West to East, see his role as essentially nomadic? Will he not see more clearly than his predecessors the Vatican institutions weighed down by marble when they should be blown by the Spirit? Once you take the Western culture out of the papacy Catholicism becomes an errant force of great potential.

ST DONATUS   ST MELLON

O ur church is having Exposition of the Blessed Sacrament today and tomorrow. It's an annual privilege for every Catholic church and prior to it a list goes up in the porch asking for watchers. The name still used in the north for the occasion is Quarante Ore – 40 hours – and it used once to be just that, 40 continuous hours of exposition. Now it has to be split into two days. A pity, because it tells us two things: first, that it's no longer safe for us to walk the streets at night; and second, that there's real doubt that we would do so.

The length of a watch is 30 minutes. The intention is that at no time will Our Lord be either alone or unguarded. When you think for a moment of the magnitude of the honour on offer – to be alone with Christ – it's a wonder we're not fighting for the privilege. Yet – shadow of the garden at Gethsemane – parishes now find it hard to fill these sentry duties and it's often the priest who has to ensure the Sacrament is not left alone.

Our excuses for rejecting this invitation are as numerous as they are facile. In the end, it's because we don't care enough. If the invitation was to meet a minor royalty or a soap opera star our names would be there. But the King of Kings – sorry, but . . .

It makes the abandonment of Christ in that garden so much truer an incident. It makes sense of the parable of those invited to the wedding party who found excuses to be absent. It makes a nonsense of our Catholic claim to revere the Person of Christ in the Blessed Sacrament. It makes a huge hypocrisy of our solemn song: 'Tantum ergo sacramentum/Veneremur cernui (Down in adoration falling/ Lo, the sacred host we hail)'.

And was I there today? Well, no. You see I had to . . .

23 October

St John of Capistrano

John of Capistrano was at one time Inquisitor General in Vienna. Now, history may not be the 'bunk' Henry Ford once thought it but for Catholics it can be obtrusive and at no time more so than at the end of the last millennium when John Paul II was doing his best to wipe the slate clean. In the end, his good intentions seemed more disruptive than creative. Even the tardy apology to Galileo did more to remind the world of the errors of the Inquisition than it did to reinstate the scientist.

When the Church was losing its grip on the secular sovereignties it came up with its own weapon – the Inquisition. But when non-Catholics – and Catholics too – voice their hatred for the discipline it is really the Spanish Inquisition which should be their target.

In Spain, Ferdinand and Isabella founded the Inquisition as a measure to exile Jews and Moors whose loyalty was ever suspect. The Dominican, Torquemada, was appointed Grand Inquisitor in 1483 and over the next 15 years was responsible for the banishment of some 100,000 suspect Spaniards.

Over the 330 years it existed it is probable that the Spanish Inquisition condemned some 30,000 to death, many after torture. Its rule – often enough criticized by Rome – lasted until the Spanish Revolution of 1820.

Nothing is ever as simple as it looks. There is a sound case to be made out that the Inquisition, and not just in Spain, did the dirty work the State wanted to wash its hands of. And there's truth in that. But then, that is an explanation and certainly no excuse. Again, you can say that it must be regarded in the light of the period – a time when a thief would be hanged, a petty criminal hacked to pieces.

But the truth is that a blemish on the Church is another wound for a suffering Christ. And we are right to have apologized for so much of our past, and equally right to crave forgiveness.

24 October

St Antony Claret

It wasn't until the Creed that he made his bid for freedom. 'Seen and unseen' found him halfway up the aisle, besieged on both sides by a phalanx of legs. He had just made the sanctuary steps when the congregation hummed, 'Through Him all things were made'. And that most certainly included a three-year-old with a sense of adventure.

But even his free spirit quailed as he saw the immensity of the altar. 'For us men and for our salvation', went on the chorus. But they had spotted the little lad and the usual roar was now little more than a whisper.

The priest was puzzled. 'He came down from Heaven,' he roared in an attempt to rally his failing congregation. Then he too saw the lad. He smiled, only murmuring, 'By the power of the Holy Spirit'. And as he spoke he reached out a hand to the boy.

Now the people had a chuckle in their voices and they smiled rather than spoke, 'He became incarnate of the Virgin Mary' – the boy allowed himself to be drawn to the priest.

About this time his mother suddenly realized that the tugging at her skirt had stopped. She looked down and became panic-stricken when there was no child there. She glanced desperately towards the door and then to the altar. And there he was, by the priest. Her momentary flash of relief gave way to embarrassment and no small confusion. What was a mother to do? Slowly she rose, followed her son's footsteps up the aisle. The boy, secure at the priest's side, smiled at her. She hastily genuflected, ran to his side and there she stood until the rousing end: 'We look for the resurrection of the dead, and the life of the world to come, Amen.' The boy released his grip on the priest's vestment, ran to his mother, she swept him up and hurried back to their pew. The people chuckled as so, perhaps, did the austere Fathers who had met in Nicaea back in AD 325.

I t says in the psalms: 'This poor man called; the Lord heard him.' It struck a chord with what had happened yesterday. I had been in the kitchen washing up (a little treat that comes my way from time to time), and outside, in the October mist, I heard my son's 12-year-old Cavalier engine spluttering. Then it gave up completely. Normally this would neither surprise nor worry me. But on this occasion he was expounding its virtues to a possible buyer and he needed the £180 involved.

As I peered through the kitchen window I muttered, 'St Joseph, please let the wretched thing start for him.' It was quite involuntary. The Catholic treats Heaven like a Citizens Advice Bureau – often the only place an answer can be found. In my mind I heard him chide me, 'Who do you think I am – St Christopher?'

Outside, the engine clunked impotently, the would-be buyer kicked a tyre or two and left. 'I'm sorry, St Joe, I shouldn't have bothered you – you're a carpenter, not a mechanic.'

There was silence from St Joseph but not from my son. He came in dolefully. 'Not a chance,' he commented as he passed through the kitchen.

I went on drying the dishes. 'I quite understand about prayer,' I explained to St Joseph. 'If it's not answered then there's a good reason for it. Perhaps next time.'

If only I had shown faith. An hour later the phone rang and my son was offered £170. He was delighted. In a way I was crestfallen – I had fallen at the first hurdle of confidence. Heaven, as always, has its own way of doing things.

I told my son about St Joseph's participation in the deal. He just looked at me. Then I knew I had failed to transmit the kind of Faith I had to my son. Worse, perhaps my Faith was wrong and had no business being transmitted to a young fellow who knew that $e=mc^2$ but saw no relevance between St Joseph and the sale of his car. What bothered me was that perhaps he was right and I was wrong.

26 October

St Cedd   St Eata

Sing psalms to the Lord who dwells in Sion.
Proclaim his mighty works among the peoples;
for the Avenger of blood has remembered them,
and has not forgotten the cry of the poor.

Psalm 9, *Grail Breviary Psalter*

You could say I was spoilt – Gregorian chant set the rhythm of my life for my early years. It washed over me before breakfast, lunch and supper. Perhaps then it was a signpost to my meals but it was also symbolic of something I didn't quite yet comprehend. It set a mood that was unhurried. The Latin was more often than not incomprehensible but soothed me in a way I've never known since. It washed over a boy's million anxieties, rattling them away on an emotional ebb tide like so many pebbles.

Today they played the first Christmas carols at my local supermarket. It was impossible not to compare their anachronistic jingle with the chant that was once part of my life. I wondered what would occur if they substituted a Gregorian tape. Would it numb desire for the beans (two for the price of one)? Would it titillate the palate for a taste of Benedictine (shop early for Christmas)?

Perhaps shoppers would stand aside as others took the last chops on offer; perhaps, without stress, we would see our neighbours differently.

Then reason told me that everything has a time and a place. The bustling market of Jesus' day would no more have welcomed Him than it does today. We're only told of one visit He made to a market and what a mess He made of it. Yet that is where His peoples are and it's where we have to try to take Him. They no longer trek to mountains for anything other than a tan. Or to churches except for a wedding. The evangelization we're committed to must be real – we have to go to where the people are, not where they ought to be.

27 October

St Odran

―――――

This day, in 1958, the Catholic world's attention was focused on Rome. The conclave to elect a successor to Pius XII had already been at work for three days and it wouldn't be until tomorrow, at the twelfth ballot, that the cheerful, rotund Angelo Giuseppe Roncalli would be chosen as a caretaker pope – he was 76 – until the cardinals could get their act together to elect a real leader. Now we all know that John XXIII was no janitor – he was to be the architect who called together the world's bishops for the Second Vatican Council (and it still went on when he died in 1963). But not until he had composed his spiritual testament.

Seldom has any pope taken so long a journey into death, or caused so much mourning when it finally came. He wrote:

> I await the arrival of Sister Death and will welcome her simply and joyfully in whatever circumstances it will please the Lord to send her.
>
> First of all I beg forgiveness from the Father of mercies for my 'countless sins, offences and negligences' as I have said and repeated so many, many times when offering my daily sacrifice of the Mass.
>
> For this first grace of forgiveness from Jesus for all my sins, and for his acceptance of my soul in his blessed and eternal paradise, I commend myself to the prayers of all who have known me and followed my whole life as priest, Bishop, and most humble and unworthy servant of the servants of the Lord.
>
> It is with a joyful heart that I renew wholly and fervently the profession of my Catholic, Apostolic and Roman faith.
>
> *The Journal of a Soul*

More than once during his long death struggle that so agonized us all in that now faraway year he said: 'My bag is packed and I'm ready to depart.' Finally the permission came – to his delight and our sorrow.

28 October

SS SIMON AND JUDE

T hey saw everything, they shared everything, they were relentlessly marked for life, yet we know so little of those Twelve who followed Jesus. About Simon and Jude we know virtually nothing, not even the manner or place of their deaths. Perhaps this is why they are paired together, partners in anonymity.

There was good reason for Jude's originally low profile. For centuries he suffered the fate of being confused with Judas and remained in obscurity – Jude the obscure – until he was rediscovered as it were and became the leading patron of hopeless causes.

Look where you will – from the *Clare Champion* to the *Daily Telegraph* – and each day you will find a few lines tucked away in the small ads thanking Jude for services rendered. For Catholics, this little thank you is an essential part of the deal with Jude. If your favour is granted you must make his name better known. It is not a foolish practice for by introducing an act of faith to a secular world you are reminding them of the power of God through Whom Jude works.

The novena prayer to St Jude is one of the most powerful prayers in the Catholic armoury of faith:

SAINT Jude, glorious apostle, faithful servant and friend of Jesus, the name of the traitor has caused you to be forgotten by many but the Church honours and invokes you universally as the patron of hopeless cases – of matters despaired of. Pray for me who am so miserable, make use, I implore you, of that particular privilege accorded to you to bring visible and speedy help where help is almost despaired of. Come to my assistance in this great need that I may receive the consolations and succour of Heaven so that [*here you name your request*] and bless God with you and all the elect throughout eternity.

It is a supplication I have never known to go unanswered.

29 October

ST COLMAN

~

Every two months or so I accompany my wife to the ophthalmic ward of the local hospital. Diabetes has severely impaired her sight. The wait is lengthy but there's literature to pass the time. A new pamphlet today read: 'Almost everyone who loses some or all of their sight goes through a period of grief, anxiety, bewilderment or depression. Each person comes to terms with sight loss in their own way.'

I had started reading it when the man next to me, he was about 40, burst out, 'It's all I need – going blind. I almost got blown away in Northern Ireland – I wish to God I had been.' His fists clenched and unclenched rapidly. 'I've got a stack of paracetamols this high' – he waved his fist at me – 'and I'll take every one if they tell me I'm going blind.'

The nurse took him off to read the sight chart. I saw that he was able to reach the fourth line – a lot better than my wife could. And then I lost sight of him as he started the journey through the various clinics – a very angry man.

Hopefully, somewhere, the surgeon was doing for my wife what Christ did for the blind beggar at Jericho. 'Lord,' he had cried out, 'give me back my sight.'

Then Jesus said to him, 'Receive thy sight; thy faith has brought you recovery.'

And, recounts Dr Luke, at once the man recovered his sight.

The surgeon will use a laser. Christ, we're told, used spittle and some dust. The laser, sadly, will make little difference. I long for Christ to be there in the waiting room with me and the very angry ex-soldier. Perhaps – no, assuredly – He was. And I did try to bring them together – the squaddy and His God. I even mentioned the man at Jericho. But the man looked at me through his dimming eyes and left silently.

Neither were my wife's eyes any better after the laser treatment. I guided her out and, in the sudden sunshine, she smiled happily. 'I think I can see the car a bit better,' she said. A little faith is as good as a miracle.

30 October

St Marcellus the Centurion

Marcellus was an old soldier – if not in years then certainly in experience. A veteran, with the command of a company of legionaries. All of a sudden he tears off his military ensignia, so hard won, and declares he cannot fight for both emperor and Christ. And his choice was Christ. Well, in justice, his commander had little choice. Marcellus was executed.

Note, Marcellus wasn't a pacifist – just a soldier changing his allegiance. He was as ready to fight for Christ as he had in the past fought for Rome.

Pacifism has never been a Catholic trait. There are countless reasons for this but the overriding one has to be that ours is a Faith of authority. Thomas Aquinas was aware of this when he wrote in *Summa Theologica*: 'For a war to be just three conditions are necessary – public authority, just cause, right motive.'

With this in mind you can see how both German and English Catholics felt justified in taking arms during the Second World War – the justification is surely in the eye of the beholder.

The Catholic movement most fervent in the cause of international peace is Pax Christi which unites a growing number in its aims for disarmament and action for peace. The Society was energetic in its support for the Campaign for Nuclear Disarmament but had to wait some time for the official Church to catch up with its enthusiasm.

Today the Church teaches that there can never be justification for the use of nuclear weapons whilst at the same time it defends the right of a state to defend itself when another seeks to impose coersion upon it. For myself, I like Pascal's definition:

> Can anything be more ridiculous than that a man has a right to kill me because he dwells the other side of the water, and because his prince has a quarrel with mine, although I have none with him.

31 October

EVE OF ALL SAINTS' DAY

H allowe'en disguises the trepidation we feel as we enter a strange two-day cycle which first honours the Church Triumphant and then the Church Suffering – those in Heaven and therefore saints; those in Purgatory and therefore suffering still.

Because these two days are the most emotionally disturbing of the Catholic year, Hallowe'en preceding them took on a weird phantom existence all of its own. It is the transition from late autumn to winter, so the associations of Hallowe'en are mostly pagan with overtones of lost spirits in search of ease. Whilst in America it has become a children's carnival, in Europe the coming winter storms create a mood of spiritual rather than physical disquiet.

Strangely, Hallowe'en has no part in either Church history or liturgy – as if we had abdicated this one night, leaving it to fantasies bred in the wild days when people had no faith but the fear of their own imagination. It is what we might still have been without the knowledge of one caring God Who holds each of us tenderly in the palm of His hand.

If there is a justification for including this odd day in this journal then it is to point out that for most children today there will be greater awareness of Hallowe'en than there will be for the two days following. They will know of the ghoulies and ghosties, the zombies and spectres, without knowing of the Spirit that gives us purpose. They will be titillated with fear without knowing the superior strength of Faith, the arcane will have more relevance for them than the truth of life.

Too few years separate us from the pagan past to encourage us to revive the bleak festivals of that era. Just as it takes so little to make a mob from a crowd, it takes but a moment for us to miss the light and be lost in the dark.

A world that has momentarily lost the scent in the search for God will all too easily pick up another that leads away from Him but promises the sensual satisfaction that pagan Hallowe'en once did.

1 November

ALL SAINTS' DAY

It means just what it says – a day for all saints, you, me, Aunt Meg and the greengrocer on the corner. Please God, one day, all saints. For the individual Catholic today's a Feast as momentous as Christmas or Easter. The day, if you like, when it all comes together – the promises, the hopes and the glory.

I've every reason to hope that amongst the great battalions of saints on parade today my own parents will be numbered and, with them, the friends I know whose lives must eventually enable them to take their places amongst the elect.

No one enters Heavens, says Catholic belief, who is not perfect. So we have the doctrine of Purgatory – tomorrow's Feast – where those who die tarry awhile before attaining the perfection needed before appearing before God.

Today's saints, then, are the great unknown – us, the little people of scant accomplishment but huge faith. Some, of course, may have attained sanctity whilst on earth. Who are we, looking around us, to say which life is or isn't wholly pleasing to God? It may be few, or everyone, or none. Thank God the judgment isn't ours to make.

Sometimes we can be excited by a glance at a face caught in prayer, almost like opening a window on to Paradise. But a face is but a face – the real window, the one that looks in on the soul, is closed to us. The souls of the holiest – and the most evil – are open only to God.

Today, as 'the saints go marching by', is the day of triumph for those who are part of the parade. We long to search the faces of those immortals we knew once as all too mortal. Yet all we can do is pray our hardest that they will be there and that they haven't forgotten us. It's great to have pals in high places. Mum and Dad – if you've made it today, spare a prayer for us still on the way. Thanks.

2 November

COMMEMORATION OF THE
FAITHFUL DEPARTED

I t's the day of the year I anticipate with unease, dread almost. It was at two o'clock in the morning in 1956 I watched my father's last agony – and it was so – as he left us. Outside that huge hospital in Birmingham rain hammered on the windows as trees bent in a gale. It was such a frightening time to die, at the start of a day when, Catholics believe, the souls in Purgatory beg of us our prayers and our remembrance.

We went out into that black morning, my mother and I, to see the leaves tumbling from the oaks; each one, we truly believed, a soul in search of peace. And now my father was one of those leaves scurrying in the wind.

Today the priest has the privilege of celebrating three Masses, each in succession. This is how seriously we take this task of releasing souls from the emptiness of that dank place which is neither here nor there but lost in time and space.

We call them Holy Souls because they are neither in Heaven nor in Hell. Their destination is Heaven; they are not amongst the damned. But their state is one of desperate longing to be in the presence of God just as soon as they have paid their debt of penance.

We believe these souls can no longer do anything on their own behalf. But we, the living, can intercede for them and perhaps hasten their journey. We can offer a Mass for their souls' ease, or do penance for them. The good they did was a part of our lives and now we can reflect that good to God.

Today, of all days, we realize that we are not one Church but three. We on earth are the Church Militant, still fighting. Those in Heaven are the Church Triumphant. Those in Purgatory are the Church Suffering. Yesterday we gloried in the triumph and our hope is that those we love have attained it. But there is no surety. So today we pray to God for their early access to Him.

St Martin de Porres   St Malachy

In a world still largely inclined to classify people by the tint of their skin, St Martin provides a bridge across this chasm of prejudice. The illegitimate son of a Spanish knight and a black woman, he was born in Lima in Peru. Abandoned by his father – who later returned to educate his children – Martin studied medicine and was able to join the Dominicans as a lay brother. He was by any measure an extraordinary man. Every day of his 40 years in the Order was spent begging for food for the hungry, then feeding them and curing their diseases, often, it seemed, miraculously.

As a result of his huge faith – it could not have been anything else – he accomplished the creation of a hospital and an orphanage which became models for the whole of the South American continent. More importantly, he recognized no difference in colour amongst those he helped. He died in 1639 but it was not until 1962, when the Church was looking for a Patron to emphasize the importance of race relations, that he was canonized.

A cult grew swiftly about his memory, not just in South America but in the blighted inner cities of the Western world. Here at last was a saint who straddled the imaginary differences between black and white, a saint very much for our times and our needs. The poor and the sick of every hue make this prayer to him:

> Most humble St Martin, whose burning charity embraces all, but especially those who are sick, afflicted or in need we turn to you for help in our present difficulties and we implore you to obtain for us from God health of soul and body, and in particular the favour we now ask . . . May we, by imitating your charity and humility, find quiet and contentment all our days and cheerful submission to God's holy will in all the trials and difficulties of life.

The poor, you will notice, don't ask for much – just contentment.

ST CHARLES BORROMEO

~

This month of the Holy Souls finds Catholics receptive to pondering matters they otherwise tend to ignore. Like St Anselm, we don't seek to understand so that we may believe, rather we believe in order to understand. Faith is to believe what we don't see and November, positively deafening us with the clamour of the unseen, links both the living and the dead.

The Catholic doesn't need table-rapping or seances – in fact, they are still forbidden to us – to keep in touch with the ones we have loved. Just as the soul is indestructible so is the bond we have with those just a little ahead of us in the climb to Paradise.

Catholics are not, as sometimes accused, preoccupied with death. However, we are conscious of its part played in the process of living. We mourn a death, thanks to our new rites, only for a selfish reason – our own sense of loss. We should never mourn a soul's natural progress to its proper destination. This we believe in order to understand the rotation of our lives.

It's always foolish to disregard the inevitable. And of things inevitable, death heads the list. Our resentment of death only occurs when it happens to the young, which seems such a travesty of the rules of inevitability. So November, like the season it introduces, is just wild enough, reckless enough, to force us to face the fact of our own mortality. None of us is stupid enough to believe we can live forever. But most of us are adept at thinking death is for someone else.

Catholicism doesn't gild the pill. In Lent we're told of the dust to which we return. In November we are shown the mud it will become. But if this month is a stick with which to beat us, it's also a carrot that proves to us that if we understand death we will no longer fear it. All things pass, and so surely will we. But, if we're sharp about it, there are still footprints we can leave.

5 November

St Elizabeth

~

nglish Catholics had every reason to welcome James I. In
Scotland his reputation for religious tolerance hardly prepared
the English for what was to come. Robert Bellarmine, when
Prefect of the Vatican Library, gave his own verdict on the
Gunpowder Plot of 1603 which was to be a watershed in the life of
the English Church:

> I excuse not the deed; I hate murders; I detest conspiracies; but no
> one can deny that men were driven to despair. The Catholics hoped .
> . . that under a new prince, who had always been noted for clemency,
> and whose accession they had cordially welcomed, they would draw
> breath again after a long persecution, and be free to retain that faith
> and religion which the king's own mother and all his ancestors had
> piously practised. But when they saw that the cruel edicts of Queen
> Elizabeth were confirmed, that crushing fines were imposed on those
> refusing to frequent heretical places of worship, and that under colour
> of accusations for breaches of the law they were being gradually
> despoiled of all their property, some among them who could not put
> up with their wrongs, driven to despair, framed that plot which we
> and you alike deplore.
>
> *Bellarmine's reply to the Apology for the Oath of Allegiance*

The plot was not forgotten by James who, three years later, brought
in an Act 'for the better discovering and repressing of popish recu-
sants'. In effect, it meant that the Catholic no longer had to affirm
that the king was the supreme spiritual authority in England, but he
did have to agree that the pope had no authority whatever over the
king who would never be subject to excommunication.

An estimate of the number of Catholics openly practising their
Faith about this period puts it at only 150,000. It was to be a long
journey back to acceptance by either government or people.
Perhaps, after all, the guy you pass today isn't worth the penny.

6 November

MARTYRS OF VIETNAM ST ILLTUD

E very so often the sheer magnitude of the universality of the
Church catches up with you and wallop! The petty bickerings
and cruelties we Westerners inflicted upon each other are
nothing as compared with the sufferings of our fellow Christians in
the East.

The Oxford Dictionary of Saints claims that during the first 200
years of Christianity in Vietnam – then the three kingships of
Tonkin, Annam and Cochin China – about 100,000 were martyred.
Most of them are nameless now, although this all happened comparatively recently, between 1745 and 1862. Many of those executed, of
course, were missionaries and the methods of death reserved for
them were especially cruel. But for thousand upon thousand of ordinary families the espousal of Catholicism meant the destruction of
their livelihoods and their eventual death. On 1 November they
were assuredly high in the ranks of the saints we celebrated.

That so many should die for a Faith so alien to their old beliefs is
awesome. But perhaps that is just what they had and we now lack in
the West – a sense of awe. With the right awe for God, everything is
possible. Without it, well nigh any sacrifice is impossible.

Before Vatican II our awe for God was largely based upon our sense
of the mystery of God. After that Council we knew Him better – of
that there is no doubt – but our awe for Him had diminished, just as
serving a public figure at close quarters will reveal his blemishes and
reduce our initial respect. It's perhaps wrong to carry this analogy to
God but the public attitude to Him has changed beyond all belief.
This is evident in our acceptance of blasphemous films, advertising,
public disdain of all kinds for the sheer majesty that is God's alone.

Whole generations are being martyred before our very eyes. They
are neither burned nor decapitated, tortured nor maimed in any
physical sense. But their awe for God is dismembered daily whilst we
do nothing about it. How those Vietnamese martyrs must weep
over us.

311

7 November

St Willibrord

N ovember nights, a time to sit by a fire and hear old tales recounted. Kate told me this in the hope I might better understand the Catholic/Protestant divide, and even the Irish Catholic/Catholic one:

65 years ago, as a small girl, I lived in a rural part of Armagh. Each Sunday we emptied from our little cottages and farms to walk the three miles to Mass along narrow lanes and in all weathers. We little ones had to keep pace with the grown-ups, all chattering as they caught up on the gossip of a week when they worked from dawn until dusk. The little crocodile lengthened until there were 30 or 40 of us walking through the prosperous Protestant fields just before the church. Sometimes I went with my mother when she worked in their homes. Neat pieces of cake would be served on little plates before a roaring fire so different from our own peat smouldering.

The priest would come visiting us on a Sunday afternoon – my Mam had no husband and I had no father – and he would give us an SVP voucher for food and my mother would get 2s 6d. One day, seeing me in trousers, Father Rice said, 'Our Lady never wore trousers.' To which I retorted, 'Neither did Our Lord.'

My mother's hand caught me a wallop that sent me reeling across the room. When the priest went I was sent to bed without supper. It was the start, although I didn't know it, of my rebellion against the Church.

It was completed when my little Protestant friend died and I was refused permission to attend her funeral in the Protestant church 'on pain of mortal sin', as I was told.

How my prayer for a little girl could have offended God I never knew and nobody bothered to tell me. But it was the beginning of the end. Catholicism I no longer understood; the Protestants I never could.'

Kate claims to be an atheist. She's not. Too much is bred in her bones for her to die other than a Catholic – however reluctantly.

REMEMBRANCE SUNDAY

I possess only one medal. It lies forgotten in a tiny cardboard box and signifies that for a time – less than three years – I once served in an area hazardous for my safety. It's not for valour, just for endurance. Or, more correctly, my inability to do anything about it. I've yet to wear it. Yet, in some perverse way, I'm proud to have it.

Today men and women will parade wearing not just my little token but many more besides. And some will be for bravery, not just attendance. Some of us will recognize their shape, their colour, and know we are watching heroes walk.

My father too had medals that showed he had slithered about in the mud of the Somme and at Ypres and Passchendaele. In most British homes you'll find these tokens of service done in some desert place, on the wild seas or in the skies.

Mostly the owners were not heroes although there is something about war that tends to produce them. They are the bane of the pacifist because it is the hero who lends veneer to the shoddy business of killing and being killed. A touch of chivalry for a brief moment during an instant of terror snatched from months of tedious discomfort. Even so, I confess to a touch of nostalgia, a recognition that war, and only war, can stimulate qualities no other activity can produce.

Those we remember today were not for the most part heroes. But neither did they reject their duty. They conformed to the pattern required of soldiers down the millennia – valiant or fearful, they obeyed, they suffered and they died.

It will be a poor day when old comrades no longer parade about the cenotaphs of our shires. But it will come, as the changing face of war chips away at all notions of chivalry inherent in the pursuit of arms. Until it comes, though, spare your tears for the long and the short and the tall whose glittering prizes entitle them to this one brief hour of glory. And spare them your prayers.

9 November

ST THEODORE OF THE STUDIUM

It won't hurt the young and it will remind the elderly that there was a time when the Church took death, judgment, Hell or Heaven forever very seriously indeed. In case you are forgetting, here are some verses written by Theodore in the ninth century:

> That fearful day, that day of speechless dread,
> When Thou shalt come to judge the quick and the dead –
> I shudder to foresee,
> O God! what then shall be!
>
> When Thou shalt come, angelic legions round,
> With thousand thousands, and with trumpet sound,
> Christ, grant me in the air
> With saints to meet me there!
>
> God comes; and who shall stand before his fear?
> Who bide His presence, when He draweth near
> My soul, my soul, prepare
> To kneel before Him there!
>
> Haste – weep – be reconcil'd to Him before
> The fearful judgement knocketh at the door;
> Where, in the judge's eyes,
> All, bare and naked, lies.
>
> *Byzantine Triodion* (trans. J. Neale)

You can only desanitize death so far. Whilst it's reassuring to be tipped the wink that we all go to Heaven, there's a little bit in all of us that reckons the journey will be longer and more fraught than the new Church leads us to believe.

If we're wise we'll take November as the month in which to hedge our bets, to bridge the gap between the solemn warnings of the 'old' Church and the hopeful messages that spring from the 'new'. In the end, our death is something too important to leave to chance.

10 November

ST LEO THE GREAT

John Paul II and Leo the Great (440 – 461) shared long tenures and both consolidated the primacy of Peter. Leo established forever the nature of the Divinity of Christ and led the action to save Rome from the barbarians; John Paul preached the gospel of life and was influential in the collapse of communism.

When the wind has weathered smooth the forgotten names of his detractors, John Paul, like Leo, will still be remembered. When, in a century to come, human beings are manufactured to a template designed by sociologists then the remnants of the human race will look back at the energetic Pole who insisted we put the dignity of humankind before our desires.

He did something else – he emphasized through his Leo-like authority the incredible difference between the Universal Church and the Church of England. As the last millennium died it became ever clearer that whilst Rome measured the future in millennia, Canterbury was counting it in decades. John Paul revealed the Church as a colossus bestriding every continent; Canterbury dealt with a Faith that was almost wholly parochial. Rome was the juggernaut to Canterbury's pedal car. The observation is neither triumphalist nor proud. It is simply fact.

The authentic leadership of a Roman pope is a reality the Christian world can ignore only at its peril. The barbarians are as close now as they were in Leo's Italy. But this time round they will not attack from outside the city but from within.

The days of triumphalist Catholicism are long since passed, replaced by a very real humility as it faces a disintegrating society. More and more often our leaders speak of Christianity rather than Catholicism. It is no time for those within that broad description to prevaricate about subtle differences of interpretation, since time is too short and the separation of Christians too scandalous. Both John Paul and the great Leo called for the peoples to rally, not on the Church but on Christ. Eventually it is what we all have to do or else deny Him.

11 November

ST MARTIN OF TOURS

H e was deliciously, companionably pickled. As his more raucous carers edged his wheelchair over the step out of the
city pub he eyed them benevolently, his face beaming and
rubicund from the tots of this and the drops of that they had been
buying him since noon.

Across his chest shone a bar of six medals or more. Their subtle
variation of colour revealed the busy war of this old sailor who had
been at the Remembrance Service at 11.00 am. The rich rainbow
indicated service in the Atlantic, on the Murmansk convoys, in the
Mediterranean.

It wasn't easy to visualize this lined face in an ice-encrusted
Balaclava or those hands – now twisted with arthritis – tussling with
snow-stiffened cables. But there he was aboard his wheelchair, cos-
seted by strangers from the public bar. Better still, it was good to see
the young lads, strangers to his horrors, looking after him so gently.

My wheelchair warrior wasn't the only one so feted in Liverpool
that day. In bars along the waterfront, the salt in the air palpable,
there were many others receiving a generous tribute in a city not
known for its gentility.

I saw it all and was glad – as was said of the Creation. Because the
very act of honouring the past is a virtue you'll only find in humanity. Not for nothing was it said that the manner in which a nation
honours its old is a reflection of its moral state.

By now the old matelot will be back at the front window of his
little home, medals wrapped carefully in cotton wool to be brought
out, please God, next year. My hope is that from his wheelchair he
will sense it is a kinder world than we sometimes think, that in the
year to come we'll look behind the wrinkles and see the young man
who was. You may think it is small recompense for two legs blasted
away some 60 years ago. But it is a start.

12 November

ST LAURENCE O'TOOLE

The art of proper dying has been lost. I can remember the days when my father would put his stethoscope into his pocket, shrug on his overcoat and tell the youngest of the family to go and fetch the priest. My father's job was at an end and the priest's was just beginning. The little messenger would do more – having told the priest, he'd scamper around relatives and friends in the area and summon them also. It was unthinkable that anyone should not be seen off at the start of such a journey.

Is it secularism, materialism or just sheer funk that has led so many of us to tuck death away in lonely hospital wards, leaving those we love to the hands of strangers, no matter how capable and compassionate?

We should not be surprised that today we have a whole new industry called bereavement counselling simply to replace what was once a simple family function. Death is too consequential an act to ignore, to sweep away behind the curtains of a stiff board of a bed in an obscure hospital. It's strictly a family matter, and as such should be conducted in the heart of the home, amongst those you wish to mention to God just as soon as you arrive with Him.

There's a practical reason, too, for wanting those you love to die at home. Those who are present with the dying share in large part not just the pain but the faith of the one dying. What sense is there, what humanity, in starting life's most interesting experience lonely, friendless, ignored – without so much as a hand to hold or a kiss on the cheek?

The grieving process should not have to start off cold, in a hospital waiting room. By sharing a death you expend a large part of your grief so that when death comes it is invariably tempered with relief both for the one gone and for yourself. And God knows that helps.

We plan so meticulously for the trip to the Algarve. Is death any less important a trip?

13 November

———————— ❧ ————————

S alt over the shoulder, duck that ladder and watch out for the black cat. Catholics are always being attacked for their super-stitious practices and the truth is that no one is so aware of the pitfalls as your average Catholic.

The Church leapt to denunciation of such habits very early on:

> Neither the higher clergy nor the lower clergy may be magicians, conjurors, mathematicans, or astrologers, nor shall they make so-called amulets which are chains for their souls. And those who wear these amulets shall be shut out from the Church.
>
> *Council of Laodicea (365)*

St Thomas Aquinas specified the types of superstition to be avoided. These ranged from the incorrect worship of God to idolatry, divina-tion and 'vain observance'. Most important to the Church – as dis-cussed at the Council of Trent – was the distinction to be made when invoking the assistance of the saints, and in particular Our Blessed Lady. Prayer to the saints is all very well providing we always realize that the prayer offered is in honour of God and it is only through God that the prayers will be effective. Even Newman tus-sled hard with the distinction.

Relics were long a subject for abuse, together with indulgences and the visions so many claimed to have had. Luther cleaned out the one stable but he was not able to change our desire to share in an experience entirely supernatural – thus the proliferation of weeping statues in the last few decades.

Witchcraft and sorcery may seem obvious targets for Church prohibition, touching as they do on the very tenets of evil, yet it is frightening how closely they follow every generation adapting chameleon-like to the mores of the times. A reminder, perhaps, should we need it, that the Devil is not dead, just changing his disguise.

14 November

———— ❧ ————

I heard of a church, a parish church, that was cleaned each week by a firm of professionals. It shone as no church had before. No spiders lurked in its corners, no dust in the chapels. The uniformed squads, the whole mighty panoply of cleansing, routed every bug, all the lingering essence of crowded humanity. Our Lady was vacuum squirted, the Little Flower was 'hygenisied' (the word in the brochure). St Anthony got the shock of his life as a mop took him unawares; polish was sprayed into every crevice of the ancient pews and a regiment of cleaners sanitized away all traces of the unhygienic congregation that swarmed there every Sunday.

Sure, the church was spotless. It was almost a pity to use it, so squeaky clean it had become. Yet somehow it was empty; it had become a pretty shell, devoid of the life that had given it purpose. You felt somehow that even God found it a strain to walk there lest He leave footmarks on the glistening carpets.

A church is not just God's home but His people's. If they are not comfortable there then neither is He. It's why so many magnificent cathedrals are fascinating to oberve for their beauty but quite impossible to pray in.

A church is the sum total of the love and reverence of the people who use it, and its condition should be the result of the loving care of those who are the parish family. They will probably be less efficient than the professionals, too old to reach the distant dust, but what they do will be done for affection not for silver.

I was told once of churches in parts of Italy where the workmen take their bread and cheese at noon and their wives and children join them for the alfresco picnic. The toddlers play games up and down the aisles and their parents gossip. I should love to see it. And how God must enjoy it – to host His people in His own home, hear their laughter and share in their presence. Perhaps the time has come to re-think our notion of 'church'.

15 November

Almost piously we say each year on Prisoners' Sunday, 'There but for the grace of God . . .' We don't mean it, it's just one of those pompous reactions we have to save us from a charge of hypocrisy. But we should mean it, for it is true. Just as the ratios of Catholics in caring professions are high, just as we seem to provide more VCs than most, so too do Catholics occupy cells in a number well out of proportion to the population.

Fr Algy, a lifelong friend, God rest him now, was a prison chaplain for many years at Risley, Durham and elsewhere. 'Believe me, Cressy,' he'd say, 'there are better inside than there are out.' And there was nothing of the sentimentalist about this Jesuit former army chaplain. He knew his men, and he knew his women. And he knew damned well that if we got our just desserts we'd all do time.

> I know not whether laws be right,
> Or whether laws be wrong;
> All that we know who lie in gaol
> Is that the wall is strong;
> And that each day is like a year,
> A year whose days are wrong.
>
> This too I know – and wise it were
> If each could know the same –
> That every prison that men build
> Is built with bricks of shame,
> And bound with bars, lest Christ should see
> How men their brother maim,
>   Oscar Wilde, 'The Ballad of Reading Gaol'

Wilde was wrong – Christ does see what goes on behind the bars. He is there Himself – taken inside by priests, nuns, laypeople of all kinds who respond so anonymously to the appeal of the greatest of the Beatitudes.

16 November

St Margaret of Scotland St Edmund

D^{ear Soul,}

ear Soul,

A splendid hack of yesteryear, Nat Gubbins, wrote letters to his tummy. I can see why he never wrote to you. Whilst a tummy is a rumbling, grumbling self-evident companion you, dear Soul, are very nearly self-effacing.

For a long time I assumed you would be resident in what the hymn calls my 'panting heart.' Then came the hospital documentaries on TV. There was no way, I decided, you were part of that red mass of pulsating muscle. Then it struck me you were part of that odd convulation called brain. Then they showed us a lobotomy. And you weren't there.

If medicine couldn't help me locate you, then perhaps the Church could. Well, it told me what you were – 'The capacity of motion from within.' As to where you were – 'the soul is immaterial yet a substantial part of the body.'

Knocking on Aristotle's door I found, dear Soul, that you would be vegetative, sensitive and rational. But again, there was no forwarding address. Plato reckoned that originally you would have been reached c/o Heaven. But even Augustine was hard pressed to establish your antecedents or your present whereabouts. In view of this, dear Soul, I'll not address this brief note. I'll just let you absorb it – just as you have absorbed so much from me in the past.

The fact is, I know you're there even if you are invisible. You've never been bottled, canned or photographed. Yet I know for sure when you are hurt, stained or even, for a time, lost.

I particularly know when you are lost. There have been times when you have completely vanished. No trace, no sign. And at such moments I too have known what it is like to be a hollow, empty thing of no substance. I write now, Soul, because for the first time I'm conscious we are reaching the end of this year, conscious too that whilst I may have revealed you a little I haven't proved you. Help me.

Your host, Norman

17 November

ST ELIZABETH OF HUNGARY
ST HUGH OF LINCOLN

A priest friend started an organization a long time ago, with the curious acronym MOMM: Movement for the Ordination of Married Men. Perhaps the initials put people off but more likely it was the description you would have to use if you were advertising a priest's job. It would go something like this:

> PRIEST required: preferably in his mid-twenties. Degree an advantage. Must be ready to work a seven-day week, celebrating Mass daily and leading other services. Additionally the applicant will visit the sick, prepare couples for marriage and pick up the pieces when they fail. He will bury the dead, console the widow, train the young, work in the school, be available for the indigent, succour the poor and needy and act as chaplain for at least half a dozen societies that will require his presence most evenings.
>
> Additionally he'll be responsible for church maintenance and should have experience of joinery, plumbing, tiling, accountancy and law. He will be required to work an average 14-hour day, Mondays off, and be on call for the local hospital three nights out of seven.
>
> Accommodation will be supplied, possibly one dank room in a delapidated house, possibly better. There can be no guarantee. He should also be an adequate cook as this service is no longer generally supplied. Salary will be in the region of £1200 – 1500 p.a. There are holidays if the candidate can find an elderly replacement and can pay him.
>
> Conditions of service leave the candidate few rights. The bishop is his immediate superior and the candidate will give him total obedience. There will be no tenure in any post, 24 hours being deemed the minimum notice of transfer.
>
> Applicants should apply in writing to . . .

As I told my friend, what woman in her right mind is going to marry a man already wed to these conditions of employment?

18 November

St Mawes   St Odo

W hen human beings could only say 'Ugh' it was probably the last time they spoke without equivocation. Since then, 'ugh' has been replaced by perhaps, maybe and whereas – and a hundred thousand euphemisms – in an effort to replicate the honest appraisal, ugh. There are those who think the Church was at its best when few in the congregation understood a word of what was being said.

The hardest task facing Catholic leaders after the Second Vatican Council was persuading people that Mass in the vernacular was valid. My generation had grown up to the gentle hum of sonorious Latin, the murmuring only occasionally interrupted by the odd 'Et cum spiritu tuo' from us. We liked it because it was not demanding and left us time to get on with the real business of saying our own prayers.

Long before the 1960s, of course, there had been constant debate over the use of the 'vulgar tongue' which was condemned at the Council of Trent. The underlying argument against the vernacular was that language isn't static – it is forever changing and so are the meanings of words. Latin was unchanging – what was meant 1000 years ago still meant the same today.

Archbishop Grimshaw of Birmingham was one of those asked to translate the Latin Mass into English. The burden of what he was asked to do literally killed him. He confided to me once his anxiety, asking, 'Will people ever accept "Hoc est enim Corpus meum" in the English – will the words ever be the same for them?' He was a holy and a good man, overwhelmed by the magnitude of what he was doing.

Whether the change from Latin to English did, as many feared it would, endanger doctrine or diminish reverence for the Eucharist is still debated. Yet the truth has to be that we could not go on worshipping God in the equivalent, for some, of 'ugh'. There had to come a time when mystery was put to the test, and when we had to move from romance to enlightenment, whatever the cost.

19 November

———— ⌒ ————

'Ye'll want to go to your church,' my Aunt Meg declared. She was from Londonderry and found it hard to say those words. Every summer I spent two weeks with her in Wallasey, just across the water from Liverpool. And she could never come to terms with having a papist nephew. But it was the Sabbath when everyone went to church – even Catholics. So whilst she and her family went to the Church of Scotland I was packed off to the Catholic church at New Brighton.

Truth to tell, it was an arrangement pleasing to the nine-year-old me. Near the church was a funfair. And my aunt had no idea just how short a Low Mass was. But once back I was enveloped in the pall of an Irish Protestant Sunday. I was despatched to the frontroom with Sir Walter Scott. There were some consolations there – a pickled brain to examine, a foetus in a jar and, best of all, the skeleton my father had given my big cousin when he qualified.

As I did my best to wade through *Redgauntlet*, I thought of those other papists – the ones across the water – who would be taking the ferry for the New Brighton Tower. They would be riding the Ghost Train, hurtling down the Figure of Eight, munching candyfloss and bashing the dodgems. It had been little relief that my mother, leaving me, had told me to offer up my Sunday tribulations for the Holy Souls.

When I tired of Sir Walter my aunt had left me a Bible open at Proverbs: 'A merry heart doeth good like a medicine; but a broken spirit drieth the bones.' Even at nine it led me to consider the differences I encountered at my aunt's. From the nearby Mersey came the haunting sounds of ships' sirens, the P&O boats and the Empresses. I longed to rush down to the prom and share their excitement. But it was the Sabbath. I didn't know it then, but already I was into comparative religion. I knew that papists laughed and the others didn't. It was slender knowledge to carry me through life. But it did.

Only if Catholicism ceases to be merry will I wonder about my choice.

20 November

St Edmund

—⟋⟍—

More than 1000 years on, you have to wonder about the mental tussle Edmund, King of East Anglia, faced when he lost the battle against the invading Vikings and was given the option of denying his Faith or dying. His execution would have been far from gentle but it was what he chose.

At Mass sometimes you can palpably feel a similar struggle being made. For, despite the gregarious thing the Mass has become, the Catholic, at heart, is still an interior person, taking to Christ those concerns which are causing anxiety.

The Church is well aware of the submerged nine-tenths of us that worries away regardless of the liturgy about us. It even has official names for our state of mind – there is the interior struggle and there is internal peace. And much of what we are taught each Sunday is intended to quell the struggle by encouraging the peace.

The struggle, says the Church, is between our desire and God's will for us. The peace comes when we finally end that conflict and then the truce which comes is called acceptance – acceptance of the will of God.

It is, of course, only a truce. For no sooner do you attain acceptance on one thing something else comes up and the cycle has to start all over again – us versus God, what we want and what He wants for us.

At school we had a punishment called lines. And each week a 'line for the week' would go up on the notice board. We always hoped it would be a short one but it seldom was. Perhaps it was a week in which I attracted more lines than usual but there is one I've never been able to forget: 'Life to be worthwhile must always be a struggle.' As, during the week, I wrote the truism hundreds upon hundreds of times I grew to hate it. But worse, I grew to despise and to query what it meant. It was only decades later, when I had passed through another frame of mind that the Church acknowledges as 'the dark night of the soul', that I came to realize the validity of the warning I had copied so many times.

PRESENTATION OF THE
BLESSED VIRGIN MARY

⁓

T oday's Feast has a slender basis. It refers to Our Lady's Presentation in the Temple when she was three years old, an event only recorded in the Apocryphal Gospels. For some centuries the Feast was something of a shuttlecock: It was permitted by Paul II, denied by Pius V, and then reinstated by Sixtus V in 1583. Finally, it was accepted and tidied up by Clement VIII in time for the seventeenth century.

Gospels or books that are apocryphal are largely to be taken with a substantial pinch of salt. There were at one time supposed to be gospels by Peter, Thomas and Matthias and any number of narratives were once in circulation giving details of Our Lord's childhood and the early story of Our Lady. Forgeries abounded in those early years and it's not surprising that Paul's adventurous life prompted an entirely fresh outpouring of imaginative tales.

We tend to forget that folk 2000 years ago were not dissimilar from ourselves – they liked a good yarn, they were intrigued by what the Gospels omitted just as we are today. And, like some tabloid editors, what they didn't know they speculated about – the diarist was as popular in Athens as he is today. And who doesn't like a good yarn?

It was once my duty to patrol the hills about the Dead Sea searching the many caves there for hidden shipments of sugar or arms. We found neither – just masses of scorpions and writhing coils of black kraits. Imagine my frustration when a young Arab searching the same caves found the Dead Sea Scrolls. But I felt something other than frustration. I felt a strange sense of humility and peace that I had come so near to touching the realities of a world contemporary with Christ. Quite suddenly the cave at Qumran, once home to a bustling, highly religious community, became a link with the Man who had certainly visited nearby Jericho and perhaps chatted for a while about the ascetic folk who lived in the mountains. There is still so much we long to know.

22 November

SOLEMNITY OF CHRIST THE KING★

⌒

S ome King this. Born in a shed, father a joiner, probably helped Dad in the workshop. Selected 12 of the most unlikely followers to be his courtiers. Rode to glory on an ass and ended up crucified like any common thief on a cross that, in a moment of whimsy, someone had decorated with the plaque: 'King of the Jews.' Some King we celebrate today.

Even Isaiah, who knew He was coming, made no pretence about His regality:

> There is no beauty in him nor comeliness . . . despised and the most
> abject of men, a man of sorrows and acquainted with grief; and his
> look was, as it were, hidden and despised; whereupon we esteemed
> him not.

Yet, King He assuredly was – King of Kings, King of Israel, King of Nations, King of righteousness; all titles given Him until we have this one great Feast in His honour, the Feast of Christ the King.

Despite His own statement that His kingdom was not of this world, this Feast establishes His supreme rule in matters both spiritual and temporal – it's a reminder to rulers everywhere that one power supersedes all others in this world.

Here in England we celebrate today as Youth Sunday. We haven't done so for all that long but it was a sound dedication. For too long we patronized the young forgetting that they, like us, were the Church. Today, in cathedrals everywhere, the young come into their own as hopefully they gather to acknowledge Christ as their King and their Leader in life. Pius XI gave us today's Feast as recently, in Church terms, as 1925 in a bid to counter the materialistic confusion of the immediate post-war years. It was time for the world to know who was Boss.

★If this movable feast does not fall today then see note on p.xiii.

23 November

ST CLEMENT ST COLUMBANUS

I n latter years an entirely new type of martyr has revealed himself – the Anglican minister. Whether in years to come he will be claimed by Protestants or Catholics remains to be seen but certainly he is valued by Rome.

It is no small thing for a man in his 50s, for example, with wife and children, no great savings amassed and only the skills of ministry, to cut himself off from all that is safe and familiar purely for the dictate of his conscience. It is, in very fact, the true stuff of martyrdom.

It's a transition of several stages, and few of them pleasant. First, the Anglican priest had to tell his family, then his bishop and, the hardest of all I'd guess, his congregation. So many confessions, and every one a severance with the past and all it had meant. This was penance on the grand scale.

When the flood to Rome started in the mid-1990s there was apprehension amongst Catholics – was this the first step towards a married clergy? The question we should have been asking ourselves, of course, was a different one. We should have been asking, is this what God wants and is He giving us the answer to our vocations problem?

Thank God for the immediate response from Pope John Paul at that stage. Told of the exodus that was moving from Canterbury he instructed Cardinal Hume: 'With such men you must be generous.' It was just the remark we needed, and surely the verdict those Anglicans were praying for. About that time some 250 Anglican priests had asked to become Catholics and many more were to follow. It was a massive act of Faith not just in Catholicism but in Catholic generosity.

But in truth Catholics received far more than we were offering in practical help. We inherited deeply thoughtful men thoroughly adept in the skills many Catholics seldom develop. They brought an appreciation of music, mood and liturgy some parishes often lack. They brought a mannered civility that was almost old Catholic. But, most of all, their huge leap of Faith encouraged our own.

St Chrysogonus St Andrew Dung-Lac

For many, the warmth felt welcoming the Anglicans to our Catholic home was slightly chilled when we thought of our own priests who had, perforce, to take the road away from us. Since the 1960s we had seen them slip so softly away to become lost in distant areas, in jobs invariably centred on social work. The mutual shame we all felt, both departing priests and the laity they left, has long since gone. Instead we wish – as many of them do – that they could return to the priesthood they abandoned.

By no means all of those who left did so for desire of the comfort of a wife and family. Many departed because their frame of mind and their specific problems were beyond the comprehension, or the sympathy, of the men then their bishops.

I know of one priest who agonized long and hard over a Church rule he found frigid and distasteful. For more than two years he hugged his problem of conscience, sharing it with only a few of his closest friends, many of whom had the same difficulty but not his sensitivity of mind. Finally he made up his mind to see his bishop. He arrived, mind in turmoil, for his 11 o'clock appointment. To the minute, he was ushered in. The bishop looked at his watch. 'I can give you just five minutes,' he told the priest.

Hopelessly flustered, the priest explained haltingly that his problem was one he had lived with incessantly for two years. 'Four minutes,' said the bishop blankly. The priest turned away and left the room. And then his priesthood. And then his Church.

Thanks be to God, such insensitivity is there no longer. But at the time of the great seepage it was common – not just from bishops but from priests themselves. Men who could have been kept with perhaps just one hour of understanding were permitted, even encouraged, to leave that which they loved and cared for best.

Many of them are still out there. Many would come home to their priesthood. They – like the Anglicans – need our generosity.

25 November

St Catherine of Alexandria

I t's probably better to be remembered for something – however trivial – than for nothing. Today the 'Catherine Wheel' firework is the sole relic of a heroic woman's life. Seemingly they tried to kill her by tying her to a wheel but the spokes broke and so she was beheaded.

So, if we're fanciful, in the gyrating fantasy of colour we see in the spinning wheel we might discern the fact of the face of the saint who gave rise to the Golden Legend of the Middle Ages.

You can feel something of this vision when you visit the sitting room in an elderly folks home, or look along the pews in your church. There is a disguise God gives us that is called ageing. No two masquerades are ever the same, nor is the age when it happens. There are the young elderly and the elderly young but, generally speaking, at that magical time of three score years and ten a veil begins to descend that obscures the past.

The sight of faces that have learned to obscure pain, passion, need, memory, is daunting. In ranks they sit about the lounge, in high chairs kind to stiffened limbs, faces turned momentarily towards you as you enter and then back to the TV or to a regard for infinity.

Behind each face, decades upon decades of living – of courting, bringing up children, of loss in war and loss in tragedy, of hopes attained and dreams lost. Every face concealing taut moments of heroism, anguished moments of shame. All masked now as the world forgets them and they themselves relinquish the world.

This hiatus the aged encounter before being summoned to death is numbing – for them and for those who watch. The modern world, as it will, has dreamed up euphemisms for the state. Elderly has replaced geriatric, senility has become contentment. There are no more OAPs, just senior citizens. The names of ageing may change but the nature of old age remains the same. The best we, the Church, can do is revitalize the past in order to lighten the corridor to God.

26 November

ST LEONARD OF PORT MAURICE

L eonard, a Franciscan, was the one who formalized one of the most rigorous, and some say, most compelling of the Catholic devotions – the Stations of the Cross. Ever since the Franciscans became the official Guardians of the Holy Land there had been concentration on the physical Way of the Cross, the prayerful pilgrimage through the Old City of Jerusalem in Jesus' footsteps on that first Good Friday.

In 1750 Leonard encouraged churches to set up Stations of the Cross which would commemorate that awful journey. Earlier, Pope Benedict XIII had attached indulgences to the practice of making the Stations, and soon enough most churches in the world displayed them – some were great art and others simple reminders. But the devotion was firmly established.

Nowadays we have 14 Stations, but at different times and in different places there have been less or more and varying in the episode they recall. For a long time the fifteenth Station was the discovery of the True Cross by St Helena.

Faber's hymn explains simply the purpose of the devotion:

> From pain to pain, from woe to woe,
> With loving hearts and footsteps slow,
> To Calvary with Christ we go.
> See how His precious blood
> At every station pours!
> Was ever grief like His?
> Was ever sin like ours?
> F. Faber, 'From Pain to Pain'

The Stations can be hugely penitential, sometimes bearing little in common with the swift ducking and weaving we do in the average parish church. At Lourdes the devotion can take up to three hours; in some monasteries six hours – the actual time of the Passion. Like the Rosary, the demand on us is as intellectual as it is physical.

27 November

St Fergus St Virgil

It seems that St Virgil – one of the many Irishmen of the eighth century who journeyed to Europe – landed in hot water with the pope for suggesting there may be other races, other suns and moons, than our own. He was way, way ahead of the times.

Rome has always had a delight in being well informed but in recent days it has also had a fear of being caught on the hop. So the possibility of UFOs created more than a passing concern in the Vatican, which is sometimes as well informed in science as it is in theology.

Not just had the Jesuits – usually foremost in the field of science – to cope with confusing discoveries in the field of genetics, they had also to devise a theology which could be adapted should the impossible happen and we discover we are not alone in the universe.

The mechanics of the possibility presented little problem. God, after all, is omnipotent and omnipresent. There is no theological reason why life should not exist elsewhere and even in abundance. That was stage one. Stage two was, and is, a whole heap more difficult – it involves redemption. Whatever the shape, appearance or texture of other beings, should they prove to be reasoning and intellectual then it has also to be presumed that they possess souls and therefore the right to eternal life. But for their right to be recognized they must, as we were, be redeemed. And there's the rub.

Would Christ, in fairness to other beings, have to die over and over again on other planets? Or was His single act of redemption on our behalf sufficient to establish the redemption of all His creatures throughout the universe?

The notion of Jesus dying on another planet, on a thousand million other planets, is noxious as well as incredible. Perhaps, in a way, it is the proof humankind needs to establish that only our own earth possesses sensiate life forms. The alternative is too bizarre to comprehend.

28 November

St Catherine Laboure

Y ou won't find 'broken heart' in a medical book. Perhaps in a tome on psychology there's a mention. But, as a physical reason for death, a broken heart does not rate. Once I was with a lady when she was told her husband had just died in hospital. Within three hours – without rancour or symptom – she died in my arms. Yet her death certificate only recorded myocardial infarction instead of broken heart.

We're familiar with the picture of Our Lady's heart, pierced and bleeding. Yet even her wounded heart revived and John was at hand to comfort her. Too often such comfort is not at hand and loneliness remains the scourge of the elderly.

Like the broken heart, loneliness is impossible to pinpoint as a disease. It isn't necessarily located in an empty house, only in an empty heart. And the best ECG going will not detect the disorder.

The Church nowadays does much more than in the past. There are nuns expert in bereavement counselling, priests wholly aware of the isolation to be found in their parishes. So too has the SVP extended its brief of care and the Union of Catholic Mothers extends its arms to the widows.

Yet, however good the intentions, there has to come a moment when the front door closes and the one inside has only the clock's incessant ticking to emphasize the futility of marking time.

St Catherine's Miraculous Medal, for no reason you can account for, helps a little in the solitude, a reminder that the saint, now at rest in Paris' Rue de Bac, once had Our Lady as a visitor. Yet, even so, it is hard to assemble the heart that is effectually broken. In the end, the owner has to take the heart and place the broken pieces before God in the hope that He will put it together again. As He made it, only He can fully repair it. Sometimes we can see the encounter between Physician and patient. And at such moments we can only pray for the success of the treatment.

29 November

1st Sunday of Advent⋆

There are few Gospel readings when we have the opportunity to place our own interpretation upon them. But today's is an exception:

> Jesus said: 'There will be signs in the sun and moon and stars; on earth nations in agony, bewildered by the clamour of the oceans and its waves; men dying of fear as they await what menaces the world, for the powers of heaven will be shaken. And then they will see the Son of Man coming in a cloud with power and great glory. When these things begin to take place, stand erect, hold your heads high, because your liberation is at hand.'

There cannot have been a generation in the last 1000 years which did not read these words and quake, for, given half a chance, we can always trim the circumstances to match the message. Yet what we are really being warned about at the start of Advent is the need for humility.

Almost by custom now I think at Advent of H.L. Mencken's cruel jibe: 'An archbishop is a Christian ecclesiastic of a rank superior to that achieved by Christ.' Sometimes the notion of a pyramidical Church suffers badly in comparison with the coming of the Lamb unless, of course, you see the pope supported by a flock of sheep. The truth is that modesty has had the stuffing knocked out of it. Modesty and leadership, in any sphere of life, make incompatible companions. The Church has not always been an exception to the rule and arrogance was once found as easily in the cloister as in the parliament.

Yet Advent is the moment we prepare to meet humanity's most perfect proponent of humility. And before we claim humility it's worth remembering that it isn't much of a virtue unless we have something to be unassuming about. Before we can 'stand erect', hold our heads high, and wait for our liberation we have to take note of George Bernard Shaw's injunction that 'the Churches must learn humility as well as teach it'. Advent is the start of the learning curve.

⋆If this movable feast does not fall today then see note on p.xiii.

30 November

St Andrew

Just as the English had to travel east for their Patron, so did the Scots. Andrew was the apostle who, like Peter, was a fisherman. And that, in reality, is all that can be said of his authentic history. Scotland bore his cross – the shape of an X – and St Andrew's was named for him although again there is no record of his prowess with tee or niblick.

Fortunately, with little taint of Catholicism to mar it, the flag was retained when in 1562 Scotland adopted Calvinism as the country's official religion. What was left of Catholicism largely prospered in the west – where Columba had founded his monastery at Iona – and later, as Irish entry increased, in Glasgow.

Unsurprisingly, the Catholic met north of the Border bears little similarity to his fellow south, unless the comparison is made in Liverpool which shares something of the wild sectarianism of the past. As with the laity, so with the priests. Typical would be the Scots' own Cardinal, Thomas Winning: tough, state educated, a Doctor of Canon Law cum laude, a character who could have stepped from one of Bruce Marshall's early novels.

He enjoys, what so many south have forgotten, the sheer exhilaration of fighting for what he believes in and what he knows his Church teaches. Like Peter, he was hewn from the granite of his own nation.

Despising the limitations debt imposes he set about settling the bills his diocese owed. He succeeded. Firmly believing in John Paul's call to life he set up a lifeline for unmarried mothers so that the abortion rate would be cut. He succeeded. When the voices down south were either stilled or muted he cried out loud enough to be heard by the London media.

Glasgow and Westminster are separated by more than a few hundred miles. The gulf between them reminds us of the individuality of local Catholic churches, even when they share an island.

1 December

St Tudwal

L ike Alice's white rabbit I'm flustered. I'm late, I'm late – here it is December with so much unsaid that matters and so much said that doesn't matter one jot. No good saying that it is always that way, that you wave from the train at someone you love and think of all the things you should have said; that you pass a friend on the other side of the street rather than make up the quarrel; that you actually die without having articulated the love or the pride you have in those you're leaving.

And here it is December and I'm landed with a saint who did nothing to inspire me. Or did he? He was a Welshman who went to Brittany with all his friends and relatives and there he stayed for the rest of his life. So what? Big deal. Isn't that just what we all do? So what made him different? Why is he a saint and we're not likely to be one? Perhaps it was because, at the end of a long life, they all still loved him. Perhaps because he was never flustered, never in such a hurry that he didn't take time to listen to them.

As a Catholic it's been dinned into my ears, driven like a stake into my heart, that what I have to do is love my neighbour and, in loving him, I love God. It's as easy as that. It reminds me of a discussion at school. Your first duty, the old monk told us, is to save your own soul. Aghast at this unchivalrous comment I cried out scornfully, 'That's the most selfish thing I've heard in all my life.'

The monk grinned deviously. 'How do you save your soul?' he next asked me. 'And don't give me any twaddle about prayer,' he added mischievously (this black ghoul who spent six hours a day propped up in a prayer stall).

I told him patiently, as he knew so little about it. By doing good, the innocence of my youth replied.

'And if you don't do good?' this crafty monk pursued.

Then I lose my soul, I said.

He had won. I had lost. Or, had I won my soul? We'll never know. Well, not for a bit anyway.

2 December

———————⌒———————

Something of a thrill goes through me when I look at *The Oxford Dictionary of Saints* and see a blank. More exactly, a day without a Feast is a Ferial day. The idea of a feria was to give priests, and people too, a day off, as it were, simply to worship God and forget for a while all earthly concerns. It certainly wasn't because the Church had run out of either saints or inspiration. So a ferial is a challenge to get out and explore – the nature of God, the essence of what He said and did, and whether the Church He founded got it right.

Go to the Cheltenham God Cup – sorry, Gold Cup – and you'll find that Catholics are indeed gamblers. Apart from the larger part of the Irish clergy you'll find priests from all over Britain. It is their big day. And the crack is good. The chestnuts are not all horses.

'I thought you blessed that horse, Father?' complains the loser.

'Sure,' said the priest, 'and if you can't tell the blessing from the Last Rites you deserve to lose.'

We are gamblers, we Catholics. Big-time ones too. Just think of the stakes. There's this one life we're given. Perhaps short, perhaps long, it makes no difference – seen in the context of eternity every life's duration is miniscule. And what do we do with it?

We spend a fair proportion of it in worship of a Being we cannot see, with one man or woman when new models are being flaunted before us every day, in modest penury because crime is an offence against that invisible Being, in contemplation only of some of the most enticing goodies the world has to offer because ... well, because of Him again.

Our Faith, properly practised, is one of the toughest you can embrace. Jew, Moslem or Catholic – we are all players in the biggest celestial game that ever was devised. And just look how, over the centuries, we have played this game – cheating each other, injuring and killing each other and all in the name of the same Being whom we love so much. Well, that's what a ferial does for you. March back the saints.

3 December

St Francis Xavier

My God, I love Thee, not because
I hope for Heaven hereby;
Nor because they, who love Thee not,
Must burn eternally.
Thou, O my Jesus, Thou didst me
Upon the Cross embrace;
For me didst bear the nails and spear,
And manifold disgrace.

'O Deus, ego amo Te' (trans. Caswall)

And there you have him – hero, adventurer, soldier, fanatic, saint. One of the original 'gang of seven' who met with Ignatius Loyola and helped form what would become the Jesuits. Francis Xavier was 35 when he left Portugal for Goa on the first step of a missionary journey that would only end when he was 45 and died of utter fatigue.

His love song, 'O Deus, ego amo Te', burned with the best of him and the worst. It conveyed his passionate feeling for a crucified Lord and exposed a theological weakness – he firmly believed that those who did not embrace Catholicism were damned to Hell's fires.

In Goa today, Francis lives as if he had never left. The one-minded enthusiasm for the Faith which he sowed there never diminished and such was the power of his conversions that in Japan, where he led 2000 to Christ, all of them later died rather than renounce what he had taught them.

He probably gave rise to the calumny that Jesuits believed the ends would always justify the means. With the poor, he was poor; approaching the rich, he was wealthy. He used his wits, his courage and his intellect – all in abundance – until there was no more to give, and then he lay down and died on an obscure island in the China seas.

The Church devotes this, his Feast day, to special prayers for the migrants of this world, of whom he was certainly one.

4 December

ST JOHN DAMASCENE

T he Church has to be on the move, a pilgrim. We've spent our days with the past and with the present. Now it's time to look to the future. Here's one possibility.

The State Examiner opened his briefcase, eyed Fr Brown sternly, and said 'A clause has been added to the Statute of States Religions, paragraph 3, sub clause 4, concerning water, holy, the use of.'

The priest hid the memory from his eyes he had just had – it was of the freedom his predecessor 300 years before had enjoyed before Catholicism had come under the wing of the Federated Western States Myths and Religions Department.

'You are performing the stipulated three miracles a day?' went on the Examiner.

'I celebrate three Masses a day,' confirmed Fr Brown. 'None of which exceeds 30 minutes or is less than 25.'

As the Examiner then counted the stock of hosts, candles, cash received and expended, the priest risked a question: 'How many priests are to be licensed this year?'

The Examiner shook his head impatiently. 'The usual as per the Rome Agreement of 2098. There will be 50.75 priests per 555,000 per capita – just as Senator Pope agreed at the Canterbury Conference.'

Fr Brown nodded sadly. He knew he should come to terms with the fact that his branch of the Civil Service was grossly understaffed but he often wondered what impact the Faith would have if permitted more help.

The Examiner seemed satisfied and left in his helicar. Relieved, the priest turned to the little plastic altar and, although he knew it was not permitted until 22:35 hours, murmured a little prayer: 'O Great Alien Being, unspecified, above, credit to my account (Brown, priest, 77084) my thanks for the possible though not proven intercession made by You – or by Your agent – on this day. And, oh, don't let the Examiner have noticed the extra crucifix illegally kept in my room.'

He felt better for the secret prayer and went off for a lunch pill.

5 December

ST CHRISTINA OF MARKYATE ST JUSTINIAN

Only God the Weaver knows how He will finish His tapestry. Yet, the truth is that He has left the design in our hands . . . The dog awoke with a raging thirst. His bowl was empty so he made his way into the church in search of water. He had already been down the High Street, picking his way fastidiously through the piled bodies, sniffing at the hand of a dead child for moisture.

Inside it was cooler, even though the church was thronged with those who had rushed there after the sirens had sounded. He smelled water and found it in the holy water font, drinking until his little stomach could hold no more.

After a while, so sick did he feel, he lay still beside the body of the priest who had led the congregation's prayers, such desperate pleas, in the moments before the bomb had fallen.

'If it be Thy will, O Lord,' the priest had cried and the people had screamed back, 'Spare us, O Lord.' And a nun, she lay beside the priest, had pleaded, 'Holy Mother of God, intervene that people's hearts might be turned from war.'

But even as they had prayed other people, as frightened as they themselves, had pressed buttons thousands of miles away and the holocaust had begun.

The dog was sick again. Sick several times until, panting, he too lay prostrate like the others before the altar. Dimly he saw the tiny red light that still flickered there before the tabernacle. With what curiosity he had left, he wondered if in some way that light might yet help him. Then, sensing he knew not what, he sat back on his haunches, whined softly and then he too died.

Only the sanctuary lamp burned on, the only movement in the church, the town, the country, the world. Behind it lay the Blessed Sacrament. Between the Host within and the lamp without lay earth's only hope for the future. But, at this stage, did it have one?

ST NICHOLAS

H ere, in the depth of Advent, a hint of treats in store. Because
so little is known of Nicholas it was easy to create from him
the Santa Claus the children love. His association with gifts
came about when he was said to have given gold to three girls to
save them from prostitution. It was the Dutch who rescued him
from oblivion and created the giftbearer St Nicholas was to be. But
in England we have always had something of a fancy for him.

I like to think that round about now Nicholas has started his trek
earthward. Ruddy already with Heaven's glow he beams at two
cherubs on their flight upwards from earth. 'Look, look,' they cry, 'it's
Santa.' He promises them that when he returns they shall have the
presents they missed in their short lives.

It's a busy route, this road from Heaven to earth. The old, the
young, the timorous, the maimed, they all line the road down which
Nicholas roars. And, as he passes, he has a wave for them just as they
have a smile for him.

As always, his first stop will be by a barren hill in the Holy Land.
There he looks back to the stars and shouts, 'I'm here, Jesus, I'm here
again and, when it comes, a very happy Christmas to You!'

Up in Heaven, the Lord God of Hosts, Creator of the Universe,
Master of All Worlds, He the Eternal One, looks down on His tubby
emissary and smiles at the vision of His own childhood.

Poor Nicholas, so much to do, so many places to visit. And the
same gift to take to all. 'Dear Lord,' he roared as he came within
sight of the outline of Asia Minor, 'open men's hearts this year to this
great love I take on Your behalf. Please let them accept it.'

He had sacks of songs – for we cannot sing and hate at the same
time; humour, because we cannot laugh and despair; even some
tears, because tears show the heart is not asleep.

All gifts freely given by his good Lord to those who would accept
them. All they had to do was accept them. Would they, wondered St
Nicholas?

7 December

ST AMBROSE

————— ✑ —————

S emantics can be absurd. Transubstantiation is the monstrously ugly word developed to describe the most sensitive action there is within the universe. It is the act of turning bread and wine into the Body and Blood of Christ. It is the epicentre of our Faith, it is the miracle that makes Catholicism unique and perpetuates the division of Christian Churches. It is an act that cannot for any purpose be compromised.

St Ambrose, in the fourth century, was one of those early Fathers who first defined with surety what was to be the unique possession of every Catholic ordained priest, the power to consecrate:

> You say perhaps, 'My bread is of the usual kind.' But that bread is bread before the words of the sacraments; when consecration has been added, from bread it becomes the Flesh of Christ. Let us therefore prove this. How can that which is bread be the Body of Christ? By consecration. But in what words and in whose language is the consecration? Those of the Lord Jesus.
>
> St Ambrose, 'On the Sacraments'

Ambrose was high-born, an intellectual, a lawyer, but not a Christian when he was acclaimed by the people. It took one week for him to be baptized and consecrated a bishop. He brought to the Church of the late fourth century a keen mind and an advocate's skills. He was one of those who established Our Lady's prominent place:

> What is greater than the Mother of God? What more glorious than she whom Glory Itself chose? What more chaste than she who bore a body without contact with another body? Why should I speak of her other virtues? She was a virgin not only in body but in mind . . .
>
> St Ambrose, 'Concerning Virgins'

Despite his learning – or because of it – he expressed his belief simply: 'A blessed life may be defined as consisting simply and solely in the possession of goodness and truth.'

8 December

FEAST OF THE IMMACULATE CONCEPTION

'J e suis l'Immaculate Conception,' Our Lady told Bernadette Soubirous at the cave in Lourdes in 1858. It was just four years after Pius IX had made the solemn declaration defining what had been believed for centuries:

> The most holy Virgin Mary was, in the first moment of her concep-
> tion, by a unique gift of grace and privilege of Almighty God, in
> view of the merits of Jesus Christ the Redeemer of mankind, pre-
> served free from all stain of original sin.

Back in the mid fourth century St Ephrem had prayed to Christ with these words: 'You and Your mother are the only ones who are totally beautiful in every way. For in You, O Lord, there is no stain, and in Your mother no stain.'

St Bernard, in the twelfth century, found difficulty with the belief that Pius IX was to make a dogma. He believed Our Lady's birth was holy but not her conception. Then he added, 'What I have said is in submission to the judgment of whosoever is wiser than myself; and especially I refer the whole of it, as of all matters of a similar kind, to the authority and decision of the See of Rome . . .'

But Our Lady found a certain champion a century on. This was Duns Scotus and he argued fervently for the Immaculate Conception to be generally accepted by the Church as a dogma. His view was this:

> Mary most assuredly needed Christ as a Redeemer, for she would
> have incurred original sin in the usual way from her parents, if she
> had not been preserved by the grace of the Mediator.
>
> Duns Scotus, Commentary

But for most Catholics such nitpicking is redundant. The vision of the Lady born without sin is too real for us to ignore or to quarrel about. And then, again, how simply Our Lady put the vexsome aside – 'Je suis l'Immaculate Conception,' she so assuredly said.

9 December

ST WOLFEIUS

~

Today it arrived – the first Christmas card. As usual it comes from a wine merchant I used just once many years ago for a great celebration now forgotten. It shows a bibulous Santa, perched on a mountain of bottles. Sadly, he looks like me even though I never drink wine.

The card will be the first of about 40. Ten years ago it would be nearer 200. But as time passes so do the people you once knew, and the reason for knowing them. Live long enough, and you know for certain that soon the cards will dwindle to fewer than ten – just one of the odd facts of life.

But at least the hopeful vintner has reminded me of Advent, given me the nudge I need to visit Jospice and buy my 40 or so cards. Most of us buy charity cards now – one of the better aspects of today's awareness. Cafod will benefit, Aid to the Church in Need and any number of Catholic charities. These cards will be purpose-fully modest, cheaply produced. But when we send them they will have a purpose other than telling someone we are still alive.

A friend of mine made a modest living writing the greetings that go inside cards. At first he was over-literary and he was ticked off. 'The message must be simple, free of any ambiguity, bland enough never to offend', he was instructed. So, no verses telling of the Incarnation, Virgin Birth, Redemption or the like. Camels and fellows with odd hats were fine; snow in abundance just great. 'A Little Babe is Born' just about acceptable but don't specify gender. 'Unto us a King is Born' was argumentative, confusing for the non-Christian and baffling for the lapsed. Finally he gave up, finding it less hassle to do the jokes for saucy seaside cards instead.

The thing is, though, that we have started to 'think Christmas'. It's a frame of mind, a curious panic that even the best of Christians cannot escape. However much we tut-tut about the earliness of Christmas we cannot escape the mood. Perhaps the perfect Catholic can spend Advent as it should be spent. How few of us are perfect.

10 December

ST EULALIA

A missioner complained to me that his Order couldn't get publicity. And without it no one would hear about the Order and vocations would dry up. I asked him what news he had submitted that the papers wouldn't print. 'We've just had two men celebrate 50 years each in Africa,' he said How did I tell him, without hurting his feelings, that was no news at all? But I did. And I hurt him – because we both knew what 100 years' service meant.

'That's not news?' he said sadly.

'No,' I said, 'that's life, not news'

News would have been the jubilarian running off with a Spice Girl, or the men betting their Order's all on a nag and winning.

Advent is all about news. It's what we call in the trade 'a teaser', a prior announcement that something big is on the way. And John the Baptist was no slouch when it came to grabbing the headlines. You cannot doubt that if Herod had a pet lizard called Humphrey then John would have made the most of it. This wild man from the desert was as shrill as any tabloid – just as truculent and outspoken He never temporized, was never in awe of authority nor pandered to a need to be loved.

Yet John knew his public, knew its cupidity and used it in spectacular fashion. In a real sense, Christ was topped by John and tailed by Paul – both master publicists. Over the centuries little has changed. The art of the herald is now that of the promoter. Their purpose is the same – to make the product better known. Virgin would be just another struggling airline without Branson, National Socialism another 'ism without Hitler, the Missionaries of Charity just a do-gooder speck without the memory of Mother Teresa.

My friend's Order presently lacks this charism. Perhaps it's up to him or another to supply it. Churches too need it – single voices and identifiable, prepared to joust for the honour of His Church and advance its cause. And what better time than Advent for Church leaders to be heard above the clamour of mediocrity.

11 December

DANIEL THE STYLITE

D aniel spent some 33 years perched on top of columns – it was a way of meditation he had learned from a more famous percher, Simeon Stylites. You have to assume that not only did they want to be alone, they always wanted to be nearer Heaven.

We were all brought up to understand that Paradise was 'up there'. And when we looked into a clear sky it was not hard to believe it. But then the scientists sent up space rockets not just to the moon but to the farther planets. And there was nothing. Just evidence of further galaxies. And certainly no sign of Heaven. As God handled us with such thoughtful care it became increasingly apparent that Heaven was not an identifiable spot in space. But, if not there, then where?

As ever, Hell was much more apparent. Hell was 'down there'. And we know with certainty that in the depths of the earth we find raging fires. So, whilst Hell is physically at hand, Heaven remains geographically elusive.

Could it be that, knowing our limitations, God made Heaven more accessible than we imagine? Could it be He placed it in a child's eyes for us all to see? No need then for meandering rockets to visit black space, since Heaven is here all the time. For every child originates in the mind of God – their very existence the result of His intention. No wonder babies look at you the way they do – their eyes are still full of that last glimpse of Him. So the vilest of crimes is the theft of that innocence.

Christmas is only a few dreams away. And the parent the child's only defence against a culture ready to snatch away their child's innocence. Christ is best put back into Christmas not by poster campaigns but by protecting the innocence of the Heaven you see in the child's smile – that same one it shares with the Baby Jesus we are preparing for.

346

12 December

St Jane Chantal   St Finnian of Clonard

C atholics still firmly believe that like gets on better with like, so mothers still tend to seek out 'good Catholic boys' for their daughters. Like certainly attracted like in the case of St Jane Frances de Chantal. Early widowed, in 1604 she met St Francis de Sales and, much later, St Vincent de Paul. They were a formidable trio but the greatest influence in this good woman's life remained the writings of St Francis on the Love of God. You can share them:

Mount Calvary is the academy of love.

All is made for charity, and charity for God . . . Charity is much stronger and more assiduous than mere natural affection.

We cannot help conforming ourselves to what we love.

We may be excused for not always being bright, but we are not excused for not being always gracious, yielding and considerate.

The love that desires to walk to God's will through consolations walks ever in fear of taking the wrong path; but the love that strikes straight through dryness toward the will of God walks in assurance.

If God has stripped you of the sense of His presence, it is in order that even His presence may no longer occupy your heart, but Himself.

The height of love's ecstasy is to have our will not in its own contentment but in God's.

The union to which love aspires is spiritual . . . The end of love is no other thing than the union of the lover and the thing loved.

On the premise of this teaching of the Love of God Jane Chantal founded the Visitation Sisters – their charism lying in their humility and gentleness. It is an Order that has survived more than 350 years.

13 December

3RD SUNDAY OF ADVENT★

S hout for joy! It's Gaudete Sunday – Rejoice in the Lord always! Whatever happened to our sense of joy? Can't you just imagine the faces around you at Mass today when this message is read?

> I want you to be happy, always happy in the Lord; I repeat, what I
> want is your happiness. Let your tolerance be evident to everyone; the
> Lord is very near. There is no need to worry; but if there is anything
> you need, pray for it, asking God for it with prayer and thanksgiving.

Even the priest will dress for the occasion, in the rose vestments reserved for celebration. And what about us today, will we join the party do you think, will we 'shout with cries of joy'?

God help us, probably not. Can't you just hear it? The priest says: 'Prepare our hearts and remove the sadness that hinders us from feeling the joy and hope.' We say: 'Will it be a fresh bird or a frozen one?'

The Reader says: 'Sing a psalm to the Lord for He has done glorious things!' We say: 'What on earth do we give Aunt Maud this year?'

We all say, with our lips: 'Alleluia, alleluia! The spirit of the Lord has been given to me. He has sent me to bring good news to the poor. Alleluia!'

Yet, deep down in our hearts, we are saying: 'However will I get around the shops in time?'

It's not the Church's fault – nor is it God's – that instead of being effervescent wine today, bubbling with the joy extended to us, we're stolid Christmas puds, weighed down and lumpish when we should be sharing in the party we're called to share. If all we know is the fear of God and not His joy in His creation then we've failed ourselves and our Church.

I've this theory – and I've seen more than one priest try to prove it – that when we find joy in church then too we find God.

★If this movable feast does not fall today then see note on p.xiii.

348

14 December

St John of the Cross

———— ❧ ————

He that seeks not the Cross of Christ seeks not the glory of Christ.
St John of the Cross, Spiritual Sentences and Maxims

Mystical theology is a branch of learning such as is a verdant island in a huge ocean. It is a 'pure knowledge of God' which a man or woman reaches primarily from contemplation and an intimacy of soul denied most of us. John of the Cross was such a mystic and, unsurprisingly, his friend and adviser was Teresa of Avila. Both Carmelites, it was Teresa who persuaded John to join the Discalced (reformed) branch, for which he was imprisoned for nine months in Toledo. There, in desperate conditions, he was to write some of his finest poetry. This extract is from his best known work, *The Dark Night of the Soul*:

> In a dark night
> With anxious love inflamed,
> O, happy lot!
> Forth unobserved I went,
> My house being now at rest . . .
> O, guiding night;
> O, night more lovely than the dawn;
> O, night that hast united
> The lover with his beloved,
> And changed her into her love.

Mostly we are not mystics. Certainly I've never met one knowingly. Even the Church has bred them but rarely. As I see it, the mystic is the person who, in pursuit of God, trips over His shadow and so is embraced by Him, absorbed by Him. Yet, even for the mystic, God remains just that – shadow.

15 December

OFFA, KING OF ESSEX

Offa was as unlike modern Essex Man as it is possible to get – he abandoned his royal rights, travelled to Rome and died a monk. But then, often enough, people are not as we think they are or should be.

A friend's son knows a man whose sister has a brother whose son is a window-cleaner called Mike. And it seems he has the archbishop's house on his round. One morning he was there early doing the dining-room windows when the High Priest (as he calls him) came in for his breakfast. Now Mike had never given thought to a high priest doing anything like eating breakfast – just posh dinners and the like. He watched, intrigued, as the prelate knocked the top off an egg, cut his toast into soldiers, and then dunked them.

At this stage, boggle-eyed, Mike had descended his ladder, lit a cigarette and meditated on what he'd seen. For not only had the bishop got egg on his nose but a watchful nun had brushed it away. My friend told me that the experience had changed Mike – it had removed the barrier between 'them' and 'us'. From then on he had listened carefully to what the bishop had said and always told his chums, 'He's one of us, you know.'

Advent serves the same purpose for us. Jesus is presented to us as a figure we can all emphathize with – a baby. For, despite what fond mothers keenly believe, one baby is much the same as another. A baby is a person we can immediately visualize. There is no 'Him' and 'us' – just a baby we recognize and can love.

In Lent we knew the Man in just as vivid a way. But it was a Man lacerated, suffering, wounded mentally and physically. We shared His hurt because we could see it. Now, as Advent draws on, we share Our Lady's delighted apprehension and Joseph's quiet pride. For all of us are faced with the reality of His humanity. Make having comprehension of the Holy Family's feelings just now one of the Christmas presents you get for yourself.

16 December

Today it starts – the deluge of canned, recorded entertainment that will last until the New Year. Mushy pap produced by entertainers long since dead for audiences long disappeared. Our external world of titillation turns in on itself, its only purpose being to satiate us.

The Church just now isn't like that – it's tense, tingling with anticipation. It doesn't want an audience of couch potatoes but congregations throbbing with expectancy of the unexpected. Because however much we think we know what is coming, we cannot be sure until the last moment. The Nativity of Christ is no tired re-run of a distant spectacular – year upon year it is different, never quite the same, because we are never the same, never identical with the 'self' that started the year so ignorant of what the months would bring.

Even the gifts we'll bring to the crib will be novel. We cannot present the identical heart we brought last year, nor the same soul. Heavier or lighter, more discerning or more abused, the heart and soul we offer Him will have altered. Just now, in Advent, we're doing the packaging. But all the finest wrappings won't disguise the value of the gift inside. The Christ Child won't tarry long with the tinsel of presentation, not when He's anxious to see what we've brought Him.

Today, at long last, we can sing the first of our songs to Him:

> O come, O come, Emmanuel,
> And ransom captive Israel,
> That mourns in lonely exile here,
> Until the Son of God appear.
> Rejoice, Rejoice, Emmanuel
> Shall come to thee, O Israel.
>
> Anon (trans. J. Neale)

Who wants to hear sleighbells ringing when the Church this week offers you the chorus of angels?

17 December

LAZARUS

Advent announces a coming – it's all about life. So here's an appropriate remembrance today, the dead man raised to life by Jesus. John's Gospel devotes almost a chapter to the raising of Lazarus, an astonishing amount of detail for a single incident albeit a miracle of astounding proportion. Perhaps the clue lies in the fact that Lazarus's resurrection almost immediately brought Jesus to the close attention of the chief priest, Caiphas, who on this occasion uttered the famous words: 'You do not reflect that it is best for us if one man is put to death for the sake of the people, to save a whole nation from destruction.'

What happened to Lazarus when he was given a second chance to live is the stuff of legends, but all of the stories appear to report that he sailed with his sisters from the Holy Land and later became a bishop.

More importantly, his name was used by St Vincent de Paul for a special 'Congregation of the Priests of the Mission' whose purpose was to give missions in the country areas first of France and then internationally. They were given the popular name 'Lazarists' for their purpose was to bring alive the consciences of the peasant folk.

The initiative came about when Vincent heard the confession of a well-placed peasant farmer who revealed that for many years he had made sacrilegious confessions – that is, omitting his mortal sins. For a Catholic, this is one of the most serious sins of all, lying to the Holy Spirit. It revealed to Vincent that the false confession was more common than believed and so the 'Lazarists' were formed, opening houses across Italy and Poland and even in the Far East.

Lazarus also gave his name to a Crusader Order whose members followed the troops, opening hospitals for lepers. They finally concentrated their efforts on the famous hospital in Paris known as St Lazare.

18 December

St Flannan St Mawnan

Y ou have to wonder when church was first associated with the great yawn. From Chaucer to Chesterton, through 200 years of *Punch* cartoons, the image persists of a dull, stolid people at prayer. Advent's plea – stay awake! – should do just that, shake us out of lethargy. The markets are awake, already they're cutting the string on an avalanche of Easter eggs ready for Boxing Day.

What about us? We have three Advent candles lit now, their flames a sight more compelling than the fairy-lights festooning the streets. And what of the Baptist? His coat of camel hair, and his diet of honey and locusts aren't the goodies you're stashing away for next week!

Years ago the Knights of St Columba made a valiant attempt to put Christ back into Christmas. But, let's be honest, our own preparation will parallel the invasive materialism around us gift for gift, anxiety for anxiety. Gifts don't buy themselves, nor do cards fly on angels' wings. Nativity concerts, carol evenings – they all beat Christ's birth to the draw.

Our Advent task isn't to take the anticipatory thrill out of Christmas – do that and we're dead in the water. Worse, we're caricatures just as *Punch* had us – morose old sobersides lost in our own solemnity. And in danger of typifying a joyous Christ as a grim old party-pooper.

We've a week left, no more, to put Christ at the centre of what's happening and to make the unchurched folk around us understand what all the excitement's about. We are the Christ Bearers – we sing His songs, spread His affection, shine His light. We bring humour, laughter, the essence of the glorious Nativity to all the chores we have to do. Our doors have His star on them, our trees His angels, our cards His message. There is still time to bring Christ into Christmas, to take His smile to those living alone, to long-term patients, to those with whom we've quarrelled. Putting Christ into Christmas is easier – and more urgent – than we think.

B ored to the tips of his horns the Devil summoned his satyrs to a general audience. It was not an invitation they could refuse. Anyway, the last one had been for the roasting of a cardinal. It had been a merry affair. But this one wasn't.

'The job's not what it was,' complained Lucifer. 'The fun's gone out of it.'

There was general clapping of trotters – this Advent had been the dullest for centuries. 'Take England,' snarled the Eminent Evil One. 'We've been so successful making their leaders fearful of accusations of hypocrisy that we've turned them into moral mutes. And in this great silence pornography goes unfettered, whilst homosexual sex is acceptable for youngsters in their teens. All the years we've spent undermining purity and now, without any effort, they've not only destroyed purity but the Natural Law too.'

A young satyr in Drug Encouragement nodded. 'In our department we know it's only a question of time before they legalize all drugs.'

The Devil nodded morosely. 'Temptation will soon be a thing of the past,' he grumbled. 'Conscience is no longer perturbed by killing the unborn and pornography is the rule rather than the exception.' He meditated. 'There was a time when morality could be relied upon to come full circle. But now, somehow, it's shot off the circle. It's headed . . .'

'To Hell?' suggested an imp hopefully.

The Devil gave it thought. 'No,' he said sadly, 'to earn Hell they have to make a deliberate choice between right and wrong. Now they don't know the difference between the sacred and the profane.'

The satyrs were puzzled. 'But if they don't come here, where will they go?' No one could come up with an answer.

Far, far, far away the Son who had been listening to the debate turned to His Father. He saw a tear fall from the Almighty One and realized His Father was about to close the experiment they had named Man.

20 December

4TH SUNDAY OF ADVENT*

~

I t was a thoughtful gesture by the Church to make today a special day for expectant mothers. It showed not just sensitivity but sound theological sense too; another way to emphasize the humanity of the divinity soon to be born. In so many ways, this prowl of ours through the Catholic year has led us to realize how precious the Church holds the humanity of Christ. Where the pre-Vatican II Church stressed His divinity, the post 1965 Church went out of its way to reveal Christ's human nature.

A consequence of this is that the Nativity scene is no longer a sentimental image – rather, it is stark reality. All that we are, He was. There is no way we can distance ourselves between Jesus who felt as we feel, suffered as we can suffer, was born as we were born.

When we leave Mass today we leave conscious that later in the week we'll be back for a birthday party. By now we'll know we cannot go to that party empty-handed, we'll need to decide upon a gift. And He asks for so little, this Babe lying in the straw. He wants no gold, apart from the glow in your heart; no rich ointments or scents. All He wants is for us to say 'Happy Birthday' and mean it.

The fourth Advent Candle is lit. So we know when we return the church will be different, strangely changed. There will be a crib in the corner ready for the children to tiptoe there to greet Him. There will be the warmth of candles, the perfume of holly, ivy and spruce. It's so right that we decorate His home for His birthday. The gift we take is reconciliation. As today's psalm implores:

> God of hosts, turn again, we implore,
> look down from heaven and see.
> Visit this vine and protect it,
> the vine your right hand has planted . . .
> And we shall never forsake you again:
> give us life that we may call upon your name.

*If this movable feast does not fall today then see note on p.xiii.

ST PETER CANISIUS ST THOMAS, APOSTLE

Because of Herod's interruption of their journey the Wise Men missed it. And so did the shepherds, because at that moment they were tending a lamb who was poorly. The ass could have seen it, had he not been chomping on a particularly sweet piece of straw at the time. As for the ox, he later claimed he had seen it. But there are those who think that dumb fellow is just a bit of a fibber.

You'd have expected Joseph to have caught the moment but, to tell the truth, at the end of what had been a very long day, he was taking 40 winks. And who could blame him? There was the innkeeper, of course, he had slipped into his rough annexe to ensure his guests were not using too much straw. But he missed the second, too, for at that moment he chose to count the pennies from the night's takings.

The one who came closest was a young Roman trooper on his first posting abroad. He'd been drinking in the inn and stopped outside the shed on his way back to his billet. But a yawn had taken him as he peered inside and so he too lost the opportunity. Strangely enough, Marcus P. Quintus was to be in charge of an execution detail some 30 years on. But he never had cause to link the events.

So it was Mary the mother – and she alone – who witnessed the first smile on her Baby's face all that time ago. It was one of the many secrets she kept all her life – until that day when Our Lord, her Son, welcomed her into Heaven. She reminded Him of the moment and He smiled, taking her into His arms.

The Nativity was so simple an event in the course of time that you'd wonder why so many learned people try to debunk it today. Many a child was born in a stable in those days; the poor invariably help the poor – so the shepherds were there. And the Magi were following a star – as the best of us do. So this week makes only one demand upon our credulity – that we accept in Faith that the Babe born to Mary was Who He said He was. Nothing more. Just that. It is enough.

22 December

ST FRANCES CABRINI

Mother Cabrini is the cold douche we need today – the reminder that whilst we're scurrying wildly in search of that last little luxury there are a whole heap of people numbly wondering where the next sip of water will come from. The world is still that unjust. Not God, mark you, but the world. He gave enough to feed and shelter all – we are the ones unable to distribute it fairly.

The Italian nun, Mother Cabrini, realized this and tried to even matters up for the thousands of Italian immigrants living in total squalor in New York. Earlier she had done what many had done before her – having been refused entry to an Order because of her health, she ended up founding her own Order, the Missionary Sisters of the Sacred Heart.

She took her Sisters to America and by the time she died in 1917 she had some 1500 nuns working in orphanages in eight countries. In 1946 (the war had delayed matters), she was canonized as the first saint of the United States of America. The little daughter of an Italian farmer had come a long way and achieved a miracle for the needy little ones.

Our Lord Himself warned us that we would always have the poor, which is a practical reason for admiring Him. He was no Utopian, no wishy-washy do-gooder who painted pictures the electorate would welcome. He knew this Man He had created, was aware of the pitfalls of human nature and was blind to the blandishments of rank or wealth. How many times did He reject both? The real privilege, He told us often enough, was possessing a soul and being able to ensure it found Paradise at the end. But, and it was such a huge but, He told us the only way to achieve that was to love our neighbour.

Was it coincidence, you have to wonder, that the twentieth century started with Mother Cabrini and ended with Mother Teresa? The backgrounds of both were startlingly similar, because they both founded their own Orders, they both lived and died for the poor and the dispossessed. Was Our Lord telling us something? You have to believe it.

I t is the day to put up the crib. Mine may be only about three foot wide by two foot high but it is a more involved task than you may think. It is – or was – a masterpiece of fretwork which must have taken my maternal grandfather many months to make. This he did about 120 years ago when he first arrived in England from Bavaria. Behind him he left a brother, a parish priest in a Black Forest village, and any number of cousins who would be killed in the German Army. It was his distaste of the Prussians which brought him to Liverpool. And there he tried his vocation for three years in the Redemptorist monastery. Excuse this biography, but it's essential if you want to understand what 'putting up the crib' means to me.

Pieces are missing, or broken. The Babe, made out of wax by my grandfather, is missing a hand. St Joseph is cracked and Our Lady's eyes are now sightless. But it has been erected in our family every Christmas for well over a century. As I put it together there will still be the faint aroma of grandpa's fat, stubby cigar; there will be the memory of so many other Christmasses and the sum total of both their joys and sadnesses will absorb me the while. For not every Christmas has been joyous – some have served only to underline the losses of the year, others have only accentuated sickness of heart and body. But, whatever the circumstances, there has always been a hand willing to erect the crib.

The Babe is not placed in the crib until the return from Midnight Mass – tradition. He is then thanked for the blessings of another year – tradition. He is then toasted in very tiny glasses of brandy – tradition. Then a night light is left burning before Him to keep Him warm during the night – tradition. So much of Christmas is just that – tradition. And in it there is security, a sense of permanence, of continuity. Tradition – a long Catholic tradition – has been the glue that keeps families together. Tradition and prayer and faith.

24 December

CHRISTMAS EVE

~

S omewhere on the very periphery of time there are just 15 minutes which are our very own and tonight we lay claim to them. When you return from Midnight Mass – or even if you are going in the morning – stand outside in the chill and look hard in the sky for the North Star. Locate it and then be still; in the silence of Christmas morn grant Him the space He's been trying to share with you all the long year through.

Today, if it followed our usual course, will have been frenetic – a series of vital tasks that, in the stillness of the night, will suddenly feel so trivial. For there is no more to do. For good or for ill we've prepared the way for the Christ Child, we've lit His path with love, marked His way to our hearts with our longing. And so soon, so very soon, He comes.

> At last Thou art come, little Savior
> And Thine angels fill midnight with song;
> Thou art come to us, gentle Creator,
> Whom Thy creatures have sighed for so long.
> F. Faber, 'Christmas Night'

On Christmas Eve we are all shepherds. However else we fill our days at other times, on Christmas Eve we are a humble folk with only one purpose in mind – to be there at the manger to see the Child. And, perforce, when we see the Child we see the mother. And in that vision we as Catholics see our Church. Not this time as a monolith planted on rock but as a fragile unity of majesty and protection.

The manger visited tonight will be all things to all people. For some a symbol of family strength, for others a dream unfulfilled, and, sadly, there are the ones who will miss the little figure of the Babe and see only the 'Fyffes Bananas' stencil on the crib roof. If any are to be pitied this night it is them – the ones who cannot see the star for the cloud.

359

CHRISTMAS DAY, NATIVITY OF THE LORD

There is no feeling quite like it – opening your eyes and ears to Christmas Day. Still fresh in your heart is the memory of the One who visited your soul only hours before in such a rapture of delight. The songs still echo in your mind of a holy night, a silent night, a chorus of angels and your own joyous trek home.

It is unbelievable that there is anyone who can live through this day without being accompanied by the vision of the Christ Child and His mother. They are there in the first break of light, in the squeals and laughter of children. They are there mirrored in the candle-shadowed table, in the sparkling baubles on the tree and the bounty of the table. They are there in the opening of the gifts and, above all, they are there in the toast to absent friends.

For if it is anything, Christmas is an ongoing kaleidoscope of memories. No Christmas is ever quite the same, no Christmas carries on to further years identical events or even faces. It is a day which marks the passage of time and people in a unique way. For, as the hours move on, the memories become that more acute. Perhaps it is the unaccustomed wine, the food's richness – whatever, towards dusk there is a remembrance of times past. Joy is tempered by a sense of nostalgia until, quite suddenly, the only priority in life that has purpose is the love of family.

Because of this, today can also be the loneliest day of the year for so many. It can be a day without voices, only echoes. And if it is like that for you today then you will need to invite three guests to your home – Mary, Joseph and their Child. Loneliness is a state of mind as well as circumstance. But with that family present you need fear neither. If you will, make a place for them at your table and be assured they will join you. Neither will they be mute companions for they are familiar friends and know you well. Be cosy in their company as they will be in yours. After all, the memories you have, they will also have shared. You have so much in common.

26 December

FEAST OF ST STEPHEN

―――――― ✐ ――――――

O f course, you gave your children the best gift of all yesterday, didn't you? The gift of a loving memory. If you didn't quite complete the packaging in time then there's still an opportunity today. You see, so rare a delight as Christmas should not be left to Disney. It shouldn't be a Pavlovian response to the demands of the marketplace, the bullying bleats of the ads on TV. We may be largely water but our mind is 100% memory.

These three days of Christmas are for the creation of memories – not the ones drummed into our minds by commercials, but memories only the families who worship at the crib will understand and treasure. You cannot start too soon giving your children the gifts that really matter, the ones that cannot run out of batteries, and don't wane.

Memories are gifts, heirlooms, that families pass on down the generations. Sure, the angel brought out year after year from her battered box is past her prime, the familiar baubles are growing a bit tatty, but Christmas would not be the same without these veterans.

Earlier and earlier children are being forced to find their memories outside the home. They're finding them on the impersonal television, the soulless Internet, in the vicarious adoration of megastars of sport and showbiz. And these are memories that are just cluttering, not memories of love.

There is a button somewhere which transforms your house into a home. You still have today in which to press it. You cannot do it on your own – you'll need the help of the Babe in the crib and all the simplicity He can give you. But then, in the years to come, you and your children will have the memory of Christmas past to help warm Christmas present.

Today the Church gives us the memory of its first martyr, Stephen, whom Paul helped stone to death. But the memory never left Paul. And just look what happened then.

FEAST OF THE HOLY FAMILY⋆
ST JOHN, APOSTLE

W̲e are back at Mass. It seems so soon and the church is still warm from the Christmas candles. Or is it the warmth from the crib in the chapel, or the greenery which now has settled into its cosy niches?

No wonder the psalm is so celebratory:

> How lovely is your dwelling place,
> Lord, God of hosts.
> My soul is longing and yearning,
> is yearning for the courts of the Lord.
> My heart and my soul ring out their joy
> to God, the living God.
> They are happy who dwell in your house, O Lord.

And we are happy. Some would say satiated, but that's not true. We are happy because we feel at one and comfortable with the Holy Family. Unlike St John, the other Feast today, the Holy Family produces no mystery, is not subject to conjecture or doubt. The Holy Family is as we would have our own family – in accord, at peace and loving.

Sadly the same cannot be said of John's authorship of the fourth Gospel. There is no doubt about John the apostle beloved of Christ, but seemingly it is possible that he was not the John whose story of Jesus seems so intimate.

But today it is good to associate John with the Holy Family – he was, after all, the one to whom Jesus gave care of His mother. He was closest of all to Jesus at the Last Supper, was at the Transfiguration and in that garden of unease, Gethsemane. Finally he was the apostle who ran with Peter to the empty tomb. He was as much a family friend as he was a disciple and no one could doubt his right to share today with the family he knew and loved so well.

⋆If this movable feast does not fall today then see note on p.xiii.

28 December

FEAST OF THE HOLY INNOCENTS

~

Without doubt, Herod was a harsh ruler. But he had cause. The Magi had told him that the Child born in Bethlehem would one day usurp his throne, would be King of the Jews. For Herod, this was not to be taken lightly, not in an age when prophets were taken seriously and rumours were a ruler's worst enemy. He had spoken at some length with the Wise Men, they had commanded both his interest and his concern. His massacre of all the babies under two in Bethlehem was therefore appalling but quite in keeping with the customs of the times.

A little over 1900 years later another massacre was to take place. The circumstances were different. For a start, those babies slain posed no threat to either ruler or government, neither had they yet been born. The cruelty of this massacre lay in the fact that the babies would be murdered whilst still in the womb and not over a short space of time, as at Bethlehem, but over years. And not dozens of babies would be done to death, but millions.

The Abortion Act roused Catholics in a manner unknown before or since. Even Catholics marginalized by their Church's rules felt bound to make their protest felt and, for the first time, Moslems and Catholics were able to act in mutual detestation of a law which condemned the babe in the womb to death.

In the case of anti-abortion measures it was the laity that led the Church's reaction. Church leaders were slow to recognize the evil taking place and perhaps felt some temerity in those days in opposing government legislation. They lost the initiative and never really regained it, the defence of the unborn resting largely upon a handful of concerned MPs and a vast network of outraged Catholics.

Today a host of organizations fight the corner of the unborn child, all of them knowing that what they do can only be a limitation of the slaughter – the principle has been accepted and is unlikely to be rejected, although it could well be soon extended to the aged. And that's something even Herod would have baulked at.

St Thomas of Canterbury

R esponsibility can play havoc with a young thing's life. Ask Thomas à Becket. Until 1162 he was as bright a gadabout as you'd wish to meet and amongst his more lively chums he numbered Henry II, King of England. For a jape – and to bring the Church more closely under control – Henry made Becket, the amiable livewire, his Archbishop of Canterbury. But alas, Becket was not to be his archbishop but God's and the pope's. And so the whole sorry affair began that ended only in Thomas' martyrdom.

This volteface won't surprise contemporary Catholics, many of whom are accustomed to seeing their clerical chums raised to high rank and thereafter strangers to them. Their reaction is not unlike Henry's, although they do draw the line at the murder which so enraged twelfth-century England, and ensured Thomas' canonization.

The mildest of Catholic clerics undergoes an almost immediate and lasting personality change when he becomes a bishop. As a priest he was a man apart; as a bishop he is a priest apart. If you are a Catholic you know – if you're going to be a Catholic you should know – that our bishops are quite unlike those of other Churches.

Since their hierarchy was restored in England in 1850 they have been individually muted – a body of up to 30 men who speak only through spokesmen or through their cardinal. It is as if they do not yet fully realize that the low profile required of them in the late nineteenth century is not what is expected of them at the start of the twenty-first. In point of fact, their profile was higher 150 years ago than it is now.

Collegiality is one thing – and we recognize its place in the modern Church. But expressing the fervent mind of an enthusiastic Church needs more than balanced documentation tidily produced by civil servants and made neat journalese by a cooperative press office.

The world will have need in this twenty-first century for inspired, individual voices – the Spirit lies uneasily on Church trying to be government.

St Egwin

―――

Fable is all that remains of the memory of Egwin, eighth century Bishop of Worcester. It is the Church's task to ensure that in the years to come Catholicism does not become just such another fable, that it remains the repository of the historical truths of Jesus Christ its Founder. And to this end Catholics are urged to a trust in God:

> Always place in God thy trust,
> Will and do what's right and true;
> Let thy soul be brave and just;
> Show thy Lord a humble mind;
> Thou shalt thus His favour find;
> Love but few and simple things;
> Simple life much comfort brings.
> Thomas à Kempis, 'In Domino semper Spera'
> (trans. D. Donahoe)

St Teresa of Jesus wrote much the same in her breviary:

> Let nothing disturb thee,
> Nothing affright thee;
> All things are passing;
> God never changeth;
> Patient endurance
> Attaineth to all things;
> Who God possesseth
> In nothing is wanting;
> Alone God sufficeth.
> (trans. Henry W. Longfellow)

In this peculiar hiatus between one year and the next the Catholic must take time to think on what is taught so often about the transient nature of our lives here. The sole accomplishment worth recording is what we have done for our neighbour who, in effect, is Christ.

31 December

St Sylvester

~

Buried cosily under the wide yews at Belmont Abbey near Hereford is the long, lanky skeleton of Brother Sylvester. Like his namesake, his past was a closed book to us boys. We just knew that he had been a Benedictine laybrother forever. He served us great helpings of revolting fish pie from which huge bones stood rampant – but always in silence and with laughter in his eyes. He chivvied us on to brave acts on the rugby field – but was there to mend us when we fell. He chased us from the rosy-appled orchard – but always had a fruit in his habit for us. He roused us at dawn to serve Mass – but had the forbidden delight of cocoa waiting for us after. He seemed always to be there, and silent. Only long afterwards did I learn just how distinguished a man he had been before entering the monastery as a lowly laybrother.

For the life of me I cannot think why he comes to mind on this last day of what has been, for me, a long year. All I can suppose is that his spirit wandered by – in the silent, effortless way he had – and glanced at the pile of words by my side. There must have been a slight shake of his head as he whispered to himself and to me: 'So many words, so many words – to say something so simple.'

He'd be right, of course, even if it would make poor pickings for a book. Jesus, faith, life, love, the best of Catholicism, all are so simple. It's only we who complicate what is self-evident and natural.

Not just a year is passing tonight but a generation, my generation of the 1920s. On balance, we did our Faith little service. We were the fag end of the 'old' Church, never wholly at ease with things of the post-Vatican II Church. Yet our vaunted discipline failed – failed to keep both priests and people in the wild 1960s, failed to imbue our children with the full glory that is the Church. Yet, even as Jesus promised, here at the start of a new millennium there are so many with a true realization of the love of God. And to them we pass the the flame of Faith that they might blow the embers into a blaze.

BIBLIOGRAPHY

W. E. Addis and Thomas Arnold, *Catholic Dictionary*, Routledge and Keegan Paul Ltd, 1960

The Broughton Catholic Charitable Society, *The Broughton Song Catechism of the Catholic Church*, Geoffrey Chapman, 1999

G. K. Chesterton, *Orthodoxy*, The Bodley Head, 1908
—*All Things Considered*, extract in *The Book of Catholic Quotations*, John Calder, 1957
—*The Catholic Church and Conversion*, Burns and Oates, 1926
—*Lepanto*, from *Poems by Gilbert Keith Chesterton*, Burns and Oates, 1915

John Dove SJ, *Strange Vagabond of God*, Gracewing, 1997

David Farmer, *The Oxford Dictionary of Saints*, Oxford University Press, 1997

Grail Breviary Psalter, Geoffrey Chapman

John A. Hardon, SJ, *Modern Catholic Dictionary*, Robert Hale, 1981

St John of the Cross, *The Dark Night of the Soul*, extract in *The Book of Catholic Quotations*, John Calder, 1957

J. N. D. Kelly, *The Oxford Dictionary of Popes*, Oxford University Press, 1992

Ronald Knox (tr.), *The New Testament in English*, Burns, Oates and Washbourne, 1947

Thomas à Kempis, *The Imitation of Christ*, tr. Evelyn Waugh and Michael Oakley, Burns and Oates, 1959

Liverpool 1980, St Paul Publications, 1981

Arnold Lunn, *Now I See*, extract in *The Book of Catholic Quotations*, John Calder, 1957

J. Neale (tr.) *Byzantine Triodion*, extract in *The Book of Catholic Quotations*, John Calder, 1957

The New Sunday Missal, Geoffrey Chapman, 1982

J. H. Newman, *Apologia pro Vita Sua*, extract in *The Book of Catholic Quotations*, John Calder, 1957

—*Sermons on Subjects of the Day*, extract in *The Book of Catholic Quotations*, John Calder, 1957

Paul Potts, *Instead of a Sonnet*, Tuba Press, 1978

John Skinner, *Hear our Silence*, Fount, 1995

St Teresa of Jesus, tr. William Henry Longfellow, *Let nothing disturb you*, extract in *The Book of Catholic Quotations*, John Calder, 1957

St Thérèse of Lisieux, tr. Alan Bancroft, *Poems*, Fount, 1996

St Francis Xavier, tr. E. Caswall, *O Deus, ego amo Te*, extract in *The Book of Catholic Quotations*, John Calder, 1957

ACKNOWLEDGEMENTS

I am indebted to Kevin Flaherty, Editor of the *Catholic Times*, for permission to revisit some of the ideas I shared whilst writing a column for that paper.

The extract from St Thérèse of Lisieux, *Poems* on p. 275 appears by kind permission of Alan Bancroft.